SECOND EDITION

THE
More-Than-Just-Surviving
H A N D B O O K

ESL FOR EVERY CLASSROOM TEACHER

Barbara Law • Mary Eckes

PORTAGE & MAIN PRESS
(PEGUIS PUBLISHERS)

Winnipeg • Canada

Printed and bound in Canada by Kromar Printing

02   03   04   5   4   3

Portage & Main Press acknowledges the financial support of the government of Canada through the Book Publishing Industry Development Program (BPIDP) for our publishing activities.

Canadian Cataloguing in Publication Data

Law, Barbara, 1950–

    The more-than-just surviving handbook

    Includes bibliographical references and index.
    ISBN 1-894110-53-6

1. English language—Study and teaching as a second language. I. Eckes, Mary, 1954– II. Title.

PE1128.A2L38 2000   428'.007   C00–920130–0

Book and cover design: Suzanne Gallant
Illustrations: Scott Barham

pp. 114–115: From *The Ghost* by Joy Cowley. © 1983, 1990 by The Wright Group. Reprinted by permission of The Wright Group. 19201–120th Avenue NE, Bothell, WA 98011 • (425) 486-8011

pp. 279–280: From *Teaching ESL Writing* by Joy Reid. © 1993 by Joy Reid. Reprinted by permission of Pearson Education. 10 Bank Street, Suite 900, White Plains, NY 10606 • (914) 993-5000

PORTAGE & MAIN PRESS
(PEGUIS PUBLISHERS)

100-318 McDermot Avenue
Winnipeg, Manitoba, Canada R3A 0A2
Email: books@peguis.com
Tel.: 204-987-3500
Toll free: 800-667-9673
Fax: 204-947-0080

CONTENTS

ACKNOWLEDGMENTS

The More-Than-Just-Surviving Handbook is a book about something we care deeply for—people from other lands and cultures who are struggling to learn our language, and the teachers who are trying to help them. We are grateful to those who have helped us in the writing of this book.

We'd like to thank Melissa Ahlers, Cathy Tegen, Mary Delie, Kelly Sturm, Cherie Mornard, Dorothy Seehausen, Bobbi Jo Moore, Jim Haese, Katrina Pearson, Cinda Pennings, Brenda Carle, Laura Herrmann, and Marisa Flores for generously sharing their expertise, their ideas, and their students' work with us. Thanks to Marcia Rowland, for her thoughtful comments on structure and to our editor, Catherine Lennox, for persevering in spite of constant changes and fretting on our part.

We also thought we ought to congratulate each other. Long ago, when we started this enterprise, we made a pact that our friendship was more important than the books, and we would never allow our egos to get in the way of what the integrity of the writing demanded. It worked, and all these years and three books later, we're still friends.

We want to thank our students, whom we've loved, who have come and gone, enriched our lives, challenged us, and made us laugh.

Mostly, we thank our families—for their unflagging love and support: for their tolerance during the endless phone calls, hours at the computer, and days spent away from home. And, above all, for their belief that we could do it.

INTRODUCTION

It can be a daunting prospect to be faced with a student who can speak no English. It might make you feel helpless, maybe even resentful. When a new student enters the classroom, you ask yourself: What can I do with this student? How can I teach him anything if he is not able to understand even the simplest words in English? How can I, who can't speak a word of his language, communicate with him? What can I best do to help him become a member of this class? Many times our first impulse is to panic and say, "Send him to someone else—anyone!—who knows what to do."

But resources are not always available. There may not be anyone in your district who can speak your student's language. There might not be an ESL specialist available. Even if your school or district has an ESL teacher, she* may be able to spare only two half-hour sessions a week for your student. Or your student may be getting ESL help, but may already have been mainstreamed into your science, math, or social studies class. Ready or not, he is there.

Many books have been written for ESL teachers, but these almost always presuppose a working knowledge of second-language theory, methods, and techniques—and that the teacher is working solely with ESL students. For regular classroom teachers these books are not helpful. You may have twenty-five students, fifteen native-English speakers, and the rest non-English speakers. This means that you must meet the needs of many types and levels of students—your regular students who can understand the language and keep up with the mandated curriculum, and your ESL students, who may or may not have any English at all, who may or may not know how to read. Being successful with this range of students requires a totally different set of strategies.

Chapter Overview

This book has been written for those of you who are regular classroom teachers, both elementary and secondary, to give you a place to start, and enough knowledge and strategies to help you cope and to help your ESL students learn. There *are* things you can do, using the resources you have in the classroom and the community to help.

---

* To retain writing clarity while ensuring gender balance, plural pronouns have been used whenever possible. When unable to avoid a generic singular pronoun, we have chosen to use masculine pronouns in reference to students and feminine pronouns in reference to teachers.

In this book we have undertaken to

- Distill the latest research on first-and second-language learning, literacy theory, and integrating the skills of reading, writing, speaking, and listening.
- Apply the latest research to the regular classroom that contains both native-English speakers and non-English-speaking students.
- Suggest activities to foster language acquisition within the context of the regular curriculum.

The activities and methods we suggest have been selected because they are appropriate for both English-speaking and ESL students.

Chapter 1, "First Days," introduces you to a hypothetical classroom made up of a range of students (both native-English-speaking and ESL students) we have known over the years. We discuss strategies for coping and for helping your ESL students get acquainted with school and classmates. Suggestions are made regarding immediate activities to occupy these students until they can pick up enough English to function as regular students. This chapter also discusses priorities—things they must know first—as well as how to set short- and long-term goals.

Chapter 2, "Testing and Placement," is of special interest to principals and counselors, as well as classroom teachers. We address the issues of placing the student in the most appropriate grade; measuring reading, writing, speaking, and listening fluency; and strategies for grading.

Chapter 3, "Language Learning—Students and Teachers," discusses the principles of second-language learning; the factors that affect the success of the learner; what the teacher can do to promote success; and behavior—how to understand and assist your student when his behavior is inappropriate.

Chapter 4, "Literacy and the Four Skills," deals with basic literacy and promoting learning in every class from English to math.

Chapters 5, 6, and 7, "Reading," "Writing," and "Speaking and Listening," discuss in detail these four skills. We answer frequently asked questions, give suggestions for teaching, and show when and how to correct errors.

Chapter 8, "Content Area Instruction," is written specifically for content teachers. We show how to modify lessons so that students, who are not fully fluent in English, can succeed in content-area classes.

Chapter 9, "Resources," discusses the most effective use of other school personnel, such as the ESL teacher, aides, interpreters, and how to tap the resources of your school and community.

Recurrent Themes, Critical for Maximizing Learning

There are several recurrent themes that we believe are critical for maximizing learning.

Language is learned best when the learner feels safe. The kind of atmosphere that pervades your classroom can make the difference between silent non-learners and eager learners. All students need

■ A classroom where all students are wanted and respected for themselves and for the contributions they can make.

■ A classroom that is as stress-free as possible, where students can feel free to attempt to use their new language without fear of correction, ridicule, or punishment.

■ A classroom that validates the students' experiences and uses them for learning purposes.

The Classroom Environment

Language is learned best when it is "whole" and in context. In an integrated approach, the focuses are on meaning in language and on using language to communicate. The four skills—reading, writing, speaking, and listening—are parts of a whole, and all four skills are essential components of each activity. Reading does not occur in isolation, but is extended to include discussion and writing; composing does not take place without a great deal of prior discussion and reading. And opportunities to learn the language arts are not limited to language arts classes, but are integrated across the curriculum to include content classes too.

Using an Integrated Language Approach

An integrated approach also means that, instead of concentrating on component parts—the alphabet and phonics before learning to read; vocabulary, then sentences, then paragraphs before learning to write; grammar and the correct pronunciation of English words before being allowed to engage in conversation—students learn to read and write by reading and writing whole stories and texts and to speak by jumping into conversations regardless of whether or not their English is correct and complete.

An integrated approach means that all teaching/learning activities have meaning and purpose. This means finding things out because the answers have real practical value, or writing well because the work is going to be shared with others.

It means the teacher has faith in the learners and sets high expectations for them, whatever their literacy level or competence in English.

Teachers recognize that there is no "right" age or sequence of learning the strands of language, but that there is "a continuum of learning" on which students learn according to their own individual stage of development.

Language is learned best when the student is surrounded by real language used for real purposes by real people. Being exposed to the language and having good models are both essential to becoming competent readers,

The Importance of Models

writers, and speakers in that language. The classroom should be set up so that communication in the new language is essential to your ESL students, and so that they are not ignored and forgotten because they have not yet mastered the intricacies of the English language.

Errors Are Just a Part of Learning

Language is learned best when errors are viewed in their proper perspective, as just a normal part of learning. Any attempt to master a skill, whether skiing, skateboarding, writing, or learning another language, involves trial and error during the course of practice. Many of us who took a foreign language in high school or college learned the hard way that errors were viewed as faults, as graphic demonstrations that something was not learned. Errors were punished and eradicated. Perfection was the goal, whether in grammar, pronunciation, reading aloud, or writing.

Research now shows that errors should be viewed as stages in the learner's progression toward competent reading, writing, or speaking in the new language. Learners start with the big issues, such as getting their thoughts articulated and their needs met. Gradually they sort out the details—the correct tenses, the word order, the right words—refining and honing their knowledge of the language. This doesn't happen overnight; it is a long slow process. Recognizing learning as a process and errors as a natural phenomenon involves an entirely different attitude toward errors. They are not signs of incompetence or faulty learning, only that something has not yet been learned; therefore, they are not to be pounced on and "fixed" immediately, but considered as indicators of progress, to be noted and tolerated.

Why We Have Written This Book

We have written this book in the hopes that the reader, knowing something about language acquisition and equipped with the knowledge that good teaching is good teaching, whether to English or non-English speakers, will feel empowered, and will be able to accept and welcome all comers to the classroom.

We have included many of our own experiences in the form of anecdotes and brief character sketches in order to make the theory more concrete and the text more real. We have found, as instructors and colleagues over the years, that once a person becomes involved with teaching ESL, it not only becomes an interest, it becomes a passion. We have found working with newcomers to be deeply satisfying, and that the rewards of teaching non-English speakers far outweigh the stumblings and the frustrations. We hope that through this book we can pass on some of our passion and make life a little easier for those in the trenches.

In the years since our book was first published, we have learned a great deal about second-language learning and about literacy. In addition, a lot has changed. Whole language came under increasing fire, and much of what teachers did in a sincere belief of what was right and good had to go underground, or take a back seat to other concerns mandated by people who are not in the know. "Back to Basics!" is the battle cry from many quadrants. We have recognized that what passed for whole language in many places simply was not. We also have recognized that "skills," once a dirty word, is important in acquiring fluency in both reading and writing. How to teach skills within an authentic environment is an issue we are still grappling with.

The world is changing, and we in the field of second-language acquisition are struggling to change with it. The questions change. And sometimes, even when the questions remain the same, the answers seem to be different. But one fact remains: children are arriving in schools with little or no proficiency in English. And whether or not we teach them in the first language, put them in special programs, or mainstream them immediately, they will, like children everywhere, march through our school systems and either graduate or drop out. Thus, the clarion call for us remains the same: we will try to better their lives and their chances for success by always looking for ways to improve our teaching. Our goal is to approach the task with an open mind—to do more than "just survive" the experience.

It is through this increased understanding of how to meet the needs of our language learners that we have revised and updated *The More-Than-Just-Surviving Handbook*. The first book was meant to be modest, forthright, and easy to access. That has become our hallmark over the years. We have done our best to maintain that accessibility in our second edition.

A Word About Labels

There are many different labels for non-English-speaking students: ESL, LEP, LES, NEP. None of these are very satisfactory.

ESL, English as a Second Language, is somewhat misleading because many of our students arrive with English as their third, fourth, or even fifth language. In addition, not all ESL students have poor skills in English or require the services of a trained professional. Their reading is often on par with our English-speaking students, and their knowledge of grammar is sometimes even better, although their spoken English may be a little difficult to understand. LEP, Limited English Proficiency, LES, Limited English Speaking, and NES, Non-English Speaking, all carry negative connotations, as if the students arrive with a deficit, needing instruction to fill the gap. In truth, they arrive with a perfectly good language of their own in which they are fluent, able to think and speak their needs with ease. They have simply been placed in a situation where the language they have is not the language they need to function in the schools and larger society.

Other terms have been promoted, such as EAL, English as an Additional Language. While we lean toward this label, in this book we have chosen to use the most commonly used term, "ESL," referring to those students whose first language is other than English and whose proficiency is not high enough to perform equally with their English-speaking peers. We use this term simply because it is the best known and most commonly understood of all the prevailing labels.

FIRST DAYS

This chapter deals with the arrival of the new ESL student and provides strategies to help the teacher cope. We focus on

- Preparing for the arrival of the new student.
- Familiarizing the new student with school and classroom routines.
- Utilizing school and community resources for support in working with the new student.
- Teaching strategies for the first days.
- Planning for the year—setting up short- and long-range goals.

The Main Characters

We have created a hypothetical classroom made up of *real* students we have known over the years as well as our own (perfect!?) children. These students represent a range of personalities, abilities, reading levels, and spoken and written English proficiency. We have chosen to do this because we feel that it makes the issues we are presenting more real and allows us to highlight and illustrate certain points within the book. We do not use the students all equally or all the time—you might find them in an elementary classroom or in a grade ten science class. Don't look for them in every chapter.

It is unlikely, but not impossible, that you will have a class that displays this range. Unless you teach in a college town, as Barb did at the beginning of her career, you probably won't have the diversity of cultures in your classroom. The decisions you make, however, will be very similar to the decisions made by the teachers we present during the course of the book.

Good luck!

Hnuku: Hmong. Preliterate, no English skills. Arrived in the United States and went to school for a few months in Fresno with the expectation of going on to where the rest of her family is located. Hnuku is quiet, but can be very naughty when she feels like it.

Fernando: Mexico. Non-literate. A recent immigrant from a small town in Mexico. He is not literate in either English or Spanish. He cannot write his own name. He tries his heart out.

Salvador: Mexico. Semiliterate. Came from a small village where he did not go to school. He has been in a bilingual program and does not have skills to function in a school where there's absolutely no bilingual support. Nice kid. Struggles. Barely keeps his head above water.

Beverly: Taiwan. Attained a very high level of literacy in her first language. Very feminine. Wears a carefully combed ponytail and glasses. Does everything neatly and with care. Says very little in class. Speaks in her native tongue to her best friend Angel. Classified low LEP.

Angel: Taiwan. Tiny, shy, does not attempt to speak English at all. Uses her friend Beverly as the buffer between her and the rest of the world. She does good work, but it's hard to tell what is her doing and what is in conjunction with Beverly. Classified as NEP.

Franco: China. Father owns a restaurant in town. Very good in math. Very sociable. His test scores classified him as non-English speaking, but his understanding of English is much higher. He pretends to know less than he really does. He's squirrely and hard to keep on task. Was not held accountable for any of his work during his first year in the country.

Yoshi: Japan. Has professional parents. Resentful of being here. Sullen and unresponsive. Refuses to participate in class. Will not join groups. Sits by himself with his chin resting on his fists. Will do work alone, but no amount of coercion or persuasion will get him to be a participant.

Newton: Vietnam. Was born in this country. Should be much more proficient, but has not seemed to learn English very well. He is the class geek. The other kids won't sit next to him and fight for other seats. He is very artistic and draws careful pictures that are remarkably accurate. He is a loner and an outsider, but it's difficult to tell if that's his choice.

Abir: Egypt. She's very shy and never talks above a whisper. She's absent much of the time. Does not turn in any homework. Conferences with father reveal that she is needed at home to baby-sit younger siblings. Her parents believe that the year they are spending in this country is a year lost academically, and they put more emphasis on her studying her subjects in Arabic. If the truant officer wasn't breathing down their necks, they probably wouldn't send Abir to school at all.

Andre: Eastern Europe. A refugee. His schooling was disrupted for several years in his country. He spent time in a western state in an ESL program taught largely by teachers of his own language group, who, for whatever reason, did not teach much at all. His progress in his native language plateaued long ago, but he has not made progress in English either. He knows neither how to read nor write in English.

Florien: Italy. Classified Fully English Proficient. Only needs fine-tuning on the writing. Because he learned British English, his spoken English is so correct he comes out sounding like a native-English speaker. He's so charming and charismatic, the girls, as well as the teachers, just love him. He gets away with murder.

Boris: Russian. Son of professional people. Speaks Russian exclusively at home and has a large chip on his shoulder. Talks out of turn constantly. Fights with others in the class. Used to the imposed discipline of his native school system, he cannot cope with what to him appears to be total lack of structure in the classroom.

Native-English Speakers

Kate: She is very bright and perceptive, not excellent academically, but is well-organized, persistent, and dedicated. Her strength is the wisdom she has that's far beyond her years. She is extremely kind, willing to try anything, and a born leader.

Ellie: Exceptionally articulate for her age. If you're doing a lesson and you want someone to have a buddy, she can explain the subject in a variety of ways. She's very sensitive, interested in other cultures, and thus will go out of her way to make friends with newcomers. Has no organizational skills.

Austin: He's very smart; has a huge vocabulary and prefaces every sentence with "although." If he doesn't see the point of what you're doing, he'll argue. He's good-natured, but everything has to be on his terms. Does not like to be touched or even have people close. Does not work well in groups.

David: This boy is musical and very bright, but don't ask him to draw anything. Ambidextrous, but not comfortable using either hand in writing or drawing. He's good at reading and math, not interested in sports. Easygoing, good-natured, and very steady. He can be an anchor.

Rory: He's a handful, the class clown who wants to fool around. He's hard to keep on task. He knows more about computers than the computer teacher and can hack his way into programs.

Ashley: Ashley demonstrates that she can be smart, but she is disorganized. Her homework is often late and often not done correctly. She's distractable, volatile, can be sweet, but very explosive. She can divide the group; she's very smart at knowing how to create dissension and hurt people's feelings. Will try to talk her way out of any trouble she gets herself into.

Jeremy: He's an average student, but really motivated; he's game for anything, the goofier the better. Any teacher is lucky to have him, because if they can't think of someone to start something, he'll start it. He gets overwhelmed if an assignment is given with too many steps. He needs to have specific instructions broken into parts. He succeeds if has a check-off list of steps that he must follow.

Nick: He is physically very coordinated and athletic, with exceptional large motor skills. His small motor skills are limited, as is his patience for activities that require their use. He will not attempt anything if he can't see the point, or if he knows up front he won't succeed. He does poorly on standardized tests, even when he knows the material. He is very much like

Jeremy in his inability to follow through on assignments that require several steps.

Robbie: He's a quiet, nice kid who is average in most things, but above average in math. He's hard to engage sometimes. He tends to be overlooked in class because he's not high profile—he's not naughty, articulate, or sparkling, but he's good at approaching problem solving from a variety of different angles. Tends to bail out on standardized tests because they're boring and he knows he can do it, so his real talent isn't recognized.

Molly: She's from an unstable home. Comes to school unprepared with many things undone. She's Kate's best friend. She acts silly a great deal of the time and doesn't stay on task, and often leads the other girls astray. She can bring out the worst in good kids. She's very creative and funny, should be in a gifted and talented program, but she struggles academically and socially. She refuses to relate to adults.

Destiny: She's very verbal and charming. Has lots of street smarts and is able to use the skills she has and the environment surrounding her to cope with challenging tasks in the classroom. Quick to catch on when given individual attention or paired with a strong student.

Spencer: He's one of seven brothers. Did not know, upon being asked, how many boys there actually were, or how to spell his last name. His mother has moved to this town to get away from the gangs of the big cities. He has very low reading skills, but he's a bright, funny, affectionate kid who's very willing to try, eager to learn. He looks out for his younger brothers.

Preparing for the Student

It's the 24th of January. The school year is almost half over. "Thank goodness," thinks Mrs. Seehausen. As she walks by the front desk on her way to pick up her mail, Mary Lou, the secretary says, "We've got another one for you. His name is Bounkham. Doesn't speak a word of English. He starts this morning."

Unless you've been through this before, the first day an ESL student arrives can be distressing for the new student, you the teacher, and the rest of the class. For the student, the day can be as traumatic as the one described in figure 1.1. At best, you might feel awkward and apprehensive;

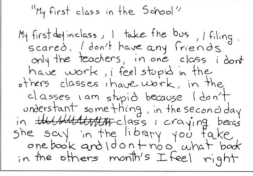

"My first class in the School"

My first day in class, I take the bus, I filing scared, I don't have any friends only the teachers, in one class i dont have work, i feel stupid in the others classes i have work, in the classes i am stupid because I don't understant something, in the second day in ~~the~~ class i craying becas she say in the library you take one book and i dont noo what book in the others month's I feel right

Figure 1.1. A student's reflection of her first day at school.

at worst, terrified and helpless. As teachers, we're used to having some degree of control, but nothing erodes that confidence faster than an inability to communicate with someone. Mrs. Seehausen was not an old hand at this, but in her second year in a low income, inner city school, she was getting used to it.

Feelings of apprehension and nervousness are natural. It is a truly intimidating prospect to be faced with the responsibility of teaching a student—or a group of students—with whom you are unable to communicate. It's only human to feel a wave of panic when that non-English-speaking student is first brought to your classroom. However, when you realize that this apprehension is only a fraction of what the new student is experiencing, it becomes a little easier to get past that first gut-level reaction of, "Oh no, why my class?" You can begin to come up with strategies to turn the situation into a positive one—for you, the new student, and the rest of your class.

What to Do First

In an ideal situation, students will come to school with their parents to register, and then return the following day, or after they have taken care of such necessities as immunizations and validation of immigration papers. This gives you some preparation time. In reality, students like Bounkham frequently arrive one morning with no notice (and often after the school year has begun), leaving the two of you to make the best of things. With or without lead-time, some very important first steps must be taken to establish a relationship.

Establish a Relationship

- Be Prepared. This is one of the most important aspects of welcoming strangers. Having both materials and ideas on-hand, "just in case," do wonders for morale (both yours and the new student's). Being prepared means being mentally ready for the task of helping the new student become part of the class, as well as having the classroom and the individuals in it primed for the potential arrival of a newcomer.

- Have a welcoming classroom. Mrs. Seehausen comments, "The physical appearance of the classroom needs to be inviting. It should say, 'come in, sit down, you'll like it here!'" Decorations should reflect not only the activities of the students, but the tastes of the students as well. ESL students have special needs to find a home in the classroom, and efforts should be made to represent all cultures.

- Sensitize the class. If you've been alerted beforehand, try to learn as much about Bounkham as you can *before* he comes to class so that you can share this information with the other students. This will help them accept Bounkham and make him part of the class. Mrs. Seehausen didn't have any lead-time for Bounkham, but she knew that it was inevitable, given the nature of the school. To prepare for that day, she had the class brainstorm and discuss how it might feel to be immersed in a new country or in the case of Native Americans, a new environment, where they don't speak, read, write, or understand the language. She read the books *Crow Boy* by Taro Yashima and *I Hate English!* by Ellen Levine to get them thinking along those lines.

- Make the student feel welcome. Even if you don't know a single word of Bounkham's language, you can show encouragement, sincerity, and empathy through gestures and body language. Smiling is universal.

- Make sure you know how to pronounce and spell the student's name. If you can't figure out the pronunciation of Bounkham's name from the intake form, ask him. Don't try to anglicize his name unless his parents have expressed this wish or he has changed it himself. Calling Bounkham "Bob" could make him feel even more alienated, as if his given name was not good enough. Identity is intricately tied to one's name, and to change it, either in the mistaken belief that the change will make him feel more part of the group or because his name is difficult to pronounce, can damage his integrity and feelings of self-worth. If he changes it, as Angel, Beverly, and Franco did, accept that too.

- Introduce the student to the class. Use a map to show the class where Bounkham is from. He may be able to point out his country and tell the class a little about it.

- If possible, learn a few words and phrases in the student's native language, such basics as "Hello," "How are you?" and, "Do you understand?" Even a simple thing such as "Hello" (in his language) will make him prick up his ears and brighten up, as well as convey that you are sincere and caring.

- Be a model of respect for the other students in the class. People of all ages can be cruel, especially when they don't understand another person's culture or dress. Showing respect for one's right to wear a turban, braids, or clothes we consider garish sets the parameters for appropriate behavior toward the new student, no matter how different he may be.

At the elementary level

- Give your new student a name tag, but make sure all the other children in the class have name tags too. Wearing the only name tag in the room can make a child feel alienated and singled out. Making name tags is a perfect classroom activity to get the newcomer and the rest of the class involved in learning each other's names. You might consider including Bounkham's parents' name, address, and phone number on the reverse side—information that would be invaluable should Bounkham become lost on the way to or from school. But use your own discretion in providing name tags that include students' addresses and phone numbers. Mrs. Seehausen's school was in a dangerous part of town; having such a label on a small person could lead to trouble. However, she decided that a name tag with information was preferable to a child wandering aimlessly about unfamiliar streets, unable to ask for help.

- Take Polaroid photographs of each student in your class, then use these to make a wall chart according to the seating arrangement of the classroom. This will reinforce the matching of names with faces.

At the secondary level

- Always introduce your new student to the class using the correct pronunciation of his name. High-schoolers, in particular, can wreak havoc with an unfamiliar name. If you can, supplement this introduction with some discussion of the geography and culture of his country.

- For the first days, ask for a class volunteer willing to help the new student with classroom procedures. In this classroom, Jeremy volunteered. He agreed to help Bounkham with such basics as the routine for starting class, providing him with paper and a pencil, sharpening the pencil, finding and using classroom resource materials, and so on. Robbie and Nick took charge of demonstrating the special equipment they had in the classroom: the computer and CD-ROM games, the tape player, and the music and reading tapes.

Sometimes a group of students will pitch in and help out. So much of what happens depends on the class makeup and the ESL student's personality. If Bounkham is outgoing and has some English, chances are that other students will help him get acquainted with no prompting from you.

At lunch break the first day, the boys found out that Bounkham was interested in soccer. This made him an instant hit—on the playing field it didn't matter if he didn't know any English at all, so long as he could kick the ball to them. By the end of break time, he already knew the names of his fellow classmates and was trying out a few words. He was friendly and willing to try to say anything, not caring if he said it wrong. The other boys really liked him and were willing to help out with anything he needed. Thus, there was a group of boys, including Salvador, Franco and Florien, who got along well inside and outside of class.

Newton, on the other hand, had arrived in October. He was shy and awkward. He wasn't into sports. He didn't seem interested in making friends. After a couple of days, the boys gave up trying. Mrs. Seehausen worked hard to make him part of the group, but it was tough going. Mrs. Seehausen had to accept that it would take time for him to join in actively. She paired him with Ellie and Kate as often as their tolerance would allow. Their effortless kindness encircled him too, so that although he rarely spoke, he was implicitly included.

As Mrs. Seehausen saw Bounkham relax, she included him in small-group activities, ones that included the volunteers who helped him. Her objective was for both Bounkham and Newton to move from interacting only with individuals, to interacting with a small group, and finally with the whole class.

■ Use an introductory small-group activity for junior-high or high-school students; for example, create a bulletin board of favorite pictures or photos that your students bring in and label. Then, in small groups, have the students share why they chose to bring in the picture they did. Bounkham will be exposed to different hobbies, pastimes, and so on, and will be able to associate the new faces he sees with activities that may interest him. This can be especially helpful when the new student is trying to get to know classmates who don't sit in the same seats every day.

Learning the School and Its Routines

As quickly as possible, acquaint Bounkham with his new school and community. He needs to know the layout of the school, the daily routines, and some basic survival phrases. Because many students have never been in a school before, or because their country's school system is radically different from ours, assume they know nothing. It is also important that parents are given some basic information about the school. In appendix A, we provide a sample information letter to parents. (If parents are not sufficiently literate in English, this may need to be translated.)

The average school day, with the routines and transitions we take for granted, can be perilous for a non-English speaker. For example, Mary's high school has a regular MWF schedule. On Tuesdays and Thursdays a block schedule is used. In a short week, Tuesday has Friday's schedule. Fernando, bewildered by the changes, came down nearly every day to ask what schedule it was and where he was supposed to be. One tense afternoon, at a junior high school where Barb worked, a new student boarded the first bus that passed. She ended up going downtown instead of to her housing project. For two hours, her parents and teachers waited anxiously until she was located.

One can only guess how many times a student has come to school in the morning only to find the schoolyard deserted and the doors locked, because neither the student nor his parents understood it was to be a holiday. Or, worse, they could not read the bulletins and had no one to translate. In a harsh climate such as where Barb lives, where the winter temperatures can plummet far below zero and schools only close when the temperature hits about -35° F, being locked out of the school, especially if parents have gone to work is a frightening and dangerous prospect. High-school ESL students are further handicapped because many announcements about the schools' frequently changing routine (e.g., assembly schedule, half-day teacher meetings, and so on) are made over a public address system often garbled by the noise of an inattentive homeroom. The English-language learner must struggle to understand the content of these messages; with no visual cues, he often fails to understand. An alert homeroom teacher would write important announcements on the chalkboard so that literate ESL students could read the messages as well as hear them. When notices are sent home, schools with available resources might consider having school communications translated into the ESL students' native tongues or enlisting community interpreters to ensure the messages are received.

The teacher can help ease the adjustment period by providing some sort of orientation. One school in northern California has put together a videotape, translated into Hmong and Spanish. Even though few of the parents own a VCR, many own TVs and either rent a VCR or gather at the home of someone who has one. They are then able to learn the routines and regulations on their own time and discuss among themselves those things that need clarification.

Things Your Students Need to Know

- How to find the washrooms (and how to tell which ones are for which gender).

- How to find their way around the school: the location of the playground, the cafeteria, the gym, and his classes. For example, if Bounkham is in junior high or high school, he will need to find his way from one class to another in the allotted time. He will also need to know the amount of time given for nutrition or morning break and lunch.

  How to Get Around in School

- How to find the main office, the nurse's office, the counselor's office, and so on. Bounkham needs to know where to bring late/tardy slips, where to go if he doesn't feel well, and so on.

- How to find the way back to the proper classroom from any of the above places. (It might help to write your room number on a card for Bounkham to carry if he leaves your room for anything; in a new place, all doors and even all teachers can look alike.)

- The names of a few key people, especially yours. In many cultures it is a sign of respect to call a teacher "Teacher," but time and time again, teachers have been dismayed that a student still does not know their names, even after months of being in school.

- How to open and close a locker, particularly if it has a lock with a combination.

- **The mechanics of the school day**
  - When must a student arrive?
  - When are recess periods or breaks?
  - When are lunch periods?
  - When is the school day over?
  - What are the dates of vacations and holidays?

- **School rules**
  - What if a student is going to be absent or late? Do his parents need to let the school know ahead of time?
  - Does he need to bring in a written excuse for an absence?

  The School Routine, Rules, Expectations of Behavior

- In secondary schools, are there absent slips that all the teachers must sign and then turn in at the end of the day? Where do these slips need to be returned?

- **Expectations of behavior at school**
  - How are students supposed to address you?
  - Does a student need to raise his hand to be acknowledged?
  - Does he need to stand by his seat, as many cultures demand, when it is his turn to speak?
  - Is talking allowed when working in small groups?
  - Is cooperative work allowed or is a student expected to work on his own?

  (Mary had a student who was constantly admonished for cheating in his content classes. When a meeting was held with Ming and his teachers, they discovered he had no idea that working on a paper with another student was wrong. At the school he had attended in his homeland, students always worked on the answers together.)

  - What is the school's policy and procedure for detention?
  - If a student has a detention after school for misbehavior, where is he to go and for how long?
  - What is he expected to do during detention? (With regard to detention or other emergency situations when the parents need to be contacted, have a list of volunteer interpreters handy for translating the message.)

- **Lunch**
  - Where do students go to eat?
  - Does Bounkham, for example, need to bring a lunch or can he buy it at school?
  - Is he aware that the food and way of eating may be unfamiliar?
  - If he buys milk or lunch, is it a cash sale, or is all the money collected on a specific day?
  - What is the procedure in the cafeteria?
  - What do students do when they finish eating?

- **Breaks**
  - Where are students allowed to go during breaks? (In elementary schools, are there special play areas for certain age groups?)
  - Are there any places they may not go? (In many high schools one area is designated for seniors only. If Bounkham is not a senior, he needs to know that area is off limits.)
  - How do the students know when it is time to go back to class?
  - What is the procedure for reentering class? In elementary school, do the students line up in a single line, or in separate lines for boys and girls? Do they stand outside the classroom door or in another

designated spot on the playground? In secondary school, are there one-way halls or is traffic designated to move in one direction on one side and another on the opposite side?

- When is a student allowed to go to his locker?

- **Getting home**
  - If a student rides the bus to and from school, where does he wait for it?
  - How does he tell which bus is his?
  - How does he tell the driver where he needs to be let off?
  - If he is being picked up by family members, where does he wait for them?
  - What should he do if they don't come?
  - Where is a phone if he needs to call his parents or other family members? Is money required to make a phone call?
  - What route does he take to get home if he must walk?
  - Are parents made aware of any child welfare legislation that governs the minimum age at which a child may be at home without adult supervision?

Use Resources Within the School/ Within the Community

As a teacher with twenty or more students (or at the secondary level, 120 or more students), you may not have time to give one new student a comprehensive orientation. Fortunately, even the smallest school can draw on a number of resources to help ease the ESL student's first day. If you are unable to give your new student an orientation during the morning break or at lunch (and face it, how many teachers really have an entire break period free?) consider these alternatives:

- Find another student who speaks the same language. A student who is already familiar with the school and its routines and requirements can explain to the new student, in his own language, what is expected of him and help him adjust to his new surroundings. At the high school, Mrs. Seehausen found another student who was released for the day to help Bounkham get from class to class. The first day of school is bewildering enough for incoming freshmen and must be many times more frightening to one who hasn't experienced North American schools before. Hnuku spoke only Hmong, but her older brother also knew some Lao. Mrs. Seehausen allowed him to sit in the class for a day or two to help ease the transition.

Use Student Help

- Assign a buddy. Put an English-speaking student in charge of showing the new student around, making sure he gets from one place to the other and doesn't get lost. Mrs. Seehausen looked at the personalities in the class. Although Kate and Ellie were responsible girls, she decided that pairing Bounkham with a boy would be a better idea. Most of the non-native-English-speaking boys, who would understand what he was going through, did not have strong enough proficiency. Except Boris and Andre. But Boris was not a good role model. Nor was Andre, who had plenty of troubles of his own. She decided not to place the entire burden on one person. She selected Robbie because he needed to take on more responsibility, David because he was steady and patient, and Jeremy and Nick because they were sociable and friendly.

■ If your school or district has an ESL teacher, she may be able to help guide the student through this first day (or days) at school.

■ A bilingual teacher or bilingual aide may be able to give the student his first-day orientation to the school.

Use Adult Help

■ In the event that you have neither an ESL or bilingual teacher available, any sympathetic and patient adult—librarian, parent volunteer, resource teacher, counselor, principal—might be entreated to adjust his or her schedule to make time for your student on that all-important first day.

■ Consider finding a mentor. Many schools have found adult volunteers who agree to devote weekly or monthly time to students to help them succeed. It can be very beneficial to a new student from another country to have an adult's consistent support as he adjusts. If Bounkham is one of the first students placed in your school and you have no idea where to find cultural support for him, check these resources in your community:

Use Cultural Resources

  ■ Cultural support groups already working within the community (for example, Lao Family Community Services, MECHA chapter, International Students' Organizations on college campuses).

  ■ The ESL department at the local college or adult basic education programs.

  ■ The telephone book—look in the "Easy Reference List of Government and Public Services" or similar listing.

  ■ Mayors' offices often have an immigrant and refugee component ("Consumer Information," "Constituent Service," "Ombudsman," and so on).

  ■ Lawyers, especially ones associated with civil rights groups, pro-bono committees of bar associations, Legal Services Corporation.

  ■ Voluntary agencies that work in refugee resettlement, such as international institutes, centers; national religious service groups (i.e., Catholic charities, church world services, world relief refugee services, Mennonite Central Committee); other voluntary agencies, such as the Salvation Army, churches, temples, the public library.

  ■ For emergency interpreters, AT&T offers a Language Line service in more than 140 languages. This 24-hour service is available in Canada and the United States. If interpreters are in short supply in your school district, this option might be critical. Contact AT&T for more information.

First-Day Teaching

Once a new student is placed in an appropriate grade, given a class (or set of classes) and an orientation to the school, you can get down to business. Bounkham has settled into his desk, and has taken inventory of his books, pencils, and pens. It's a fairly safe bet that he's not going to bolt for the neighbor's yard. It's social studies time. The other students are getting their books out; he sits, hands folded, quietly watching you. He's ready to learn. But he doesn't speak English, and you don't speak Lao. How will you teach?

If Bounkham speaks no English, it may take a while for him to start to participate. However, this does not mean putting him "on hold" until he talks. As time goes on, you can use different alternatives for individualizing instruction so that your student will be learning at least some basic subjects. But for now, you can help him adjust to the classroom and begin to learn English.

Things to Do to Help the Student Adjust and Begin to Learn

- Give him a place of his own. For younger children, this may be a cubby to keep things in. For older students, it may be a desk or an assigned seat. If the students select their own seats each day, you may have an area where students keep supplies. Show Bounkham where to keep his materials for use in your class. This sense of a personal "space" will make him feel included, which will help prevent him hovering in the doorway until everyone else is seated and ready for class, and allow him to slip to his desk without feeling self-conscious.

- Give him something definite to do. This activity does not have to be elaborate, just something to occupy him so that he doesn't have to sit doing nothing while the rest of the class works. Make it a simple task that he can enjoy and achieve some success at.

  Many elementary schools that frequently have ESL children drop in during the school year keep an "emergency kit" of things for a newcomer to do when he first arrives. This kit is filled with magazines, pictures to cut out and color, and items to sort and identify. Many of the manipulables we discuss on page 135 are appropriate for this kit, which may also be used by the student whenever he cannot participate in a particular classroom activity.

  For older students, magazines or books with interesting pictures, such as *Life, Time, Sunset, Ranger Rick*, even old calendars are useful. The students can copy or create labels of item categories, or practice writing their names, family members' names, addresses, and so on. They can also label different items found in a classroom. In content area classrooms, students can label such things as equipment or materials. We advocate supplying students with picture dictionaries, such as the *Oxford Picture Dictionary*, so that they can begin learning new vocabulary immediately. The realistic pictures depict everyday life in and out of school. While this dictionary is acceptable for older children, the number of items on a page might be overwhelming for lower elementary children.

Don't be dismayed if Bounkham only sits and watches for the first few days or so. It is important that he be able to choose whether or not to become involved. The main thing is to be prepared. Have a kit of worthwhile activities planned and ready as discussed earlier—so that he doesn't have to sit doing nothing, only to get bored, frustrated, or disruptive. It doesn't take long to put an "emergency kit" together, and it will save you a great deal of anxiety and guilt when your new student does show up.

- Establish a routine. We cannot overemphasize how critical this is to a student. Knowing exactly what he's to do first, and where he's going to go next, makes life simpler for students like Bounkham. For a non-English speaker, everything has to be learned by observing, so routine is essential. Bounkham will feel less self-conscious if he can anticipate what is going to happen in class. And as the process becomes familiar, he will become more inclined to risk error by speaking. It also makes your planning easier because you will follow the same steps each time.

- Include the student in activities. The first few days and weeks of school are lonely times when ESL students may feel alienated and alone. Being part of a group will help Bounkham overcome those feelings. Even if he cannot participate fully—or at all—he will benefit from the exposure. A buddy system may decrease the possibility of anxiety and alienation.

- Seat the ESL students with care. This is another instance where Mrs. Seehausen had to think strategically. Seating had to be judicious. And flexible. Hers is a lively class with many strong personalities. Frankly, we struggled with this part as all teachers do. It's not enough, with ESL students in your classroom, to arrange them in alphabetical order. They need access to you, and to each other, as well as to students who can and are willing to help them.

  To help us think this through, we gave the list of students' personalities to preservice teachers (who are planning to teach all different grade levels and classes) and asked them what they would do if they had this class. The results surprised us, as well as helped us see the possibilities. Some teachers were willing to gamble. One group put Boris and Ashley together because they "deserved" each other. Another group put Boris in a corner by the door so he could leave whenever necessary, without disrupting the class. Yet, they all worried about Angel and Beverly. And they worried about Boris and Ashley.

The personalities of the different students, their personalities as teachers, and their teaching philosophies had to be taken into account. The layout of the room and the purposes of the class also figured into the seating arrangements.

We found there is no one right way to seat ESL students. Still, we found it exciting and fun to watch the thought processes of the preservice teachers and the care they took in thinking the problem through. We have replicated some of their suggestions, as well as their rationale, so you have a model upon which to base your own decision making (figure 1.2-4). Where would you seat Bounkham?

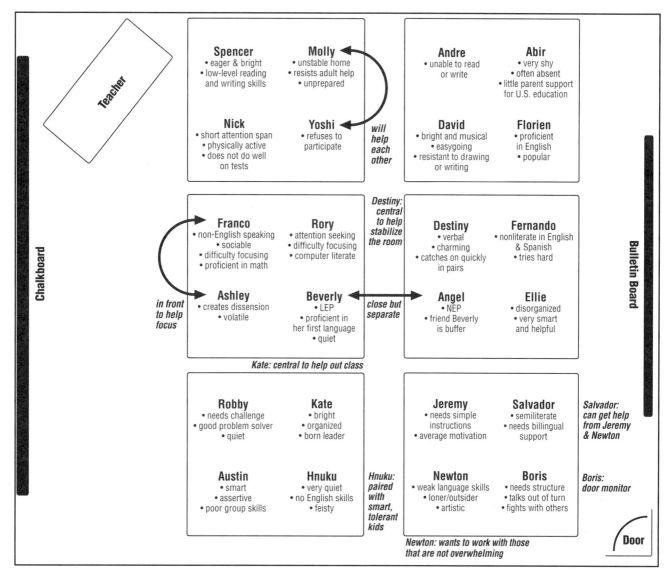

Figure 1.2. In this seating arrangement Angel and Beverly are close, but not together. Two anchors are at every table, along with second-language learners and/or students with behavioral issues. Boris was by the door. He was given the job as door monitor, with the idea that if he had a specific job he would attend to it with diligence, and it would make him more responsible.

Planning for the Year

Setting short- and long-term goals is a good remedy for curing the panic you may feel when a non-English-speaking student is assigned to your class. Mapping out your objectives helps you see that you can achieve realistic goals with this new student; making sure your goals fall into short- and long-term categories keeps you from overwhelming yourself or him! But don't make any long-term goals for the first few weeks. Bounkham will be adjusting to all the people and things he encounters at the school and may seem to know less English than he actually does. Only when you know you have a good sense of your student and his learning style should you make long-range plans for his curriculum. The following steps will help you to manage.

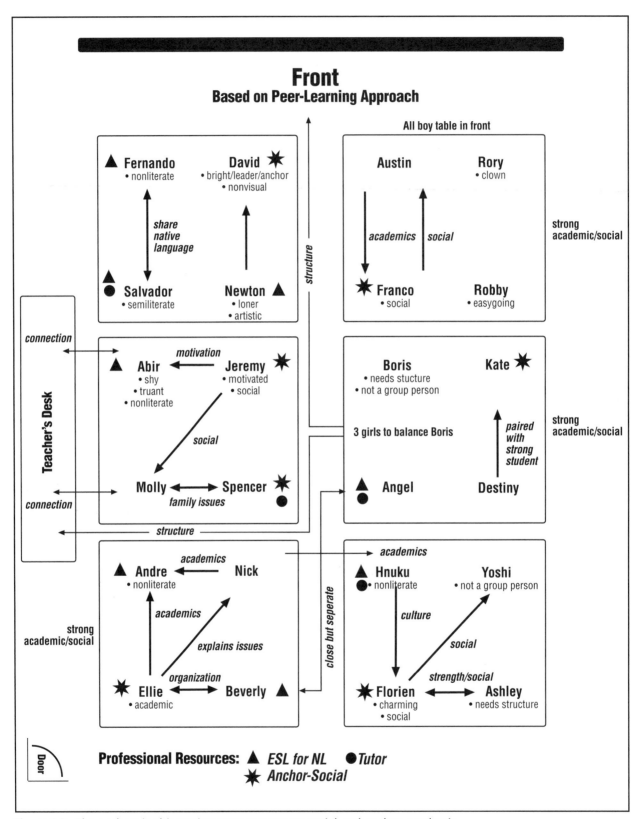

Figure 1.3. The anchors in this seating arrangement are social, rather than academic.

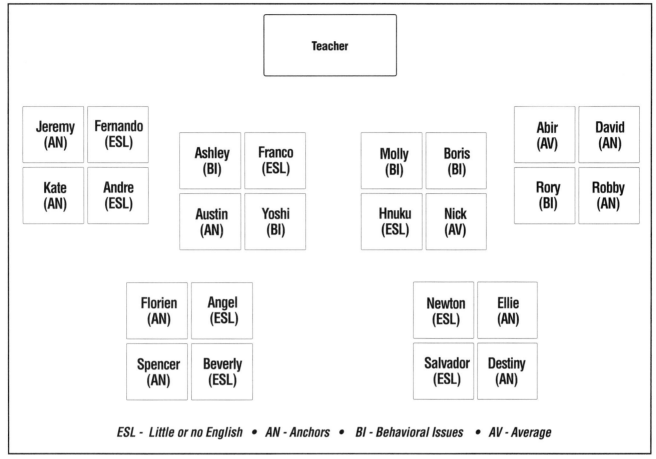

Figure 1.4. In this seating arrangement, one well-behaved or average student was put into each group. Beverly and Angel are seated together, but not next to each other to give stability.

- Have a game plan. It is not enough to assume that the student will "pick up" English on his own. Bounkham needs you to help him make sense of the new language so that he is able to catch up and work at grade level with his peers.

- Have expectations. Not just expectations, but HIGH ones. Expect the student to learn. Learning does not stop because he is grappling with a new language. Although he may not speak a word of English, Bounkham is capable of sophisticated and penetrating thoughts in his own language. We need to guard against underestimating his potential for making serious contributions to classroom discussions. Bounkham can learn new words, and he can learn concepts from the activities he participates in. Your expectations of him are positive encouragement that you believe in his potential.

- Accept the fact that the ESL student will be behind. If you feel anxiety because you believe Bounkham has to be up with the rest of the class in four weeks, you are setting yourself up for some real misery. Understanding that he will be filtering content through limited-

Prepare Coping Strategies

language proficiency allows you to focus on the bigger picture and helps you to appreciate his little successes.

Establish Short-Term Goals

■ Write down what the new student can and cannot do. Mrs. Seehausen discovered that Bounkham did not have strong reading skills. Over the next few days, she watched, in a variety of situations, how much he was able to communicate. He could write full sentences. He was able and willing to interact with the other students. When partnered with another, stronger, student, he could handle the assignments; he watched to get a feel for things, then took off on his own. She watched to see if he was able to demonstrate any prior knowledge in the content area. He knew math. He didn't have formal background in science or the social studies units they were working on. It was her task to figure out whether this was due to lack of vocabulary or concepts that he had not encountered during his previous schooling. She needed to figure out if he would be required to adjust to a new learning style. He did. Bounkham did not know that if he did not understand a concept, it was appropriate to ask for help. She found that he simply pretended to do work, wrong or right, rather than ask for clarification. Having Hnuku explain as best she could helped him realize what he could do and what he needed to do. You should keep records of his starting points and progress. That way you will know what he needs and you will know how well he is doing.

■ As you are getting acquainted, set some short-term goals for your student based on your observations. For the first week or so of class, Mrs. Seehausen focused on getting Bounkham to participate in the classroom routine and to begin to use English. This included anything from acknowledging instructions to turning in a written assignment. She tailored the goals she had set to her perception of his abilities.

■ When teaching the new student to communicate, teach vocabulary that will be useful. Teach him words and popular idiomatic expressions that he will hear and be able to use immediately. Don't teach vocabulary-list words that have little to do with this student's everyday life. These words are meaningless memory-eaters, and time could be spent more fruitfully on a vocabulary that will give him instant feedback. Mrs. Seehausen taught Bounkham important phrases such as "I don't understand" and "Where is the…?" (bathroom, library, and so on), and other survival words to get him through the day. The boys taught him how to say, "Whatever." She also gave him small assignments, such as mapping the school. This was an area that he could work on while others were engaged in tasks beyond his language abilities.

■ Teach essential content-vocabulary. For example, Mrs. Seehausen was teaching a unit on matter. The words *matter, air, solid, liquid, gas, weight,* and *space* were fundamental vocabulary to this unit. This was vocabulary that could not be simplified. Even if Bounkahm could not read the text, he needed to know these words to participate in the experiments and understand even the rudiments of the lessons.

- Use audio-visual materials, which are wonderful tools for language learning. Films, recordings of popular songs, videotapes of educational TV shows, photos, slide shows, and comic strips can all help to develop communication skills. All kids think movies are a treat, a break from the daily routine, and they pay attention. It especially helps Bounkham and the other less proficient students.

- Find out the new student's favorite activities and interests, and develop related assignments that will encourage and advance his attempts at the English language. English is most effectively learned when generated from attempts to communicate, not from a focus on perfect grammar and syntax. Mrs. Seehausen found that Bounkham was a sunny, friendly, likable child who took everything in stride and liked video games, soccer, and music. He was willing to attempt anything. He was particularly adept at using his hands. He liked working on the computer and could often fix problems that arose, simply because he had a knack for knowing how things worked, even though he didn't have the language for it. Like many of the other boys in the class, he was not good at doing seat work; he was continually up and around. Rather than have him plod through workbooks, Mrs. Seehausen planned activities for Bounkham that were short in duration or required an active role, making the most of his strengths.

- Encourage extracurricular activities as springboards for English acquisition. Many school clubs and after-school activities can provide firsthand exposure to all kinds of vocabulary in a variety of contexts. If your student wants to play on the school's soccer team, he will be exposed to English vocabulary used for a game he probably already knows how to play. Whatever club or activity the student joins, the motivation to learn English will arise from the need to contribute to his chosen interest and communicate with others involved.

- Develop an overall plan. Now that you know something about your ESL students, develop strategies for the long run. This step might seem self-evident, but it is a critical one. Rather than have "getting through the book" as your objective, envision the course as a whole. What do you want them to learn? (We discuss this further in chapter 8, "Content Area Instruction.")

Establish Long-Term Goals

- Select themes for teaching/learning units. For instance, in history at the junior-high or high-school level, you can use themes such as expansion, waves of immigration, the Colonial era, the Civil War, and so on. (Be sensitive to certain topics/themes that might evoke traumatic and negative emotions.) For science, Mrs. Seehausen decided to examine a nearby plot of ground as the seasons changed. She planned for students to gather data at specified times each month, keeping careful records of plant and animal life, the effects of various types of weather, as well as other activity on the land. They would classify species and varieties of life, speculate on changes that might take place, and revise their predictions based upon new data gathered. Each successive observation would improve everybody's skills, and they would all benefit from the repetition involved in the study. Repetition gives the course a coherent structure and makes each segment successively easier to understand—not only by the ESL students, but by other students as well. Repetition also gives a course shape and symmetry. Often, history or science courses seem little more than a jumble of unrelated facts and dates that are memorized for a test, only to be forgotten immediately afterward. In an integrated, thematic approach to instruction, students can see the course as a comprehensive whole, related to the world outside and to the people who live in it. This isn't always feasible, but offers a lot of fun possibilities.

- Establish minimum competencies. When you know what you want to cover by the end of the semester, decide on a "bottom line" set of concepts your students must learn to pass. You can then evaluate your ESL students, using this list. It is easy to assess ESL students in terms of how much they are missing the mark, how much they *don't* know when compared to your regular students. In establishing basic goals, you can measure, instead, how much they *can* do.

Mrs. Seehausen was teaching "matter." This concept is one that is studied in several grades in school (second grade and in greater depth in junior high). If Bounkham is in second grade, you can be sure that he will get this again later. If he's in eighth grade, and missed it the first time, you can look at some of the activities at the lower levels and adapt.

Mrs. Seehausen wanted all students, including Hnuku, Bounkham, Angel, Beverly, Fernando, and Salvador, to understand

- Basic vocabulary.
- What matter is.
- Matter has weight and takes up space.
- Matter exists in different states.
- Steps to conducting experiments.
- How to predict and write up findings.

Prioritize your list. Mrs. Seehausen decided that understanding the vocabulary was important. She also wanted all students to be able to understand that gas changed to liquid to solid and back again. Conducting the experiments and writing up the findings in articulate ways was beyond Bounkham and Salvador, but the others could try.

- Adapt your lessons to the levels of the students. Mrs. Seehausen had tried this unit the previous year and was not particularly happy with how it had turned out. It seemed that whatever she did, many of the students didn't "get it." She needed to gear the lessons more closely to the literacy abilities of Salvador, Fernando, Hnuku, and Angel, as well as Destiny and Spencer. She also had to make it challenging enough for Katie, Ellie, David, and Ashley.

This year, she decided that a lead-in was important, both to grab students' attention and to get them thinking about the subject. The first

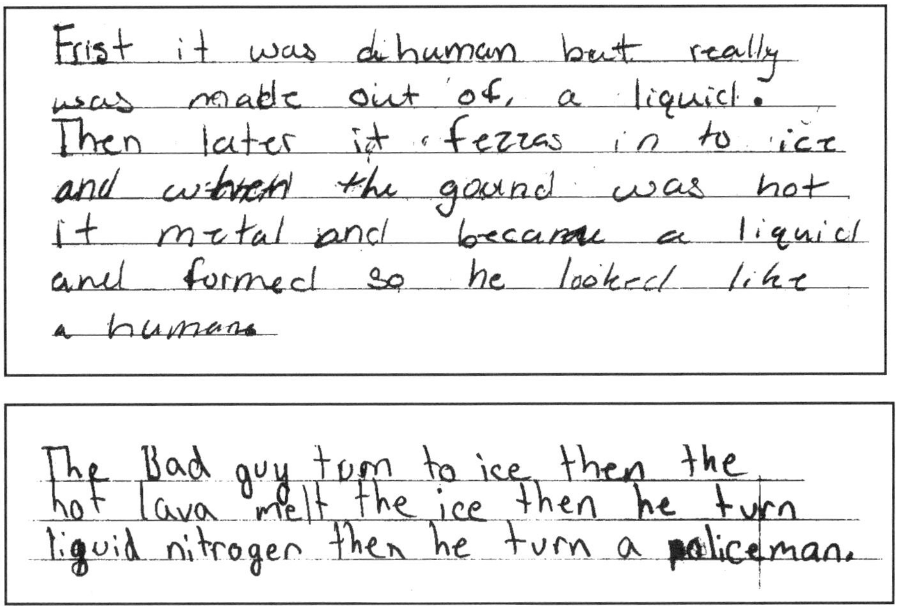

Frist it was d human but really was made out of, a liquid. Then later it fezzas in to ice and w the goand was hot it metal and became a liquid and formed so he looked like a human

The Bad guy turn to ice then the hot lava melt the ice then he turn liquid nitrogen then he turn a policeman.

Figure 1.5a-b. Students' descriptions of what they observed.

thing she did was show a clip of *Terminator Two: Judgment Day*. In this clip, the "T-1000 model terminator" overturns a tank truck filled with liquid nitrogen—the terminator freezes solid, then explodes. As the heat from the nearby factory thaws the solid particles, they melt into a liquid state that runs together and re-forms into the T-1000 model again, another solid shape.

The students watched the film clip three times: the first for fun and the second to observe the changes. They wrote down how they saw the terminator change form (figure 1.5a-b).

During the third viewing, the students assessed their writing for accuracy and detail. Those students who were satisfied with their writing were given the option to read it aloud for the group, giving the struggling students the opportunity to hear a model of good observation, and a chance to reevaluate what they had seen and written.

While her English-speaking students were reading the textbook and answering questions, Hnuku, Salvador, and Fernando were making posters. Mrs. Seehausen gave them magazines and specific instructions for finding twenty pictures of solids, ten of liquids, and five of gases. They were instructed to make a collage and identify the various states (figure 1.6). The more proficient students (Abir, Newton, Angel, and Beverly) labeled the different items. This allowed the limited-English-speaking students to participate, to demonstrate their understanding, and to continue along with the unit at their own level.

When students made charts of the properties of the various states of matter, the less-proficient students listened and copied (figure 1.7).

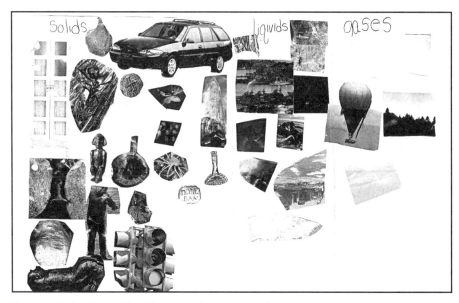

Figure 1.6. Students identify the various states of matter.

Solid	liquid	Gas
•you can feel it	•moves easily	can not se easily
you can broach it	•It's wet	you can feel it whe it moves
The shape can not be changed easily	•stays together	
	•It can make other things wet	some gas smalls chang it's shape
We use solids for a lot of things	•can change temperatures	you use air in tires
you can see solid easily	•when you add color to a liquid the whole liquid changes	
can change temperatures	•liquid take the shape of the container you put it in	
	liquids can changes in to solids	

Figure 1.7. A student's chart showing the properties of states of matter.

In many of the experiments Mrs. Seehausen did with her students, she included the less-proficient students. By pairing them with or putting them in groups with more proficient students, they could watch, take part, draw their understanding, and, if possible, write up their findings.

Requirements for ESL Students

■ During the first nine weeks, literate ESL students are accountable for
   ■ All math.
   ■ All work done in ESL assignments or with their tutor.
   ■ Tasks modified for the ESL student, such as book reports that require the student to take the book a chapter at a time and do a simple retelling of the story.
   ■ Contributions to group work.

■ During the second nine weeks, literate ESL students must
   ■ Take all work sheets.
   ■ Put their names on them.
   ■ Do as much as they can.
   ■ Hand them in.
      (The more advanced students can be graded after the second nine weeks.)

■ During the third nine weeks, the students must
   ■ Be able to do almost all the work.
   ■ Be graded with others, with some allowances (for instance, if they didn't finish a test because they needed to make constant references to a dictionary, they can finish later in study hall or after school).

Figure 1.8. An example of a grading structure for literate ESL students.

- Develop a grading structure for literate ESL students. Mrs. Seehausen designed an evaluation system to mark the progress made by Bounkham, which reduced the gray areas during grading time. As an example, we have included the format one junior high school has adopted for grading within specific marking periods (figure 1.8).

  This format is ambitious, but if the ESL students are aware that they will be accountable for certain things they have certain goals to shoot for, rather than a vague "when they learn English."

Conclusion

The first days with a limited-English speaker in the classroom are the hardest for everyone concerned. At times you may feel that the going is slow, and results are few and far between. Chances are your student feels the same way. Nurture attitudes of patience, compassion, and a sense of humor to encourage the student's process of assimilation. Celebrate the successes no matter how small they may seem. In spite of the frustrations, this can be a rich opportunity for all of you.

CHAPTER 2

TESTING AND PLACEMENT

In this chapter, we provide practical guidelines about

- Testing issues.
- Where ESL students should be placed.
- How to test them.
- How to make use of the test scores.

Tomás arrived in the middle of May from a small town in Mexico. He was nine, but was placed in a third grade classroom. He was a darling boy, with smiling eyes and a front tooth that was chipped twice. He spoke not a word of English. Barb, who had been testing all incoming children in that school for the past year and a half, came with her usual materials for testing reading and writing—graded reading passages in English and a writing prompt. Barb's Spanish comprehension is fair at best; she can follow along when she knows the topic of conversation, but when faced with the need to communicate the Spanish gets mixed in with French and finally dribbles away altogether.

With a lot of goodwill and a few false starts, they established that Tomás was nine, he was born in September, and he had three brothers in town with him and two more in Mexico. He would not attempt to read in English, but willingly wrote what he had communicated in a manner that revealed that he was literate in Spanish (figure 2.1). His handwriting was neat and well-formed, and he wrote easily.

But that was all they accomplished, so they gave up and went back to the classroom.

It was, altogether, an uncomfortable and less-than-revealing encounter that took Tomás away from the classroom and probably left him wondering what the heck all that was about. And Barb was frustrated because, had she had the right materials (a selection of reading passages in Spanish and an appropriate writing prompt he could read and respond to), she could have found out more information that was useful to Tomás's classroom teacher.

The questions that arise from such an encounter are

- What do we want to know?
- How do we find out efficiently and accurately?
- What do we do with that information once we've obtained it?

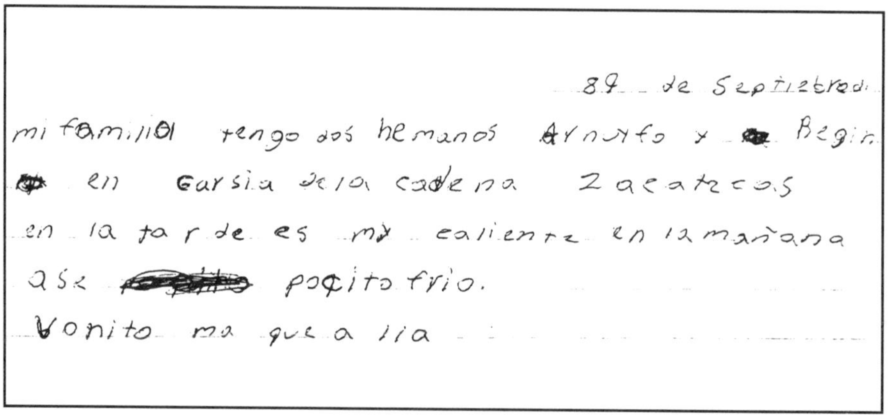

Figure 2.1. Tomás's writing sample.

Testing Issues

In the U.S., federal law requires that all students coming from a non-English-speaking background

- Be surveyed within thirty days of enrollment to determine if they speak a language other than English.
- Be tested within ninety days of enrollment in their native language, if they are not sufficiently fluent in English.

Note: There is no equivalent federal law in Canada. Policies for ESL students are the responsibility of school divisions/districts or, in some cases, individual schools.

Many school districts do not test because they don't know how, are unaware of the test choices they have available to them, or they have no tests translated into the students' native languages.

There are many tests available. Even in those cases when no standardized tests have been translated into the languages your students speak, it is possible to learn much about your students and their proficiency levels. You can then make competent decisions about which classes and grade levels to place them in.

Initial Decisions

Ideally, your school will have been given prior warning that a new ESL student is coming, and whoever is responsible can make unhurried decisions about his placement. Unfortunately, this is often not the case. Parents or guardians will bring the student to the school, medical papers in hand, and leave him there, forcing placement in a classroom without any type of assessment.

The person(s) responsible for the initial testing and placement of ESL students vary remarkably from school to school. Ideally, testing and placement will be the responsibility of an ESL specialist, or in cases in which no specialist is available, a counselor, special education teacher, or principal. The reality is that these people are often overextended, so the job of testing and placement is handed over to someone else—a teacher, an aide, or a parent volunteer. This is regrettable, as these people are often not provided with the necessary training and sometimes lack the sensitivity for this task.

Before the new student comes to school, or as soon as possible after his arrival, a home language survey should be administered to determine whether he speaks a language other than English at home. In appendix B, we illustrate a sample survey. An older student can fill this out at school with an adult's help. Younger students are often unreliable about the languages spoken in their homes, so the parents or legal guardians can be asked to fill the survey out. The help of an interpreter/translator is often required.

Placement

To illustrate the issues involved in placement and evaluation, we will track the progress of five students.

Hnuku is brought to school by a church sponsor. Her father was killed and her mother died in childbirth. She is here with her uncle. The scanty records that arrived from Fresno seemed to be for another child named Hnuku. Her uncle says she is nine.

Boris, thirteen, is a confident boy with a swaggering manner and a loud voice. His parents are college educated, and he has studied English in school.

Newton, whose parents were refugees, is sixteen. He has lived all his life in this country, but speaks little or no English.

Spencer is five and has just moved here from a large, inner city. His mother has moved to this town to escape the ghetto after his older brother was killed in a drive-by shooting. He speaks a non-standard variety of English.

Charlie Bill is a six-year-old from a reservation. His parents have moved temporarily to this district to seek medical help for a younger sister. He is fluent in his native language and has learned some English, but is not proficient.

The Grade-Level Issue

The school's first job is to place each student in the proper grade with the right teacher. Hnuku is tiny and appears much younger than her nine years. She smiles shyly, but will not speak. The principal is tempted to place her in the first or second grade. Boris has had some English, but does not speak it fluently. The counselor argues that he be placed in the sixth grade rather than the eighth grade because the content is less demanding, and he will have an easier time learning the language without the pressure of studying new subjects he has not encountered before. Newton's parents think that he would do well in the tenth grade. Spencer and Charlie have not had any preschool experience at all. Their placement is relatively simple: because of their ages they can be put into kindergarten with their peers. Charlie's main limitations are his lack of fluency in English and the challenges associated with adjustment to a new culture and environment.

Boris and Hnuku's lack of content knowledge and required skills are not reason enough to warrant placement in lower grades. These students should be placed with classmates of their age group for several very important reasons:

- Their emotional and social needs can be met only by being with their age-mates. Hanscombe (1989) asserts that social integration is much more important than language needs. It may be devastating to Boris's ego to place him with younger students, severely affecting both his motivation and self-esteem. Students adapting to a new language and culture are quick to model the behavior of their peers. Sharing common interests with their age-mates encourages and enhances language development. Depriving students of the opportunity to interact with their peers can hinder adjustment to their new life.

- Lack of fluency in English does not indicate limited intelligence. Even though the students' lack of English makes them unable to cope with grade-level work at first, they are not necessarily behind in cognitive development. What is more, the English spoken in the eighth grade is not appreciably different from that spoken in the sixth grade. Many students experience boredom and frustration when required to repeat the content they have gained in their first language. It may well be that Hnuku, Boris, and Newton are perfectly capable of doing work at grade level. But you need to find out.

- Students beyond the primary grades can often learn to read faster than younger children, simply because they are more mature.

- More than any other factor, success with ESL students depends upon a commitment by teachers and administrators to acknowledge and meet the students' special needs. Academic achievement is directly linked to the quality of instruction, not just the placement of the student.

At the elementary level

As noted, Charlie can be placed in kindergarten with his peers. Most kindergarten curricula blend the development of prereading and pre-writing skills with an exploration of the child's world. Activities at this level are predominately hands-on and rich in language-learning opportunities. The teacher will need to allow Charlie more time to demonstrate his mastery of lesson concepts, because he is juggling language learning at the same time as he is adapting to a new culture. For example, Charlie and Spencer do not have much experience and may take longer to learn how to read. First they will need to connect print with meaning. Charlie must learn words for concepts and his alphabet. The teacher must be sensitive to Charlie and Spencer's unique learning curve and assess their progress appropriately.

With Hnuku there is some flexibility. Under certain circumstances and with careful consideration, it might be permissible to place a child such as Hnuku one grade lower than her age-mates (but not more than one). If the school has split or multi-age classes, this would be the best option, as both her affective and cognitive growth would be ensured. Placing Hnuku in a class made up of third- and fourth-grade students would allow her to work with the younger children *and* socialize with her age-mates in the fourth grade.

What if subsequent testing reveals that Hnuku has no skills at all? With no prior schooling, she will be starting at square one. It is very difficult to teach a child who is at the prekindergarten level when there are twenty-five other students in the class. The experience would be frustrating, not only for her (because she can't do the work), but for the teacher (who won't have the time to help her). One solution would be to place Hnuku in a first-grade classroom where the teacher would be better equipped to handle her needs until she learns her basic skills. However, this choice is not best for the student. For a child like Hnuku, being with her age-mates is the most important consideration. She will be able to participate with them in phys. ed., art, music, and during recess and lunchtime make the friends that are so critical for second-language learning (not to mention, for happiness). But she will need to work with her reading and math peers in those skill areas. This might necessitate going for math and reading to the first-grade classroom or to the school's learning or resource center (if the school has one), or working one-on-one with a tutor, with resource assistance, or with part-time ESL support. Pulling her out of class or separating her for special help is, admittedly, not the ideal situation, but does offer a balance that responds to her varied needs. Some elementary schools coordinate their "centers," having reading and math at the same time throughout the school. In this way, students can move from center to center according to their needs without missing out on other classroom activities.

At the secondary level

The placements of Boris and Newton involve other considerations. For the same reasons outlined previously, both students would benefit from placement in the grades appropriate to their ages with careful selection of the classes they take. There is some leeway in placement depending on (1) whether there is an ESL teacher and (2) what tests reveal about Boris's and Newton's skills.

If the school has an ESL teacher, Boris and Newton could be placed in an ESL classroom or with the ESL teacher for one or two hours a day. If there is no ESL specialist, then other arrangements—aides, peer tutors, and/or volunteers—will have to be made.

If Boris and Newton can understand, read, and write English, consider placing them in regular classes all day with some support from tutors during study periods or after school. Here are some course options:

- Math, a course where ESL students tend to do well, because it is, in many ways, "language and culture" free.

- Science, a "hands-on" course with many opportunities for ESL students to watch and participate with their classmates.

- Art, which allows non-English speakers to express themselves in ways other than the verbal.

- Music, particularly choir, which relies on a great deal of repetition and provides an emotional outlet.

- Phys. ed., which is in many ways language-free (in games such as football or basketball, verbal instructions are "context embedded," that is, the activities are rich in visual cues, and the language the student hears or the instructions given are accompanied by gestures and demonstration).

English is the most important class for instruction in reading and writing. Although we insist elsewhere that reading and writing should take place in all classes, this class is the one in which ESL students will receive the most direction in the acquisition of English skills. In language arts, students must be involved in more than simply learning language; they must learn how to use language to learn. According to Chamot and O'Malley (1986), ESL students need to learn study skills that help them succeed in content areas in which course concepts—not the language—are the focus.

For Boris and Newton, courses such as history and social sciences should be added later. These courses are "context reduced"—the students cannot rely as much on visual cues to determine the meaning of the content matter. What is more, these subjects require a great deal of reading. When Newton and Boris have gained more English proficiency, these courses can be added.

If ESL students' skills are poor, or they come to school illiterate, then remedial help in some form is the only alternative. In Newton's situation, extra help is probably needed. He will need time to adjust, gain fluency, and complete his required course work. He can take grade nine and/or grade ten courses without shame, and catch up as his proficiency grows. Some school districts have implemented five-year programs for their ESL students. As some students don't begin to function in class for a year or more, a five-year plan allows them the time they need.

Be sure to consult parents about placement. Many feel strongly that their son or daughter should be placed with their age-mates; others will go along with whatever recommendations you make, as long as they are based on sound assessments. Some parents may even want their child placed a grade ahead, believing that the schools in their country of origin are academically ahead of the new school. That's what Boris's family thought. They argued that the schooling in his country was of such rigor that he would be bored and, should they go back, he would be a year behind in his studies.

Placement, then, is a tricky business. Each placement should be dealt with on an individual basis, taking into consideration the student, his schooling history, his parents' wishes, and what administered tests reveal about his skills.

Assessment Through Testing

Testing is a complex and difficult issue. At the risk of oversimplifying matters, we have established some basic guidelines to help you through the maze of testing procedures and jargon.

Many commercially produced tests are on the market. Some common ones are the LAS (Language Assessment Scale); the BINL (Basic Inventory of Natural Language); the BSM (Bilingual Syntax Measure); and the IPT (Idea Proficiency Test). Others are also available.

Deciding Which Test to Use

Language competency is a very murky area—it is difficult to measure scientifically. Whether or not standardized tests are valid is a matter of controversy. Reliable tests should

- Demonstrate who should be labeled ESL, i.e., who are in need of language services because their English proficiency is low.

- Be consistent. If one test shows Boris needs ESL services, it should be possible to corroborate this by other tests.

- Highlight skills students have mastered, thereby predicting the students' ability to succeed in regular academic programs.

- Identify the students' specific linguistic and academic needs. Do they speak well, but need help in writing? Do they write well, but speak haltingly?

- Tell you the students' proficiency levels with the various skills: what grade level they read at, how much they can write, what vocabulary they know, and how much they understand.

- Have "high content validity"—do these tests measure what they claim to measure? Often, the validity of tests is confounded by the language proficiency of the test-taker.

You may have heard complaints about commercially produced assessment tests: that they are useless—or worse! We feel it is important for you to understand why these complaints are often based on reality. Frequently, the test results are ambiguous or incorrect; they do not accurately reflect students' English language abilities. These tests fail for one or more of the following reasons:

Why Tests Fail

■ Many of the tests are culturally biased. One test asks students to identify pictures of an elephant, a dinosaur, a submarine, and a watermelon. Hnuku might not know the English word for *house* or *table*, but at least she has them in her own language and understands them because of her own life experience. Unless she has seen a watermelon or a submarine (even in pictures), she does not have the equivalent in her own language. Asking her to identify something she has never seen or experienced is not a fair measure of her English vocabulary.

■ Many tests are linguistically biased—the instructions are not translated into the appropriate language. For example, when the instructions, "When you hear two words on the tape tell me if they sound the same or different," are not translated into Amharic, or Hungarian, or Urdu, you have no way of telling whether your new students actually understood what they were to do—if their answers accurately reflect what they know, or if they are a response to their inaccurate perception of the instructions.

■ Some tests are too ambiguous; you cannot determine exactly what they are telling you about your students' competence. For example, if Newton leaves blanks on a cloze test is it because (1) he did not know the appropriate vocabulary word in English, (2) he did not know the grammatical structure of the word he wanted to use, or (3) he did not understand the context of the sentences he was to complete?

■ Other tests, because they include testing on very small discrete points, giving equal scoring weight to these sections, do not give the speaker from another culture a chance to show what he can do in English. For instance, one tests the students' ability to distinguish between minimal pairs and phonemes, the discrimination between the smallest units of sound in English, such as /v/ and /b/ or /sh/ and /ch/. This will only tell you which sounds a student does or does not hear. Knowing that Charlie cannot distinguish between *very* and *berry* is of little use to you and of negligible importance in the overall task of learning the language.

■ Many tests have arbitrary cut-off scores, so they don't necessarily measure students' competency. For example, they might state that a score below 80 percent indicates that the student functions at the "limited proficiency" level. The companies that design these tests use nice, round figures because they are easy to work with. However, there is no direct relationship between the score and the student's actual ability level. Newton may score 81 percent on the test, above the test's stated limited proficiency level, but in actuality may function on a limited basis in English. In a similar vein, Boris may achieve a grade of 100 percent on a test and still not be able to compete with his English-speaking classmates. The test may measure Boris's skill "at a fourth-grade level," but it does not measure Boris's ability to cope in the classroom.

- Many tests provide incomplete information. Commercial tests should be used only to provide guidelines for placement and to determine if an incoming student will require ESL or bilingual services. These tests are designed to differentiate between those who have enough English to function in the classroom and those who are truly limited in their English. Not all foreign students are ESL students, nor are all Native Americans. (Boris might actually know enough English to keep up with his English-speaking classmates.) Use these tests to help with placement, and go elsewhere to find more specific answers to your questions on how well a student reads or writes.

Supplemental Tests

Although you are required to use one standardized test, in the U.S. supplemental tests can be developed to find out other information that teachers really need to know. These supplemental tests should be given by the classroom teacher as this is the person who requires the information.

Individual students' proficiency levels in listening, speaking, reading, and writing vary depending upon their experiences in North America and their own countries. Some might have advanced speaking and listening skills, but poor reading and writing skills. Others might be proficient in reading and writing, but will be able to understand little spoken English or speak well enough to be understood by others. Therefore, you need to test all skills to determine how much your student knows. For example,

Can Charlie speak any English? How much does he understand?

If it is established that Boris has some literacy in English, can he handle the classroom assignments?

Can Hnuku read and write?

What specific areas does Newton need help with?

Once you have this information, you can decide the course of your instruction and monitor your students' progress. All four language skill areas—listening, speaking, reading, and writing—must be tested.

Testing Hints

Before testing, you must have a list of things your students need to know. In the Student Vocabulary Test (appendix C), we list some survival words and concepts that are important; you can start with these. But vocabulary is just the beginning; you also want to discover whether students can understand and produce extended discourse-speech beyond the word and sentence level. Students' proficiency refers both to their knowledge of the language and their ability to use it.

- Try to make test situations as low-key and stress free as possible. Put your students at ease. Take the time to explain why you are testing them and why you are taking notes; some students will be nervous anyway, but this helps to create a less threatening atmosphere.

- Don't take students away from the class for testing when their classmates are involved in "fun" activities.

- When testing, try to ask students to do at least one thing they can succeed at. If students can't get through the oral section of the test, don't assume they will be unable to do the written section. Many students who have studied English in school in their country of origin can read and write much better than they speak (and often put native-English speakers to shame with their knowledge of grammar).

- Stop testing when the students indicate fatigue or frustration. You can always come back to do another segment later.

Testing Listening Comprehension

Test your students' "receptive proficiency"—how much English they understand. When testing identification of vocabulary, we suggest the following:

- Use real objects as much as possible. For example, use a desk rather than a picture of a desk.

- Use photographs (cut out of magazines or catalogs), not drawings or paintings. Many children, even those from literate North American families, cannot make sense of little whimsical figures or line drawings. Students from nonliterate cultures often have great difficulty making a connection between what they see in real life and two-dimensional drawings or paintings.

- Using photographs, ask test questions about things that are fairly universal, such as boys, girls, children, trees, clouds, and so on, not about culturally laden objects such as hamburgers.

- Ask only one question at a time—don't combine questions. Test for colors, then shapes, but not both at the same time. Have the student look over a page of colored squares, then ask, for instance, "Which is the red square? Which is the blue square?" Don't ask complex questions like, "Where is the red triangle?" then "Where is the black pen?"

- Use simple commands. Find out if they can understand simple sentences so that they can follow classroom instructions. In appendix C, items 12 and 17, we list a number of commands they will be expected to know.

Testing Oral Language Ability

Spontaneous speech will elicit a language sample that is most representative of your students' oral language ability. This is best accomplished through an informal interview. Many students are shy and self-conscious, so you need to think carefully about how to elicit speech. While working in several programs that needed a "fast sorting" mechanism to determine oral language proficiency, Barb devised a series of questions designed to elicit an increasingly sophisticated command of the language:

What is your name? Simple fact. This is an easy one and shows interest in the student. But it isn't always that easy. Several students Barb was working with had chosen their own English names from a book. Horace, who was an extremely naughty little boy, didn't pronounce his name correctly, nor did he write it in a form that enabled us to guess what name he really intended (he spelled it Hosense). He also did not recognize "Horace" when he was called upon. It was frustrating to be shouting at a child who was flailing at another boy, when he didn't even know he was the one being yelled at. But if they understand and can answer, they have at least some English.

How old are you? Another simple fact question. However, if the student answers, "I'm fine," you can tell the limitations of his English. This answer usually means the student has memorized an answer to a question he has been taught and is not listening to the sense of the question, but is picking up parts of it.

When is your birthday? This can tell you, in many cases, the level of the student's English proficiency. In other cases, the student may simply not know, which can be an indicator of gaps in education, cultural difference, problems in transition, or lack of linguistic and cognitive input. Spencer, for instance, did not know when his birthday was; he knew that his birthday came when the weather was warm. His family life had been extremely disrupted and he had moved often. Not knowing his birthdate was perhaps understandable at the age of five. But when he moved into another district at the age of twelve, he still could not tell the teacher.

Tell me about your family. Again, this question demonstrates interest on your part and gives students a topic that they are familiar with and have feelings about. The complexity of a student's answer gives you an indication of his level of functioning. Angel, for instance, looked confused by the question and answered, "I am little English." This revealed that she was just a beginner and the question was too complex for her. Florien, on the other hand, talked confidently and enthusiastically about his two older sisters and his younger brother, revealing his command of the language.

What would you do if...? This conditional and much more advanced question requires speculation on the part of the student. When Barb was in California she would ask, "What would you do if you saw a bear coming through the door?" Often she would have to mime a bear. If the question was greeted with a shrug, she knew the student didn't understand. If a smile appeared on the face of the child, she knew she had communicated. Answers that revealed understanding ranged from "run" to "I would go RARRRR! and run away." Another possible question to be used in a school is "What would you do if the school caught on fire?"

It doesn't take much more than that to get a sense of how conversant a student is in our language. In fact, it's so informal and so deceptively simple, it's possible to overlook the richness of the information you can get. If you take the attention away from yourself and the "testing" situation and put the child at ease, you can glean a great deal of information.

Testing Reading Proficiency

First, you need to find out if the student can read at all. Once it has been established that the student is literate, you can determine his level of proficiency.

Although the home language survey should have given you a good indication of the students' level of education, confirm this by giving him something like the written instructions for a writing sample. Place the instructions sideways on the table. If he turns the paper right side up so that the words can be read, he is probably literate. Now ask the student to write his name, watching to see how he does it. If he holds his pen awkwardly and writes with difficulty, the student probably has little experience with reading or writing.

Give the student a brief questionnaire similar to the home language survey (appendix B) that asks for name, address, date of birth, and age, as well as some personal questions, such as those in the oral language assessment. (See appendix D for an example.) The way in which the student answers the questions and fills in the blanks will enable you to make rough assessments of reading and writing skills.

The following tests each focus on specific areas of language acquisition and should be given by the teacher. While these tests are helpful when trying to determine an appropriate grade level, they by no means provide definitive results. They are most useful for the teacher who must plan short- and long-term learning objectives for the students. Again, observation of the student while taking the tests is invaluable.

Story Retelling

If you have been trained in miscue analysis, you can use it with your student. If not, you can have the student read a story by himself, then retell the story to you. His retelling will give you a fairly accurate picture of how much he has understood. As with the oral retelling test, you may have to help the student with prompts. Once again, key questions that lead, but don't give the answers away are useful.

We don't recommend having students read the story aloud to you for several reasons:

- Reading aloud is a separate skill.
- Being required to read aloud when they are unsure about their reading skills and may be self-conscious about their accents makes the situation uncomfortable. It can often cause students to pay more attention to their pronunciation than their understanding.
- Students' oral mistakes often don't reflect their comprehension. Many students who make errors may actually be able to understand the majority of the story.

■ As the test-giver, it is easy to get frustrated and be tempted to jump in and help when you listen to students trying to read a passage aloud. It is best to avoid this situation.

The following example contains a story retelling by a high school student whose first exposure to reading was in English. Somaly read *Jacki* by Elizabeth Rice, a story about a cat who raises a baby rabbit with her kittens. The rabbit thinks she is a kitten too until she sees another rabbit, a "stranger," hanging around the barnyard. After seeing her reflection in a water trough, the little rabbit discovers that she is like the stranger, and when she sees him again, knows it is time to leave with him and lead a rabbit's life.

Somaly's retelling:

Story about a mother cat was one. He had her baby born—you know— coming out from her. Then about one week or two week they try to open their eye. And then a mother cat had seen rabbit—the little rabbit—and she took her home and living with her family together. You know, and then they live at—in a mother cat home together and rabbit be a cat baby too. And then one cat and one rabbit that stay on the new "starger"—it kind of thing different you know—rabbit and cat stand in the moonlight and they looking something in the moonlight and they saw it. That's it!

Somaly understood the story line about a cat adopting a little rabbit into its family of kittens. She remembered the details of the kittens opening their eyes and the mother finding the baby rabbit. However, from the point in the story where the "stranger" is introduced, Somaly lost the thread. She was not able to guess the meaning from the context, so she did not understand that the "stranger" was another rabbit. She "fudges" in her retelling: "starger—it kind of thing different you know" and tiptoes around the ending.

Somaly demonstrated she had understood many parts of the story. She also showed some language skills when she retold part of the plot involving the rabbit's relationship with the cats. Somaly's retelling would allow the assessor to see that she had some basic reading skills, but that she would need much more reading practice and vocabulary exposure to develop those skills. This information would help her teacher find a starting point for class work.

Story retelling requires that students use English to repeat the story they've heard or read. As their poor speaking skills may not allow them to communicate what they actually understood, the tester must keep in mind that story retelling is not a precise measuring instrument, only a tool that will provide some insight into students' reading abilities.

Testing Writing Proficiency

Writing samples help determine students' ability to communicate coherently in writing.

Obtaining and assessing a spontaneous writing sample, which reflects the student's genuine response to a subject he has an interest in or experience with, is the best way to assess the writing ability of students.

Give students several topics to choose from and a set amount of writing time (fifteen minutes for younger students; thirty minutes for older students). Topics might include writing about "Something you like to do," "Your family," "Your first day in this school," or "Something frightening that happened to you." (See chapter 6, "Writing," for a more detailed discussion of writing assignments.)

Your scoring criteria for this sample should be prioritized beginning with the most important writing skills—those that involve communicating the message—and ending with mechanics. It is easy to be dismayed by a paper filled with grammatical or spelling errors, but these surface errors should not outweigh more critical factors.

The following writing samples are from students who came from Taiwan to take a summer school course in English (figure 2.2-6). They had studied English formally in an after-school program for varying lengths of time. Their work samples were chosen as examples because the students are all roughly the same age, but display very different skill levels in both speaking and writing. Please note that the questions we asked were specifically geared to their experiences; we had learned beforehand that they would be touring the Southwest prior to their arrival at the school, and we could gear our questions, including the writing sample, to those experiences. Also note that we changed the questions, partly in response to their varying levels, but also because we found that we were getting less proficient students giving the exact same answers as more proficient students. This led us to conclude that those who went before were coaching the ones who came after! Test anxiety was running high.

James

- What's your name? *My name is James.*
- How old are you? *Hello.*
- How long have you studied English? *Yes.*
- Tell me about your family. *I don't know.*
- (We skipped the last question because it would be too confusing.)

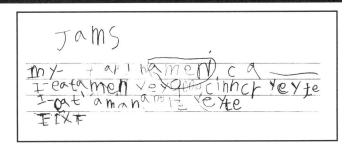

Hereafter, he was affectionately known as "Jams." It is obvious that Jams is a beginning writer and speaker of English. His sentences are almost unreadable. The letter formation is awkward and elementary. The letters don't always rest on the line, and words do not always have spaces between them, demonstrating that he has not had much practice yet. There is little organization and only a few recognizable English words. But he does know how to write English letters, and one sentence, which looks like "I eat many very good things," shows an understanding of English syntax.

Content
- Topic is not fully developed
- Two specific details are provided

Organization
- Opening sentence is included

Vocabulary
- James uses a few words correctly. Most others are not distinguishable.

Language Skills
- Many errors, no evidence of knowledge of past tense
- Very basic sentence structure: I + verb

Mechanics
- No punctuation

Level
- Ranked as a beginner

Figure 2.2

Royal

- What's your name? *Royal*
- How old are you? *12*
- How long have you studied English? *2 years*
- Tell me three things you like about California? *Here is very good.*
- If you saw a bear in the window what would you do? *(Shrugged)*

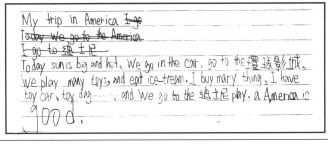

Royal shows experience with English. He uses a very good strategy of writing the Chinese for words he hasn't learned in English. This demonstrates his mastery of his native language and is a valuable clue for testers, even if they are not fluent in the other language. His answers are relatively simple, but he pays attention to detail, lists a number of things, and shows organization.

Content
- Topic is developed
- Specific details are provided
- Description given

Organization
- Opening sentence is included
- Very orderly, moved from one example to the next
- Transitions used
- Closing sentence is included

Vocabulary
- Effective word choices made and correct use of word forms

Language Skills
- Royal sticks to the present tense
- Grammar is simple but accurate
- Little sentence variety used

Mechanics
- No spelling errors made
- Has control of most punctuation (commas, periods)

Level
- Royal is a beginner, but shows more skills than Jams and can be asked to complete more difficult tasks

Figure 2.3

Matty

- What's your name? *Matty*
- How old are you? *12*
- How long have you studied English? *five or six years*
- Tell me three things you like about California? *no answer*
- If you saw a bear in the window what would you do? *no answer*

Matty's oral skills are not much better than Royal's. She wrote less, but demonstrated, through her writing, a better command of English. Her sentences are more complex. She uses sophisticated connectors such as *so* and *but* correctly.

Content
- Topic is somewhat developed
- Specific details are provided
- No description given

Organization
- Opening sentence is included
- One transition (*than*)

Vocabulary
- Effective word choices made and correct use of word forms

Language Skills
- There is overall control of agreement, etc.
- Good sentence variety used
- Effective use of word forms, connectors

Mechanics
- No spelling errors
- Commas and periods used correctly

Level
- Tentatively placed in a level higher than Royal

Figure 2.4

Lady

- What's your name? *Lady*
- How old are you? *12 years old*
- Why do you choose the name "Lady?" *Because my teacher call me Lady all the time.*
- What do you like about California? *I like Los Angeles. They have many many funny things and many people.*
- If you saw a bear in the window what would you do? *Climb up tree and loud help me.*

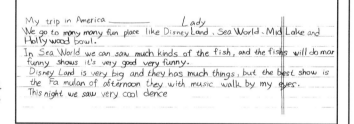

Lady wrote much more than the others. She uses connectors such as *and* and *but*, creating complex sentences. She uses adjectives such as *many, funny,* and *cool*. This shows a much broader range of English experience and proficiency than the others.

Content
- Topic is well developed
- Specific details are provided
- Adequate description given

Organization
- Opening sentence is included
- Very orderly, moved from one example to the next
- Transitions used

Vocabulary
- Effective word choices made and correct use of word forms

Language Skills
- Mostly sticks to present tense
- One grammar error (*can saw*), but there is overall control of agreement, etc.
- Good sentence variety used
- Effective use of word forms

Mechanics
- No spelling errors made
- Has control of punctuation

Level
- She has reached a level of proficiency at which she can be expected to do grade level work with assistance

Figure 2.5

Alice

- What's your name? *Alice*
- How old are you? *12 years old*
- Are you glad to be back? *Yes*
- What do you like about California? *Traffic is very good in California, the air is good. Here is so cold.*
- If you got lost what would you do? *To go to ask a policeman.*

My trip in America is very funny. we go to very good place, last week, we go to seaworld, in there, have many fish and fish show. we play very happy. I want to go there again. And we go to disniland. we saw mickey, oh! god! is so so funny. And we go to hollewood. in there has E.T. ...... many many. last day. we go to shopping. we cost many money to buy something. toys. is so quit. And I like here, here is very good. Los Angeles is a good city. The trfic is so good. The air is trible. but is better than Talwain. Twain's trfic and air is very bad. Yestoday, we go to shopping move. there is so big. and some body is get lost. There sails many so things. And afternoon we go to this summer camp

One can tell by the length of her essay that Alice has a good deal of proficiency. Compared to Jams' paper, for instance, it is obvious how much more practice she's had in forming her letters and writing in this language. She does not need to insert Chinese characters where she doesn't know the English word. She exhibits voice in her writing when she talks about seeing Mickey Mouse and compares America to Taiwan.

Content

- Topic is developed
- Specific details are provided
- Adequate description given

Organization

- Opening sentence is included
- Very orderly, moved from one example to the next
- Transitions used
- Closing sentence is included

Vocabulary

- Effective word choices made and correct use of word forms

Language Skills

- One grammar error is made, but there is overall control of agreement, etc.
- Good sentence variety used
- Effective use of word forms
- Her own voice shows through the writing

Mechanics

- A few minor spelling errors made (*sails, trfc, trible*)
- Good control of most punctuation
- Very good description given

Level

- Alice is capable of much more difficult and challenging tasks than Jams and Royal. She needs less ESL intervention from the teacher and needs less accommodation in terms of language. Alice has begun to approximate what we might expect from a native-English seventh grader (in fact, she has done better than many)

Figure 2.6

Making Use of Test Scores

The standardized assessment tests, in addition to the school's own supplemental tests, can provide information about what your students are capable of understanding and producing. However, it is unrealistic to think that scores from these tests will tell you everything you need to know about the new students. The main purpose of the test is to give the teacher a sense of how to begin to plan for the newcomers in the classroom.

Categorizing Students

The State of Wisconsin has defined English proficiency in terms of both oral and reading proficiency. We believe this is of singular importance. We have seen, too many times, students exited from programs solely on the basis of their oral proficiency. They enter regular classrooms, flounder, and often fail because they have not achieved academic language proficiency. As we have stated earlier, the labels students are given (NES, LES, LEP, FEP) are frequently inaccurate and do not take into account each student as an individual. We believe the following "Levels" are more useful. They allow you to prescribe goals and objectives for your students based upon their English competency. If you feel overwhelmed by all the data the test scores generate, but need a place to start your planning, you can begin with these definitions:

Level I

Students in this level do not understand, speak, read, or write in English with any degree of fluency, but may know a few words or expressions in English.

Strategy: These students need a great deal of support. They need to learn survival English to

- Function in the school environment.
- Understand routines and rules.
- Function in everyday situations.
- Adapt to climate.
- Adapt to a new culture.
- Understand holidays.

Oral skills

- Begin conversations.
- Communicate needs.
- Follow directions.

Reading Skills

- Recognize the alphabet.
- Begin literacy activities.

The ESL support teacher (if you have one), can coordinate with you and work on beginning reading skills, background and concept building, and vocabulary. Assimilate these students into the school routine. Use one-on-one tutoring, "buddies," and concrete vocabulary. Chapter 5, "Reading," lists many strategies for students such as Hnuku and Jams; although Jams is very low, he is much higher than Hnuku.

Note: See appendix E for an example of a checklist designed specifically to assess emerging readers.

At the high-school level, the student derives little benefit from being in mainstream classrooms such as social studies, science, and so on. At this level, oral and reading skills are too low to understand the language of the classroom. The student would benefit from intensive work with an ESL teacher and classes that build basic core vocabulary.

Level II

Students in this level understand simple sentences in English, but speak only isolated words and expressions. Students are at an emergent level of reading and writing in English.

Strategy: These students need less intensive support than students at Level I and know more basic knowledge that we take for granted. Students usually have BICS (Basic Interpersonal Language Skills). Students benefit only minimally from regular classroom instruction without a great deal of support. If you have bilingual support, they can continue working in the first language, building concepts and vocabulary, as well as skills in the second. Students can be mainstreamed for art, math, and so on. Students need to learn content and reading. At the secondary levels, students would benefit from learning the same content material at a pace geared to their language skills.

Level III

The students understand and speak conversational and academic English with hesitancy and difficulty. With effort and assistance, students can carry on conversations in English, understand at least parts of lessons, and follow simple directions, but make noticeable errors in grammar. These students are at a beginning level of reading and writing in English and need assistance in reading/writing in content to achieve at an appropriate level for their age and grade.

Strategy: Students at this level are usually able to function in the classroom, but need considerable assistance, especially in the content areas. Students need a wide variety of learning experiences that stimulate and encourage language use. The emphasis of your instruction should be on moving students closer to grade level. Your academic expectations should be higher than those placed on Level I and Level II students.

Level IV

The students understand and speak conversational English without apparent difficulty, but understand and speak academic English with some difficulty. These students are at an intermediate level of reading and writing in English.

Strategy: Cognitive academic language development is essential for success in content areas. Oral language proficiency, by itself, is not an accurate measure of holistic language proficiency nor is it a predictor of academic success. In the high school, these students can be mainstreamed for classes such as science and held accountable for schoolwork in art, math, and science. Students still need help and support.

Level V

Students understand and speak conversational and academic English well, but need assistance in reading and writing in content areas to achieve at a level appropriate for their age or grade.

Strategy: Fully mainstreamed with extra help as appropriate. Even at this level, students are not free from error or free from lack of background knowledge and/or gaps in reading skills.

Full English Proficiency

Students understand, speak, read, and write English, and possess thinking and reasoning skills to succeed in academic classes at or above their age or grade level.

Complete proficiency in English can take a long time. Collier (1989) speculates that it can take as long as seven years. Staying on top of what your students know, and balancing their needs with your high expectations, can move them forward to success.

Note: In appendix F we give a detailed form to use when rating writing samples. A student whose writing sample receives the "beginner" rating in any of the five categories is significantly limited in his or her ability to write English.

Follow-up

Be prepared to informally re-evaluate ESL students as they become familiar with the school and class routine. Because students are often apprehensive about tests, or feel inhibited in a new environment, their abilities in English may seem weaker than they are. They often show their true colors only after they relax and feel more secure. You may find you have to adjust your materials up a level or two as your students adjust to the daily routine.

Note: To demonstrate how to plan a course of instruction, we have included sample IEP (Individualized Educational Plan) forms for the students we have used as examples. (See appendix G.)

Conclusion

Testing and placement are issues with lots of "gray areas"—no clear-cut, foolproof answers. Remember that evaluation of test results must be based on the particular student being assessed. Be prepared to be flexible. We have attempted to provide some guidelines, but most decisions must be made on a case-by-case basis, depending on what you and your administrators, the students, and their parents feel are best.

LANGUAGE LEARNING— STUDENTS AND TEACHERS

In this chapter, we discuss principles of second-language learning. We focus on

- What we know about language learning.
- A quality program—the factors that influence how fast and how well a newcomer learns English.
- Behavior and what affects it.
- Facilitating cultural adjustment in the classroom.
- Teaching strategies that help to maximize learning.

A Comparison of Two Language Programs

We wanted this chapter to be more than a simple presentation of facts and theories, so we decided to illustrate the principles of second-language learning in the form of an anecdotal history of Barb's experience as an elementary and secondary level ESL teacher. Although much of the discussion centers on her experiences at the lower levels, the principles can be applied to the secondary level as well.

For three years Barb taught ESL in a small midwestern town adjacent to a large university. The foreign population in the university's married housing complexes was so large that each "village" had its own elementary school with its own resident ESL teacher. Barb was responsible for ESL in all the other schools in the district—five elementary and two middle schools.

With twenty-five to thirty students in eight grades in seven different schools, Barb had only limited time available to spend with each student— pulling the younger children out of their regular classes for perhaps an hour and a half each week, the middle schoolers for an hour each day. With such limited access to an ESL specialist, each student was integrated within the classroom working alongside his classmates. When the newcomer could not keep up with his English-speaking peers, Barb would supply the teacher with supplemental activities to keep him busy. All students were mainstreamed and took part in regular classroom activities as best they could.

Although the pull-out program had its drawbacks—particularly as the students had limited time with a trained ESL teacher and were mainstreamed immediately without any survival English—the students, by and large, did very well. The teachers worked hard to provide them with the best opportunities for learning English.

During her third year, Barb was transferred to a position as full-time ESL teacher at one of the university housing-village schools. This school, instead of using the same kind of pull-out program found in the other district schools, had implemented a self-contained classroom. All ESL children needing assistance spent half the day there, returning to their classrooms in the afternoon for math, phys. ed., music, and art.

On the surface, this program looked ideal. There were several positive features:

- All ESL children were given half a day in the self-contained classroom to work specifically on their English.

- Class size was considerably reduced for regular teachers by having the ESL children spend the morning with another teacher. Thus, classroom teachers could concentrate on their English-speaking students without being held back by children who did not have the understanding to keep up with the mandated curriculum. They were not burdened by the extra preparation and explanation time required when working with ESL children.

- The ESL students were able to work with a teacher who was specially trained in teaching ESL. This appeared to be preferable to remaining in a class for most of the day with a teacher untrained in ESL methodology.

- The ESL classroom provided a safe haven for the children, with a teacher who could give attention to their needs. It was a place just for them, where they could feel secure, wanted, and cherished, rather than being lost in the crowd competing against children who could speak the language of instruction.

This school's program is similar to many others, and many schools searching for ways to meet the needs of ESL students find it an appealing option. A teacher with a third or more of her students unable to speak English is faced with a double load: trying to meet the needs of both groups, but at the same time being required to finish the mandated curriculum by June.

Although there were many positive features to this program, there were also many negative effects due to the reality of the classroom situation.

- Barb was responsible for more than thirty-three children, from grades one through five, from nine different language groups: Spanish, French, Portuguese, Chinese, Japanese, Korean, Hindi, Farsi, and Indonesian. Some, like first-grader Guillermo, had been in the country for over a year, having come to school as a kindergarten student. Others, like fifth-grader Chatphet, arrived in the middle of November, having spent five years in an Indonesian school. Six-year-old Vaji was slow to catch on to the concept of reading though she spoke well. Ten-year-old Helga, a smart aggressive learner, was ready to take on content material in the new language. Third-grader Yoichiro could read well in Japanese, but resented being in America and fought against learning any English. Quiet, gentle second-grader Laban, who could read Chinese, rarely spoke, but made the transition from Chinese to English with stunning ease.

This range in age, in needs, and in students' ability to speak and read in English made planning extremely difficult. Thirty-three students meant thirty-three different challenges. Grouping was the obvious answer. But how? According to age? Competence in speaking? Grade level in reading? And what would Barb teach them? How to say hello? What an umbrella was? Colors? Helga and Chatphet were going on to the middle school the following year. Spending time making cut-outs of umbrellas on a rainy day was a waste of their valuable time. They needed to do more than learn only grammar or vocabulary. Barb needed to fill in the academics that were being missed while they were away from their classroom, because a year spent learning only English was a year lost to subject matter.

Barb had two bilingual aides, Spanish-speaking Emma and Midori from Japan. Both were intelligent, dedicated women who worked hard to make the atmosphere pleasant and the learning experience a successful one for each child. Neither, however, was a native-English speaker, and neither spoke perfect English. This meant that for the majority of the day, the children listened to English spoken either by their classmates who had not fully learned English, or by adults, two of whom had not fully mastered English either. The models the children were exposed to were not adequate or appropriate for their needs.

The friendships that formed in the ESL class extended to the playground and after school. For example, Japanese boys played only with each other, talking in Japanese. Several of the little girls in the class made friends, but only communicated in rudimentary English sentences, which were rarely extended and enriched by exposure to the English of their peers.

The solution to meeting the needs of all students was grouping, which was a compromise between age, reading ability, and language competence. However, since each child was working at a different level, all needed constant supervision. The student-teacher ratio was about eight to one, larger than the optimum ratio for a situation such as this when each student was working on a different level.

Most important, these children were isolated, segregated from their peers, away from the mainstream for that portion of the day when most of the content and skill development took place, listening only to their teachers and the imperfect English of other newcomers. Lack of access to fluent English models significantly slowed both their English acquisition and their assimilation. The process of acquiring enough "coping" English took much longer.

What We Know About Language Learning

Even though the self-contained program was set up with the best of intentions, the teachers who originated and supported it were operating under certain assumptions that run counter to what we know about language acquisition. We have outlined some of these ESL learning myths:

Incorrect Assumptions

- Language must be taught.

- Input in the new language must be sequenced and carefully controlled.

- The language teacher is in the best position to decide what vocabulary and concepts to introduce, and when to do so.

- Newcomers need to master English before they can learn any subject matter.

- Once students have learned the language of instruction—in this case, English—their problems in the classroom are largely over, and they should be able to handle their academic assignments with no difficulty.

- Regular classroom teachers are not equipped to give their ESL students the best opportunities for language learning.

Research Results

In the past twenty years or so, a great deal of research has been done on first-language and second-language acquisition. This research has revealed that

- The second language is learned best when the setting is natural. Communication is a two-way street; there is a speaker who has something to say and a listener who wants to hear it. Without these three components—speaker, listener, and message—there is no communication. Learning a language is much more than just learning the vocabulary or the grammatical rules; it's knowing how and when to use those rules— even in ordinary conversation. This may seem self-evident, but much of the second-language teaching that has gone on in schools ignores this fact and teaches only vocabulary and rules. The result is students who can conjugate verbs, but cannot carry on a simple conversation.

- Students learn from their peers. Because the use of language is first and foremost a social activity, students learn best from those they work, live, and play with every day. They learn to make sentences and interact in order to meet their social needs: to make friends, to be included in games, to express themselves. No matter how dedicated and resourceful the teacher is, she cannot provide the kind of input that learners need so that they can learn how to use the language in real-life situations. The language that students learn from their peers is a *living* language; they have learned it only by and through communicating within situations that are important to them.

- Although second-language learners usually learn certain forms in a set order (such as the *-ing* ending on verbs before they learn the articles *a*, *an*, *the*), presenting language in a sequence (such as the present tense first, then the past tense) is *not* the most effective way of teaching. This method ignores the needs of learners by limiting their exposure to as much grammar and vocabulary as can be easily presented and practiced at one time. Students may need to say things such as, "I took my mother to the doctor yesterday, so I couldn't come to school," or, "I am going back to Mexico for a few weeks. I'll be back after Christmas." They may need to comprehend advanced language forms such as "If you don't hand in all your assignments, you'll get an F." Sequencing forms rigidly, teaching structures one at a time, and proceeding only when the structure is learned (the way many of us were taught foreign languages) limits students' ability to function within all the situations they might encounter.

- A new language is learned best when the primary focus is on the meaning, not the form. In other words, students learn how to make friends, satisfy their own needs, and learn new things by *using* the language, not by perfecting grammatical forms (such as tenses) one at a time. Learners make mistakes; this is a natural part of learning anything. However, with practice, they gradually get better at figuring out the rules. Communication comes first, then grammatical rules are learned as a part of learning to communicate effectively, not the other way around.

- Non-native-English speakers do not need to master English by studying it formally as an isolated activity before they can begin regular class work. Language should be learned through content material as long as the material is understandable.

- There is a misperception that speaking English well will equip ESL students to handle regular class work. Research has shown this is not necessarily so. It often takes five to seven years to achieve sufficient fluency in academic English to compete on a par with other English-speaking students. To hold students in ESL classes or special programs until they are fully proficient in all areas is unrealistic, impractical, and, in the end, impossible.

- Although support from bilingual or ESL personnel is helpful and important, it is not enough. The classroom teacher, provided she employs appropriate methods for teaching non-English speakers, and supplies both understandable situations and opportunities for the student to interact with classmates, is a key factor in the success of the ESL student.

A Quality Program

The two programs Barb taught—the pull-out program and the self-contained ESL classroom—were vastly divergent solutions to the challenge of teaching ESL students. Each had positive features, but neither was ideal. The pull-out program provided small-group tutoring on gaps in learning and individual help with class work. The self-contained program attempted to deal with the linguistic needs of the students in an intensive way.

ACCELERATORS AND ROADBLOCKS TO LANGUAGE LEARNING

Accelerators	Roadblocks
It's easier when...	It's harder when...
■ The purpose of using language—reading, writing, speaking, and listening—is real and natural	■ The reasons given or situations created for using language are artificial
■ The focus is on communication	■ The focus is on the form, not on the function (communication)
■ There are lots of opportunities to talk and interact with native-English speakers	■ ESL students are isolated
■ Talk is about interesting topics	■ Talk is dull and uninteresting
■ Mistakes are part of learning	■ Mistakes are bad, and it's more important to get it right than to get a message communicated
■ Language is always used—or studied—within a context, not as isolated letters, words, or sentences	■ Language is studied out of context
■ Language has a purpose for the learner	■ The particular use of language studied or assigned is irrelevant for the learner
■ Students speak only when they're ready	■ Students are forced to speak
■ Sufficient time is provided	■ Students are pressured to complete work or make progress
■ Students can talk to each other in their own language	■ Students are not allowed to speak and converse in their native tongue
■ The first language is viewed as a valuable resource	■ The first language is not valued, is denigrated or forbidden

Figure 3.1. What we know about language learning.

Barb's experience may not be anywhere near your own. You may be teaching in a district with one or twelve students whose first language is not English. The school district might be ignoring those issues. You might be teaching in an area that has large numbers of ESL students, and the schools have mounted a full-scale program with many bilingual or ESL teachers.

But no matter how many students are in your class or district, the issues remain the same. Over the past several decades, the number of non-English-speaking students arriving in our schools has burgeoned. It will continue to increase. At this writing, students who are learning English as an additional language are the fastest-growing segment of the school age population in the United States (reported in Echevarria 2000). In 1994–1995, over 3.1 million school-aged children were identified as limited-English speaking, about 7.3 percent of the school population K–12 (reported in Waggoner 1999). In many places, one in four students are limited-English speakers. In other places, 95 percent speak little or no English. Rural areas are experiencing an influx of immigrants. School systems and community support systems are straining to meet the needs of these newcomers. We must strive to put together quality programs.

How? What constitutes a quality program? How are students' needs best met?

Handscombe (1989) writes:

> A quality program for second-language learners will neither segregate all students until they are "fit" to join their peers, nor will it place them in a regular classroom with the expectation that they will learn all they need to learn on their own….The ideal is a program that supports second language students' learning for the entire day.

What often happens in the range of choices for services—be it pull-out, push-in, self-contained, or bilingual—is that the language teacher assumes the responsibility (and the blame) for the limited-English students. The time spent with this specialist is regarded as the "real" learning time. During the remainder of the day (and we have found this, unfortunately, to be true at all levels, from kindergarten through college), the students simply mark time until they are proficient enough to participate fully in classroom activities. This happened when Barb began teaching twenty-five years ago, and, to our dismay, continues to be a major battle that is fought daily. Much of ESL teaching is simply "Band-Aid" work.

The Cooperative Roles of Language and Content Teachers

In the face of the growing population of non-English-speaking students, the traditional roles of the classroom teacher teaching content and the language teacher teaching language have become rigid, artificial, and inefficient.

What are needed are

- A common agenda.
- Partnerships between stakeholders.

In reviewing this section from our first edition, our assertion seemed, at first blush, to be hopelessly naive. However, upon reflection, and after examining others' research (Kuhlman et al. 1993; Lucas 1993, 1997; Gonzalez and Darling-Hammond 1994), we remain committed to these two foundational principles. They underlie everything else. Even though they seem simple, they are punishingly difficult to achieve. Why?

- Endless bickering between ideological factions.
- Political agendas that supercede the needs of the students.
- Inadequate attention and funding that has relegated these students to a corner and, at best, second rate status.

Regardless of the choices that are made in terms of programs, courses, and curriculum, the needs of the students *must* come first.

The entire point of educating *all* children, including immigrant children, is to prepare them to function within the larger society. Lucas (1997, 164) writes: [to] "participate fully in... business, government, and education, all residents must have a command of English... A primary goal of everyone associated with the education of immigrants and English language learners is to help them develop English skills strong enough to move into mainstream classes, where they will be integrated with native-born students and where they can participate in the regular curriculum and instruction." The majority of the contentiousness among educators and other stakeholders has been how we achieve that goal. If we keep this primary goal firmly in mind, however, perhaps we can transcend the squabbling that has crippled programs and hindered progress. The first priority should be the child. What does he need? Where is he now, in terms of learning the curriculum, of English proficiency? Where does he need to go? One size does not fit all. This means that the program model cannot take precedence over the population at hand. Any and all programs have their merits and can be successful if they are based on the particular needs of the students within that school or district.

A Common Agenda

Language is everybody's business and everybody's responsibility. This means:

- All teachers are prepared to accept and teach immigrant students.

- Classroom teachers adapt their curriculum and their teaching style to include students who are less than proficient in their English.

- Schools are responsive and flexible to the needs of these newcomers in terms of access to academic concepts and skills, time to learn English, trained personnel, and alternative and multiple pathways to achievement (Lucas 1997).

- A recognition that there is no one best way.

Partnerships Between Stakeholders

Stakeholders include the ESL teacher, the bilingual teacher, the classroom teacher, and parents. ESL and bilingual teachers can offer their expertise on language learning and second-language methodologies, while classroom teachers can offer their knowledge of the content to be covered and skills to be learned. At the elementary level, this means (unless sheer numbers preclude it), children are integrated within the classroom with their English-speaking peers, and the ESL or bilingual teacher works within that classroom or with small groups in another locale on concepts that the rest of the class is learning. In some schools, the ESL teacher team teaches with content teachers. Regular meeting and planning times are priorities to ensure that both the students' language needs and content needs are being met, and that both teachers are making maximum use of their time and energy.

High school students have needs that are different from elementary students, and they require different programs. They are making multiple transitions: from a known cultural milieu into an unfamiliar one, from childhood through adolescence into adulthood, from the protected insular one-teacher classroom of elementary school to the sometimes overwhelming array of classes at the secondary school (Lucas 1997). High school students have less time than elementary students to learn English and master the academic content required to graduate from high school (Chips 1993). Traditional high schools are often not equipped (and resistant) to adapting their structure or programs to the needs of these students. At the high school level, bilingual support, or one or more ESL classes per day is probably the minimum newcomers need at first. The ESL teacher can reinforce concepts taught in the content classes, or if trained teachers are available, content can be taught in the first language. Once again, the coordination of objectives is paramount.

In addition, partnership means collaboration within the school and outside the school: students and teachers, among students, between schools and families, with community-based organizations and institutes of higher learning. (See in particular Lucas 1997.)

Content teachers should define and identify the minimum amount of knowledge and competency a student needs to receive a passing grade for the class-knowledge of essential vocabulary and concepts (see chapter 8, "Content Area Instruction"). Armed with this knowledge, the ESL teacher can review with the students, accurately diagnosing content and language deficiencies. Language structures can be taught within the framework of these lessons, making them both usable and useful: for history classes, they can work on correct use of the past tense; for science classes, they can work on cause and effect, and *what if* questions.

One method now widely practiced is the "Sheltered English" approach.* This instructional process teaches subject matter in an understandable way to students whose English is not sufficiently proficient to manage in regular content courses. It is not "watered down" content; it is content offered at the language level of the student. History, for instance, is taught to ESL students in high school using a lower grade-level book. The ESL students study the same content as students in regular history classes do and receive credit for completing a requirement for their high school diploma. While Sheltered English is strictly for ESL students, you can use many of the strategies in your regular content-area classes without sacrificing the needs of your regular students. (We demonstrate how in chapter 8.)

---

* In California: Specially Designed Academic Instruction in English (SDAIE). For more detailed discussion of this approach see Echevarria and Graves 1998; Echevarria et al. 2000; Lucas 1997; Short in Faltis and Wolfe 1999.

Learners and Teachers

Language learning is a balance between the learner and the language-learning environment, between "input" and "intake." *Input* is the language the student hears and encounters daily. *Intake* is how much of this input the student actually processes and acquires. On the input side of the equation, there is the teacher, the amount and quality of her training, the materials and methods used, and the manner in which (and how often) the teacher corrects errors. The climate within the classroom is important: do the learners feel accepted and free to try out their new language without fear of ridicule and punishment? Another factor is the amount of exposure students get to the language: do they hear it only at school, going home to speak their native language? Do students get input only from the teacher? Or do they have English-speaking friends who will talk to them and guide them through the linguistic maze?

A teacher can provide an optimum environment and still have her students learn at different rates and with varying degrees of success. This is because so much learning is dependent on the students themselves. Regrettably, input does not necessarily equal intake.

Intake—The Learner

On the intake side, there are many factors that influence how much language the learner is able or willing to learn: factors within the learner and factors related to the learner's culture. First we will discuss several of the most important variables within the learner. The psychological factors that allow in or screen out the incoming language are called "affective filters" (Burt and Dulay 1982).

Important Factors

■ The learner's personality. Is this student outgoing and confident, or withdrawn and shy? Bounkham is very talkative and attempts to make himself understood by using gestures and examples. He is very motivated and interested in opportunities to express himself. He participates in any activity gladly, studies hard, and jumps into conversations, laughing when he stumbles or makes mistakes. Newton, on the other hand, is shy and quiet. He doesn't seem to be very active outdoors, except that he enjoys the solitary activity of riding his bike. He needs to be coaxed to talk and to become involved in activities. By the end of his first year in his new school, Bounkham is able to take part in all classroom work, while Newton is just beginning to make headway.

■ Motivation. Does the learner really want to know this new language? Andre tells his tutor time and again that he doesn't *want* to learn English. He anticipates going home very soon. His progress is very slow and he forgets what he learned the day before. Fernando, however, wants to learn English in a hurry. As the eldest son, he must help his family adjust to life in America, interpreting at the doctor's office or with the landlord, buying groceries, and paying bills. He also wants to make friends and get into the swing of things as quickly as possible, and one way to speed this process up is to learn English.

■ Age. Mary knows of one family of seven that came from Laos. The children's ages ranged from eight to thirty. They had all been in the United States for the same amount of time and had all attended English classes. The younger ones were able to speak well enough within the year to translate for the older ones. By the second year, they had little accent and were making great strides in catching up with their peers in class. The older children did not progress nearly as well.

Teachers intuitively sense—and they see this in their classes constantly—that younger learners learn better and faster. But some researchers claim that older learners are more successful over the long haul. Others, such as Stephen Krashen (1982), believe that what is operating is the difference between "acquisition versus learning." Younger children simply learn differently from older ones. Little ones acquire their second language much like they do their first: by listening, understanding, and eventually speaking—largely an unconscious process. They aren't aware that they are learning the language; they are simply aware that they are communicating. While older learners do a great deal of "acquiring" too, they also seem to need to learn language consciously, sometimes painstakingly, by learning vocabulary and the grammatical rules.

The age factor in language learning is a murky area that has not been satisfactorily clarified by experts. Partly because they are motivated to make friends and have few inhibitions about making mistakes, young children jump right into learning the new language. Older learners, however, have many other things on their minds. They have responsibilities to school and family and cannot devote the same amount of time to focus on learning. Older learners are also less willing to experiment with new forms, and more interested in "saving face," playing it safe with linguistic structures they are sure of, rather than embarrassing themselves in front of native-English speakers. Older learners also have more linguistic demands placed on them than younger ones. Young children are usually only required to communicate orally, and their language skills can grow along with their minds as they grapple with more and more sophisticated ideas. Adolescents and adults are required to use more complex types of language to coincide with the complex reasoning processes demanded by school and society. These language skills take much longer to acquire than the usual interpersonal language skills that are needed to get by on the playground or in the street.

■ State of mind. Mary had a student who came dutifully to class, never missing a day. However, soon after class got underway, Boua would rest his head on his hand unwilling to participate in class activities. If asked questions, he would politely answer with a smile but still seemed to hang on the edge of things. When Mary finally found an interpreter, she discovered that Boua had suffered head injuries fighting in his country. The bullet, still lodged in his head, caused horrendous headaches. He came to class because he wanted to learn English and felt some comfort by being able to participate, if only marginally.

How your student is feeling, how stable his life is, how preoccupied he is with emotions such as loneliness, homesickness, and culture shock, or with outside distractions such as family responsibilities, profoundly influence his ability to absorb and use the input he is receiving.

This last variable is extremely complex. Often the things that affect your student's state of mind are either beyond his control or operate at an unconscious level. These factors are so important that we have devoted the entire next section to them.

Behavior and What Affects It

Moving is difficult under any circumstance. For some of us, moving across town, away from familiar scenes and faces, can be a wrenching experience. How much more those feelings are magnified for students who come from halfway around the world! The changes ESL students have to cope with are many and great, and these can have a far-reaching effect on their assimilation.

In this section, we'll focus on the struggles of three very different students who are having trouble adjusting. One of them, Boris, you have encountered in *Assessment and ESL* (1995). In addition, we are adding Yoshi and Andre.

Boris is the son of professional people who came here with his family for religious freedom and better opportunities. He speaks Russian exclusively at home. He comes from a very rigid home and school environment. He has a large chip on his shoulder, talks out of turn, puts others down contemptuously, particularly shy Beverly and Angel, as well as Newton and Salvador. Because he's used to the imposed discipline of his native school, he cannot cope with what to him appears to be the total lack of structure in the classroom.

Andre is a refugee. His schooling was disrupted for several years in his country. He spent many years in a western state in an ESL program taught largely by teachers of his own language group, who, for whatever reason, did not teach much at all. His progress in his native language plateaued long ago, and he knows neither how to read nor write in English. He has many emotional problems, some of which, we can speculate, resulted from the trauma of war in his country and the many moves. He lies, steals, tries to organize gangs, and picks fights with others. He wants to go back home. Because he has a "transient mentality," he doesn't try to grow roots here. What's the point if he's going to leave soon?

Yoshi has professional parents. His mother is here on an exchange program, leaving Dad behind. He is resentful of being here and is rude and disrespectful to his mother. In class, he is sullen and unresponsive.

He refuses to participate, won't join groups, and sits by himself with his chin resting on his fists. He will do work alone, but no amount of coaxing or coercion will get him to be a participant.

We are not suggesting that all students who walk in the door are a problem, or, for that matter, all boys. But let's face it, the ones who drive us crazy, make us and their fellow students miserable, act out or don't do anything at all are the ones we spend our time dealing with. Understanding what's going on is part of the key to coping.

- A change in geography and climate. Students from tropical Southeast Asia, for example, who are located to places such as Minnesota, are unprepared for the severity of the winters. Barb remembers wearing mittens and a winter jacket to go trick-or-treating with her children and seeing many of the neighborhood children of newly arrived immigrants running around in sandals and tee shirts.

  One boy, relocated from the refugee camps in Thailand wrote, *The weather was so cold and snowing. I never saw the snow before. I thought it was ice. I asked my dad how can you live here? Everything was dead. I said the big tree was dead too what else is going to be safe.*

- A change from rural to urban settings. Refugees from the farms of Cambodia and Laos have found themselves thrust into inner city tenements with few trees or birds, without even a tiny plot of land to till. Native Americans from reservations find themselves having to adjust to the big city.

- A change in the size of the living environment and/or the economic situation. Many refugees, often farmers or previously well-to-do businessmen, have lost everything and arrive in this country with only the clothes on their backs. Andre's family is crowded into a tiny apartment, and his parents work long hours at minimum wage just to survive.

- A change in the culture of school. Schools are different in North America from most other parts of the world. In many other countries students wear uniforms, they sit in rows, they are not expected to render their own opinions, or to talk among themselves. The student-centered learning of many classrooms today seems chaotic and ungoverned to those who come from the "transmission approach" to education. Many students are at a loss about how to function in classrooms such as these, and, like Abir, avoid school as much as possible, or, like Boris become almost uncontrollable at times.

- A change in social status or opportunities and goals. A number of refugees, such as many of the Cubans and Vietnamese, were the elite, well-educated professionals in their home countries and now find their licenses or degrees not valid in North America. Doctors and dentists often can find work only as gardeners or factory workers, unable to make the most of their skills. Boris' mom was a physician. In order to get a license here she will have to start over completely. She works as a

Changes ESL Students Experience

cashier in a gas station. Boris finds this very demeaning and is ashamed of her.

- **The reason for the changes.** Although many new immigrants come to the United States or Canada to find a better life, others like Andre and his family fled their countries out of fear for their lives, not out of a desire to live elsewhere. For them, the move was a forced choice. In the words of one expert, "An immigrant leaves his homeland because the grass is greener; a refugee leaves because the grass is burning under his feet." Thus, refugee students often have emotional ties to their homeland and continue to nurture the hope of returning there, only allowing themselves to become marginally involved with their new home. Andre's mother refuses to learn more than the rudiments of English. There's no point, she argues, when she's going home any time.

  One student wrote, *I do not know how well others are doing in term of trying to adapt American's culture. My family is not doing well; my parents are giving up trying to make living from scrap. They said that they are too old. Both of my parents has no education. As they begin to live a comfortable life with stable income and properties, they had to fled to a totally different country with almost everything different. Very few people who live in their country for many generations understand the pain and suffer immigrants have build up inside.*

- **The change itself.** For many, the move has been traumatic, if not life-threatening. One can only guess at the experiences Andre and his younger brothers have been through. They won't talk about it, nor is it our place to ask. Some have seen their parents murdered or their families separated by war. Some must deal with the guilt of being the child chosen to live, while their siblings were left behind to face certain death. Many have lived through days at sea on unseaworthy boats without food or shelter; others have walked hundreds of miles to safety. Many have left loved ones behind and are faced with the anxiety of not knowing whether these people are still alive. They live in a sort of limbo, waiting for their lives to right themselves somehow.

  One boy wrote, *When I was a small boy, my mom died. I was crying every day looking for her. Because the enemy killed her. We didn't have food. We didn't have clothes. Because the enemy came to fight at my country, I'm not happy for the one that make my country fall down to another hand. They called mine was their. Now, we are just like the chicken. I think the chicken was more important than we are. We have a language, but we don't use mine. We use another language. Its too hard, when I think about that. It makes me cry. Do you know how hard we study English?*

- **A change in the language.** This element compounds the loss of a student's lifestyle and homeland for all our students. Being unable to speak English slows students' ability to adjust to North America. They can't understand the school routine. They can't make friends easily. They can't fit in. They have no one to "show them the ropes" and, most important, no one who is able to provide the emotional support and reassurance that they are accepted.

One student wrote, *I have an advantage over many other ESL students because I have had a lot of instruction in English and the textbooks that I used in the Philippines were often in English. My biggest problem is I still feel shy about using the language. I find it difficult to understand everything that is said in class, so when I get home I have to read everything in my textbook to make sure I understood. I probably won't ask questions, and you probably won't guess that I'm still struggling with the language.*

■ A change in the way language is used. Another widely researched issue is the linguistic cues and patterns of interactions used by different language and ethnic groups. (See Au 1980; 1985; Heath 1983; Michaels 1981; Philips 1972; Wong Fillmore 1986.) School, particularly in the areas of reading instruction and assessment, can serve as a gatekeeping organization. Mismatches between what teachers assume is correct and the linguistic styles of the children can result in frustration and, possibly, negative attitudes toward one another. Teachers who are culturally sensitive can adjust their styles of interaction to those of the students. This isn't easy, and when you have a number of different language backgrounds and styles within one classroom, you can go crazy trying to accommodate them all. At the risk of oversimplifying an enormously complex issue, we want to state that over the years we've found that an open mind and a genuine liking of the kids can go a long way to overcoming these sorts of hidden barriers.

■ A change in their relationship with their parents. Often younger children find themselves shouldering many of the responsibilities that were traditionally designated to adults. Andre has found himself translating at the doctor's office or the license bureaus; he writes the checks; he steers his bewildered parents and grandparents through the maze of bureaucracy. This has caused an imbalance in the power structure within his family, and the roles are reversed or muddied. His father is not the head of the family anymore: in many ways, Andre is. The fallout that occurs has been acute in some families, leading to rebellion and disrespect, and, at worst, a rejection of the old culture. In addition, the emphasis on freedom of thought and the encouragement to discuss his point of view has led Andre to openly rebel against the very strict hierarchy of his traditional society.

Facilitating Cultural Adjustment in the Classroom

The following charming letters, written by students and responded to by another student who is wise beyond her years, exemplify some of the issues that confront our newcomers.

Dear Señorita Fix It:

I have a serious problem. I am Korean and I'm living living in an apartment with two Americans. We are having a desagreement about food. My roommates don't like the smell of the Korean food. They don't like the smell of Kim Chee and the sauces I use. They won't let me cook. They say; "Eat sandwiches," but I'm bored with American food. I eat it for six month and I'm loosing weight. What can I do? Please, help me.

—Getting Thin Fast

Dear Getting Thin Fast

You must know that there is a lot of oriental people here especially form Japan. I know that Japanese food is similar to Korean food. It's a good idea join whit these people and to cook together. In this way you can make friends and resolve your problem at the same time. And you can remember to that there is no damn for 100 years and there is no body that can bear that.

Dear Señorita Fix It:

I am a exange student. My only idea when I came was to study hard and make a major, but I meet a girl here. We started being good friends, then we started going out and finaly we fall in love each other. We both know than I need to come back to my country as soon as I finish my major, but I really love that girl. What can I do? Please, help me.

—Signed: Heart Broken

Dear Mr. Heart Broken:

Do you know What the word preocupied means? PREOCUPIED, PRE-OCUPIED means to be ocupied in something before it happens. Many times we do that. We are extremly worried about something that we think is going to be to hard and wasting energy thinking about that and when it comes it doesn't bring any problem. I think that you are having an extremly beautiful experience in your life. Sombody who share with is one of the best things in the word that somebody can have. How can I thing about tomorrow if I have not resolve my today's problems? Time solve everithing and luck has the last word.

Dear Señorita Fix It:

I'm a exchange student. When i knew about the program, I thought that it was a great oportunity to come tu the United States and to learn English and other classes at the same time. I worked hard and safe money to come and now I'm here. But things are not as I expected. I've got problems with the language. Is hard for me to espeak and to understand English. I've got a job, but I dont like it and I need to do that because I need the money. Dormitories are to far from bars and others fun places and you can't go if you don't have a car. More than I've got problems with my roommate. He use my food card and drink my juices!! So, now I wonder my self, what am I doing here? PLEASE HELP ME!

—Signed: Loosed

Apreciated loosed:

Many, many times we blame to our family, or school, our teachers, the country, the weather, etc. about our "bad luck". Here, there and anywhere life is hard and we need to fight to be better. I just wanna ask you. Is mom here? Is somebody of your family 10 miles around or 100 miles?

While students are individuals, they are also members of the particular culture they were born into. The culture of a society embodies elements that are tangible: the clothing, food, festivals, social customs, and so on. It also encompasses the intangible elements: the values of the society, its world view, its attitudes concerning life and death. Our culture helps define us mentally and spiritually. It also dictates how we interact with society.

Many students from other cultures—including Native Americans—are confronted with the awesome task of functioning in a society they don't understand. There is a mismatch between our culture and theirs. Their own culture has a different set of norms for simple things we take for granted, such as how to address the teacher, how close to stand to the person they are talking to, how loud to talk. Many times what they see and hear in North America is in direct conflict with their own set of cultural values: people sitting with their legs crossed so that the soles of their feet are showing, dating, displaying affection in public, openly questioning a teacher's point of view. They often feel confusion, conflict, and helplessness over the wide disparity between what they have hitherto unquestioningly believed was right and what they experience in everyday North American life. These feelings are defined as "culture shock."

One boy from Ethiopia put it this way:

I come from a culture and a language very different from yours. In fact, our whole way of making our society is very different. The school I went to is also very different in many ways. I'm still having culture shock. Yes, my parents chose to come to canada to make a better life for us, so I really want to try hard.

Faced with the task of coming to terms with this new culture, students such as Boris, Andre, and Yoshi, as well as Beverly and Angel must decide for themselves how they want to fit in and what kinds of compromises they are willing to make in order to succeed.

Becoming acculturated to the mainstream North American way of life can mean conflict. Many feel that they must abandon the old ways. Children, more adaptable than their parents, embrace our culture more readily, which can lead to tension between the generations. Hibe, for instance, began school at five. She was outspoken and sociable, expressing her opinions in a forthright manner. This was a cause of real worry for her parents, who believe in the submissive place of women in their society. What North American schools encourage and what her parents believed was acceptable were in direct conflict. Gaida, who came at age eleven, threw herself into the North American lifestyle, becoming a cheerleader and a star on the girl's volleyball team in high school. By the time her parents returned to their country when she was nineteen, she could no longer fit into the traditional society she had been born into, and chose, against her parent's wishes, to stay in America.

Different Cultural Behaviors

Sometimes our customs conflict with theirs, and we are not always quick to notice the mismatch because these are automatic behaviors—things we do without thinking. Cultural behaviors that differ significantly from ours include

- Avoiding eye contact. This is considered polite and respectful behavior in some cultures, such as Laotian, Hmong, or Hispanic. However, a teacher might consider a student who looks down at the floor uncooperative or sullen. How many times do we say to children we are scolding, "Look at me when I'm talking to you!" Avoiding eye contact can have serious consequences for older students and adults. Mary had several high schoolers who were turned down for jobs they were qualified for because the employer thought they weren't listening or paying attention to what he said, although they were merely showing respect by keeping their eyes downcast.

- Different attitudes about cooperation. Some students come from cultures that are based on the premise that people help each other in all areas. They are unaware that in our schools helping a fellow student with a problem may be construed as cheating. Many Polynesian, Native North American, and Southeast Asian cultures are this way.

- Fear of making mistakes. For some students, making a mistake is a greater error than leaving a question unanswered or asking another student for help—ultimate correctness is always the primary objective. For example, Mary's beginning English class of Vietnamese students became deathly quiet when state senators came to observe the classroom. This usually rowdy class was proper and silent. They were afraid of making mistakes in front of the visitors and therefore shaming their teacher.

- Fear of being singled out for individual praise. In many cultures, such as Southeast Asian and Native American, the group or the family is always seen as more important than the individual.

- Different role expectations for boys and girls. This attitude is most prominent among students who come from countries that have ascribed different roles to women and men, such as the Middle East. Problems arise if the students are unused to having a teacher of the opposite sex; they may react with some awkwardness toward the teacher or they may be openly disrespectful.

- High or low motivation to achieve academically, based on gender. This is related to the item above. In some cultures, only males are expected to do well; the females simply mark time. They are in school as a formality, not to achieve any real learning goals.

- Uneasiness with the informality of classroom atmosphere. Public behavior in certain cultures is always formal. Many European schools, such as those in Germany, or Asian schools such as those in Japan, are very strict—to us, almost militaristic. They often view North American schools as bordering on chaos and the informality an invitation to misbehave. Teachers who wear jeans, sit on their desks, and put their feet up are viewed as extremely impolite.

- Uneasiness with our North American school system. Related to the issue above, newcomers are often uneasy about the learner-centered, process-oriented curriculum and educational practices of our school systems, as opposed to the more traditional subject-centered learning environments found in most countries of the Old World and the Far East.

- Taboos toward certain physical contact. For some religions, the area around the head and shoulders is sacred, and it is considered impolite for another person to touch these areas. Therefore, a reassuring pat on the shoulder from the teacher may be interpreted as an affront by the student.

- Beliefs about the propriety of certain kinds of dress. Certain cultures have rigid customs as to what is proper and improper dress, particularly for girls. As a result, for instance, the clothes students must wear for gym and the requirement to take showers may cause a great deal of distress for students. Abir objected greatly to wearing shorts and gym uniforms. She would hide in the bathroom during the entire class period.

Anyone who moves to a different area, whether it is within their immediate neighborhood, town, state or province, or country, experiences to some degree the same four stages as they become adjusted to their new surroundings. There are many names for these stages, but the easiest to remember are the four Hs: honeymoon, hostility, humor, and home.

The Stages of Acculturation

- Honeymoon. This stage takes place when people first arrive. It is characterized by extreme happiness, sometimes even by euphoria. This is especially prevalent with refugees who have finally arrived safely in North America. For them, their new home is truly the land of milk and honey.

- Hostility. After about four to six months, reality sets in. These people know a bit about getting around and have begun learning the ropes, but this new place is not like their home: they can't get the food they are accustomed to; things don't look the same; they miss the life of their home country, the familiar places and faces and ways of doing things. Gradually they begin to feel that they hate North America and want to go back to their home country, no matter how bad things were there. This stage is often characterized by complaining; wanting to be only with others who speak their language; rejecting anything associated with the new culture, such as the food, the people, even the new language; feeling depressed and irritable or even angry; having headaches or feeling tired all the time.

- Humor. Gradually, the newcomers work toward resolution of their feelings and their sense of being torn between the new and the old. They begin to accept their new home. They begin to find friends, discover that there are good things about where they are living, and adjust to their lives by coming to terms with both the old and the new ways of living. This is a long process, fraught with feelings of great anxiety in some, because to many, accepting the new means rejecting the old.

- Home. Finally, the newcomers become "native" in the sense that where they live is their home, and they accept that they are here to stay. This last stage may be years in coming and for some will never take place.

Thus, what is happening in students' minds and hearts as a result of the drastic changes in their lives has a direct influence on their ability to cope with life and succeed in school.

Behavior in the Classroom

How your students cope with the emotional upheaval in their lives is often reflected in their behavior in class. The affective factors discussed above greatly influence their adjustment. Some students can make the transition from one culture to another with relative ease. Franco, for instance, is a happy, sunny-tempered boy who likes everybody. It doesn't matter to him whether he can speak good English or not; he jumps right into games, discussions, and activities, making the most of the little bit of English he has. Salvador uses his prowess at soccer to win him friends. Because he is a good player, as well as a congenial, outgoing kid, everybody likes him, and he slipped smoothly into his new life in North America.

Other students react to the upheaval with hostility and act out their aggression, rejecting anything constructive the teachers plan. Yoshi, for example, managed to make life miserable for everyone, talking loudly in Japanese to his friends, crawling under tables while the teacher was trying to lead a lesson, picking fights, ignoring all instructions as if he didn't understand (even though his teachers knew he did), and refusing to respond to anyone but the Japanese aide.

Other students react with passive-aggressive behavior and selectively decline to participate in activities. For instance, Mary taught a group of students who were upset that they had been transferred to her class, having to leave their teacher of six months. These students were refugees who were brand new to this country and had little control over any facet of their lives. They were comfortable with the teacher they had, and when the system demanded they move up a level to a different teacher, they withdrew. No matter what Mary did for the first few weeks, no matter what adjustments she made to accommodate different levels of abilities, most of the students declined to participate. It was apparent that they were making an attempt to control something in their own lives, and only gradually did they begin to relax and take part in activities.

Some students choose to withdraw completely, effectively shutting out anyone or anything that represents the new culture. Abir withdrew into her lonely self, spending most of her time complaining how unlike North

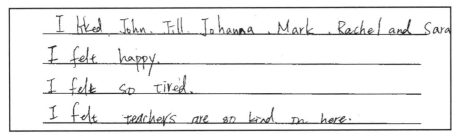

I liked John. Till. Johanna, Mark, Rachel and Sara
I felt happy.
I felt so tired.
I felt teachers are so kind. In here.

Figure 3.2. Nina's reflection shows the importance of teachers in her life.

America and Egypt were. She never made friends and continued to be unhappy through all of her years at high school.

All these factors add up to myriad forces that are at work within the learner. Upon reviewing these variables, it may seem an impossible task to help some newcomers learn our language. However, what you do as a teacher is critical to their success, and there are many positive things you can do to assist in making their adjustment to this country (or in the case of Native Americans, to their new environment) and to the English language successful.

Teaching Strategies That Help Maximize Learning

Input—The Teacher

Although language is not necessarily taught, it is not enough to assume that, given enough time, students will just "pick it up" on their own. Conscious and direct input from you is necessary.

There are five major things you can do to maximize learning:

1. Provide comprehensible input.
2. Make the environment as stress free as possible.
3. Provide numerous opportunities for students to hear and speak the language.
4. Provide a network of support.
5. Have clear and unmistakable guidelines.

Provide Plenty of Comprehensible Input

Comprehensible input comes from the language students are exposed to that they can understand. Your students will only learn when the information you teach is meaningful.

Communicate Effectively

■ Use clear, predictable, "guessable" teacher talk. Researchers have noted that the way native-English speakers interact with those who don't speak the language is very similar to the way mothers speak to their infants. When adults or native-English speakers speak to each other, their speech is full of stops, starts, and incomplete phrases. When mothers speak to their children, however, they adjust their speech and talk "motherese." Making similar adjustments in your speech to your ESL students is the most helpful way to speak to them.

- Talk more slowly. This means at a relaxed rate, not unnaturally slow. Don't overdo it.

- Reduce the use of idioms. Idioms are notoriously "untranslatable," that is, if you try to explain them word for word their meaning is lost. Think of trying to explain such expressions as "off the wall," "out of the blue," "grab a seat," "keep it under your hat," or "give me a ballpark figure."

- Use the active voice and positive sentences. The passive voice is much more difficult to understand because students have learned that "the subject of the sentence is the actor." For example, "There will be no homework assignments handed in after January 10" is harder to understand than "You must hand in all homework by January 10."

- Monitor your sentence length; don't make your sentences too long. Lengthy and complex sentences are often too hard for students to sort through.

- Simplify your vocabulary whenever possible. But this should not include technical vocabulary. Content areas have many technical words that are central to concepts being studied. You should not substitute these words for simpler ones; the students must know them to grasp the central meaning of the lesson. In other cases, finding simpler synonyms for words can make your speech easier to grasp.

- Use linguistic cues, or attention getters, such as "look" or "watch" to direct the students' attention to important points. These signals alert listeners to the fact that you consider those points particularly important.

- Use key words. Choose several words that are critical to the current lesson, write them on the chalkboard, and use them frequently during the discussion so the students will get exposure in several different contexts. Use phonological cues, such as tone and stress, to emphasize these words and call the students' attention to them.

- Focus the exchange on the here and now. Abstract concepts are very difficult to understand or express in limited English.

- Expand the one-word or two-word sentences that students produce. When a student says, for example, "Book home," you can respond, "Oh, your book is at home. Here, use this one."

Other Suggestions   Another way to provide comprehensible input is through nonverbal cues. You can accomplish this by doing the following:

- Use plenty of visual cues, such as concrete objects, charts, maps, pictures, photos, and collages.

- Act out your material or use gestures to help get your meaning across. Point, mime, role-play, demonstrate an action. When you direct the learners' attention to features of the object you are talking about, you are providing them with additional clues to meaning. Students can then see what you are talking about, rather than being solely dependent upon translating everything in their heads.

■ Use contextual cues. Words and sentences are more comprehensible when they are used in a context that is understandable. Concepts, such as larger, smaller, fewer, and more, are easily understood when they are demonstrated with real objects (such as coins) rather than explained.

■ Use more than one method. Give assignments and lectures orally as well as by writing them on the chalkboard. Show a movie or a filmstrip on the same material as your lecture. Have a hands-on project in addition to reading assignments.

■ Check often for understanding. Stop to see if your ESL students are comprehending the material. Watch for body language, facial expressions, or signs of frustration that will alert you to whether or not the students are understanding. Simply asking "Do you understand?" is not enough. Many students will not admit they don't understand, either because they are ashamed or because they have been taught that their failure will be a sign of disrespect and an affront to the teacher. They often tell you they understand even when they are completely lost. Find alternative ways to check their comprehension, such as asking them to paraphrase a key point. Encourage them to tell you when they don't understand. Develop signals—such as a little throat-clearing—so that they can alert you without overtly stating so. If you teach in chunks, plan an activity to allow them to demonstrate their understanding in nonverbal ways before you go on to the next section.

■ Allow some "wait time," time for the students to hear, understand, and formulate their responses. Often students have to translate your thoughts into their own language, then re-translate their answer back into English. Native Americans have a longer wait time in their own language; you might have to wait even longer for them to translate and re-translate.

■ Give feedback, such as a nod, a frown, or a look of bewilderment, so students know how well they are getting their attempts at communicating across.

Set Up a Stress Free Environment

Students who are relaxed and self-confident learn better and faster. You can help reduce the stress your students are under and nurture self-esteem.

Reduce Stress and Nurture Self-Esteem

■ Show genuine interest in the students, their language, and their culture.

■ Make your students feel secure. Even if you can't speak their language, you can reassure them and demonstrate interest and concern through gestures and tone of voice.

■ Allow them to verbalize in their own language. Many teachers feel that allowing students to talk in their own language will slow their language growth. Some schools even go to the extent of fining or punishing students for talking in their native languages. However, trying to understand a foreign language—in this case English—for hours at a time is physically and mentally exhausting. Students will often do better if they have some "jell time," time when they are not constantly forced to translate information in their heads. Allowing students time to discuss topics together in their own language can actually facilitate learning, because they can focus solely on the content, unimpeded by their lack of fluency in English.

■ Avoid forcing your students to speak. Research shows that forcing students to respond orally before they are ready is a major cause of poor articulation and grammatical control, as well as stress overload. Your students will talk when they are ready.

■ Accept gestures, pantomime, or drawings whenever possible. These can often demonstrate whether the students understand the concept involved and relieves them of the stress of trying to articulate their thoughts.

■ Make your students feel that they should never be embarrassed or ashamed of their errors. Errors are a part of learning anything. If students are given the message that errors are bad, or if they are laughed at because of their mistakes, they will clam up. They will only use forms they are perfectly sure of, thus closing the door to learning new forms through practice. Look at mistakes from an analytical perspective rather than a corrective perspective: use them to tell you what your student needs to learn in the future.

■ Don't correct grammatical or pronunciation errors. Again, meaning is more important than form. Research has shown that correcting errors has little or no value. Corrections can actually impede progress because (1) the students are given the message that being correct is more important than what they have to say; (2) students are distracted from the task at hand—communicating. If the meaning of what the students say is unclear, ask for clarification; otherwise, accept the responses as they are given. Learners start with large issues such as the correct words. As their fluency increases, they will iron out the finer points such as word endings and tenses. Trust learners to work these things out. You can model the correct form when you respond.

■ Continually reinforce the students' progress. Keep charts, save their early papers in cumulative folders, and show them how far they've come: "This is where you were; this is where you are now. These are the words you've learned."

■ Encourage your students to share their backgrounds and cultures. ESL students often long to talk about their homelands and cultures and are seldom given this opportunity. For example, asking students to speak about their homelands—perhaps during geography or history lessons—not only provides them with the chance to talk about their countries, but also to use English, speaking about topics familiar to them. And other students in your class will benefit from immediate exposure to a variety of cultures. A welcome by-product is that allowing students to ask questions about the various cultures can help prevent or reduce friction that might be building in the school, because a forum is provided for an open discussion of sensitive topics.

Maximize Students' Exposure to Natural Communication

The best language learning comes from students' genuine attempts to communicate. Encourage your students' participation in activities within and beyond the classroom.

Encourage Participation

- Promote friendships. You can help promote friendships by introducing students to others who share their interests, by encouraging the student in the class who loves to "parent" to take up the cause of the ESL student, by putting together two lonely shy kids, and by prevailing upon all members of the class to be extra sensitive and friendly. As a teacher, your time and energies are limited. You cannot possibly provide students with all the educational input they require as well as meet their social and emotional needs. Everyone wants to have friends and be liked. By promoting friendships you are

  - Easing the transition for lonely, often heartsick, students.
  - Providing the students with the kind of social relationships in which "getting along" is the most important issue, and learning the language is part and parcel of being a friend. They learn the vocabulary and grammar that is important and useful, while getting feedback that is essential for refining their new language. Put them in "play" situations, whether this involves playing in the sandbox or on the playground (at the elementary level), or competing in friendly games (at any level).

- Integrate the ESL students within the classroom. Make them feel part of the group. Give them duties, perhaps with another student, such as cleaning erasers or feeding the fish (at the elementary level), or turning in roll sheets or checking equipment (in upper grades).

- Make cooperative learning an important part of every class. Students do not need to work alone to become independent learners. Cooperative learning is a strategy in which a small group of students is involved in an activity or project with a common purpose. Cooperative learning is much more than simply lumping students into a group to work together; often when students are grouped without any ground rules, one or two carry the weight of the assignment.

  For effective learning, both groups and tasks must be carefully structured. Cooperative learning involves task specialization within teams; the task cannot be completed without important input from each team member. Heterogeneous grouping, in which one or more ESL students may be in each group, is an important part of cooperative learning. Research has shown that all students—both English speakers and non-English speakers—make substantial gains in their command of the subject. Students get feedback on their attempts to represent problems, have background knowledge supplied by native-English speakers, and profit from discussing problems and observing others' thought processes in tackling issues. Cooperative effort is particularly relevant to some cultures that stress working for the common good as opposed to striving for individual recognition.

Your Role As Teacher

We cannot overstate the importance of your role as teacher. You are on the front line helping these students make the difficult transition from one culture to another. Often you spend more time with them than their parents do and can see changes or behaviors that family members cannot (or do not) recognize.

■ Your most appropriate role is to teach ESL students English and to give them a means to become functional members of the community.

This means doing the job you are trained for: teaching. It also means, conversely, not trying to solve all their problems. You are not the counselor, the psychiatrist, or the physician. It is inappropriate to try to be. Teachers can get in over their heads, or burn out fast if they try to solve all the problems of their students. This is, admittedly, a very fine line to tread. We went into teaching because we like people, and we want to help make the world a better place. But if, for instance, you urge a traumatized student to tell you things that have happened to him, thinking that simply unburdening will make him feel better, you can make things worse. You can become traumatized. You can become so overwhelmed that you can't do your job. The student may feel so badly afterwards that he will shy away, and the gains you have made will be lost.

■ You are also a model of appropriate behavior. Many of them have lost the leadership of their parents; immigrant or refugee parents are often confused and baffled by our culture and cannot effectively interpret society and culture for their children as most parents do. By modeling correct behavior and setting limits, you are making it possible for them to learn how to act in ways we consider acceptable.

Teachers Should...   ■ Adopt a policy of "a little more." Take the initiative in trying to understand your students, to be aware of the problems they face and the adjustments they're making. A little extra time invested in finding friends for these students, observing how they act and react, and making sure they understand what is expected of them can make the difference between success and failure.

For example, Spencer had the saddest eyes Barb had ever seen. It broke her heart to look at him. His older brother had been murdered in a drive-by shooting. The four brothers in school all had different last names. He had a hair trigger temper and was often in detention, but he responded like wildflowers to rain to special attention, and his smile could light up a room. By knowing what was going on in his life, we could be sympathetic yet firm in our guidelines.

■ Learn a little more. All Southeast Asians are not alike, just as all Native Americans, Europeans, or Africans are not alike. Ongoing wars and political unrest have divided regions for decades, and the memories of violence, on both sides, create tensions that transcend country boundaries. (For example, at the end of the school year, one student told Barb he had slept with a knife under his pillow for the entire year; the roommate assigned to him was from a country he considered his enemy.) Some ethnic groups are very class conscious among themselves and will not associate with those they feel are inferior. Culture, religion, and family patterns all influence your students profoundly. By learning about these, you can be wary of the pitfalls, and be better prepared to understand why and how your students perceive the world. This puts you in a position to modify your classroom to meet the needs of all the students in the class.

■ Be aware of the danger signals. ESL students fall into the category of "fragile" learners. Fragile learners aren't necessarily those from low income or single-parent families, although these circumstances can be part of newcomers' situations; the fragility refers to the many stresses, traumas, and concerns beyond the students' control, which assault their senses and drain attention and energy. Overcome with feelings of loss and emotional anguish, your students are often "in crisis." Knowing the stages of grief and loss—shock, denial, anger, depression, bargaining, and finally acceptance—as well as being aware of inappropriate behavior such as laughing at sad stories, crying at a joke, being extremely irritable or suspicious, will help you see beyond the students' behavior and look for causes rather than focus on the effect and instantly judge or blame.

■ Learn about resources within the community. Depression among refugees is very high. Knowing who to turn to when you spot danger signals or behavior problems can relieve untold stress in your students' lives, as well as make your own life easier. Recognize that you are an important member of a team. There are many agencies to help immigrants and refugees. Find out which ones are operating in your area so that you can turn to them when your students need counseling, answers to questions, or help wading through the mire of bureaucracy.

Provide a Network of Support

■ Keep the lines of communication open; be a listening ear. Some of our students have lived through horrors we can't begin to imagine: perhaps they saw their parents blown apart in mine fields, or family members tortured, raped, and murdered by the enemy. The burden of their memories is always with them. Don't probe or openly ask them about their past. Someday something—a smell, a word, a picture—may trigger the memory and they may "tell their story." When that happens, don't try to stop them; it is important to allow your students to share this memory. (Use your discretion as to whether or not it's appropriate for the rest of the class to hear.) Your place is simply to listen and to validate the memory. Let them maintain power by authoring their own story. But then steer them to a professional who can help them in their healing process; it takes a trained professional to help them along the difficult, complicated road to wholeness.

Coping With Misbehavior

Shaker was a huge guy with a huge attitude. On the first day of class, when Barb was reading aloud "notes to the student" from the front of a book, he raised his hand and said, "Teacher, we can read that for ourselves." Clearly, he was setting out, not just to undermine Barb's control, but to topple it. If she didn't react fast and with force, all was lost before the semester began.

Boris could be defiant. "No, I'm not gonna do that." Andre had a friend call in sick for him; he was caught in the parking lot smoking during second hour. During class he prowled the room, asking to go to the bathroom every ten minutes, talking with other students, messing with their papers, copying work.

Behavior is an issue every teacher wrestles with. Problems can be compounded when there is an overlay of language barriers. Discipline can be difficult and time-consuming when your students can't understand what you are trying to say. There are established procedures for dealing with abusive, defiant, or aggressive students, and it's not our place to review those here.

Ideally, you should do as much as you can to prevent misbehavior before it happens. Both students and parents from other cultures may benefit from a sensitive introduction to the learner-centered approach to discipline, i.e., leaving the students' integrity and self-worth intact, as opposed to the more traditional punitive approach to discipline that they may be accustomed to. But, as in the case of Shaker, Boris, and Andre, more often than not, the ball of dissension comes out of left field and knocks you on the head before you're ready.

Have Clear and Unmistakable Guidelines

Make your classroom rules very clear. Explain them well, using an interpreter if possible. So much of what we consider acceptable behavior is implicitly understood by North Americans, and yet is not necessarily clear to those from other countries. For instance, one classroom's rules were (1) Students will respect all school rules and (2) Students will use acceptable language. Those of us who have grown up in North American schools will know what these rules mean. But those who are coming from a different culture may not. They hear their classmates swearing all the time. How are they supposed to know that this is not acceptable within a teacher's hearing? Unless the rules are explained to them, how will they know what "respecting" the rules means?

We also have to be sure that the consequences for misbehavior are explained to the students. One teacher we interviewed told us she had kept a student in through lunchtime because he had incessantly talked out loud to another student. The teacher used the method of discipline that gives the student warnings by putting checkmarks on the chalkboard. When the student accumulated five checkmarks, he was kept in during lunch break. She later found out that the student did not understand this discipline method. He did not know that his talking was disruptive to her, or that the checkmarks on the board were meant for him. Ultimately, she found out that he did not even understand why she had kept him in class while the other students were allowed to go to lunch.

If you have students who are acting up, the first place to start is by reviewing the following:

When Things Go Wrong

- The physical setting. Where are your students seated? Can they hear, see, observe properly? Do they need the support of students of the same background? (Or do they need to be separated from these students?)

- The amount of contact for feedback, clarification, and so on. Are the students aware of what you want them to do? Do they know how to go about doing it? Do they have opportunities to work with you one-on-one? Can they ask questions and get the answers they need to do the work?

- Your level of expectation. Was your assessment of your students' abilities accurate or are they getting frustrated?

- Problems with assignments. Are they overwhelmed because the assignment is too complex, or have you broken it down in components with each part containing a clearly stated objective? Part of Andre's problem was that he felt he could not do the assignments and spent much of his time avoiding them.

- Students' emotional states. Are you beginning to see some of the danger signals—inappropriate behavior, aggression, withdrawal, or apathy? Spencer was near to giving up, and his temper often got the better of him. Finding a counselor for him helped him work through his grief.

- Cultural mismatch. It may be, for instance, that some students come from cultures where classes are tightly structured. In our less formal classes, students may be unable to figure out what rules are in effect and how they should behave. They may be frustrated at the contradiction between those behaviors they believe are acceptable and your behavioral expectations. This was part of Boris's problem; when the rules were stated clearly and unequivocally, he was on the road toward learning how to cope in the classroom. He had to be told exactly how to speak with the teacher, and so on; he was unable to infer these rules.

If no problems exist in your setup, and you don't believe culture is a factor, then confront students individually with the problems. Communication may be difficult, so try to get the help of a translator. A student may be able to recognize that problems exist and may even be able to tell you what would improve the situation. For example, he might be able to say, "You talk too fast and then I don't understand how to do the assignment. Could you write it on the board?"

More likely, however, the student will deny that any problems exist. He may even react with hostility and end up blaming you for all his problems, or he may withdraw and say very little to enlighten you.

*Resolving Behavior
Problems*

We are living in an
imperfect world, so there
is no such thing as a
paradise with no pain.
As long as we are still
alive and well, we should
not give up trying to
make world a better place
to live in. As a philophy
put it, "Stay hardiness is
the best human can do."
I am here to stay.

Figure 3.3. Chome's summation
of life as an immigrant.

Working through the following steps can help resolve behavior problems,
because, in the end, the student will know exactly what is expected of him.

1. Review what the correct behavior is.

2. State clearly what he can and cannot do, using language that he can
   understand. For instance, "Stay in your seat when I am talking."
   "No crawling under tables," or "No sharing of answers." While we
   want to be positive and provide positive models of behavior, the word
   No clearly sets the parameters of what is acceptable and what isn't.
   It often helps to learn those commands in the students' language.
   The first word Barb learned in Chinese was NO! The first phrase was
   NO FIGHTING. Horace and Rex, two great kids when they were
   separated, could not get along. Barb even has video footage of Horace
   walloping a blindfolded Rex during a game. Our final shot of Rex is
   at graduation, glowering as he accepts his diploma, because he and
   Horace were fighting in the stands. Knowing phrases such as
   Wakarimasuka? (Do you understand?) and *Que Pasa?* (What's
   happening?) are essential to have available when needed.

Figure 3.4. This lovely drawing, made by a student as a reflection of her ESL experiences,
captures the essence of what a positive and joyful experience meeting new people, sharing
cultures, and becoming friends can be.

3. Avoid putting yourself in a position that you can't change later, such as stating unequivocally that all plagiarism will be awarded with instant failure. Your student may not have any idea what the word plagiarism means, thus may not understand that copying directly from a book or his classmate's essay is wrong.

4. Tell the student how he can correct the problem. If he is in high school and has the language capabilities, he may even be able to plan strategies for correcting the problem himself.

5. Detail the consequences if the student does not comply with the resolutions you have established. Be flexible. Be prepared to negotiate, but hold on to reasonable standards. Nobody in the class objected when the teacher negotiated with Andre that he could go to the bathroom whenever he wanted, as long as he kept it under two minutes and as long as he stayed away from the others so they could do their work.

Conclusion

Dealing with students from different backgrounds entails much planning and research on your part. However, the benefits in terms of the enrichment each newcomer brings to your class far outweigh the negatives. By creating plenty of opportunities for interaction, providing appropriate feedback, and being sensitive to the types of changes your students are coping with, you can set up the optimal environment for learning.

We do not want to suggest that all students have bad experiences. There's hope. Sooner or later, most of them break through the struggles and make a home for themselves here.

CHAPTER 4

LITERACY AND THE FOUR SKILLS

In this chapter, we discuss learning language within what we call a "balanced literacy and language program" and its importance for second-language learners. We focus on

- Approaches to teaching literacy.
- Different types of ESL literacy.
- Our assumptions about literacy in an era of change.
- Strategies for promoting literacy in the mainstream classroom.

Authentic Approaches to Teaching/Learning

In the past several decades, teachers and researchers have learned a great deal about reading. How it should be taught is less clear—and the source of a great deal of bitter controversy. Many states have mandated by law that all teachers should be trained in the use of phonics.

In our first edition, we operated under certain assumptions that we still stand behind:

- Opportunities for reading, writing, speaking, and listening must be "real." Real situations—reading to enjoy a story or to find out how to fix a bike, writing a letter to complain about a canceled TV show— are intrinsically motivating because they have purpose. For example, ESL students often pass driver's education with flying colors in a remarkably short time. They learn to read the driving manuals and understand the instructions so that they can pass the test and get their license. Because driving is often important, not only for them, but for their families (frequently the students are the ones who do the ferrying, the bill paying, and the grocery shopping), they are intensely motivated to learn.

- The situations must be meaningful, i.e., meaning-full. We communicate in order to accomplish something: to learn, to have our needs met, to get along with other people, or just to play. We have a purpose and an audience. Infants do not learn to talk by learning that we put the subject before the verb or add *s* to nouns to make them plural. They learn words like *bye-bye*, *juice*, and *milk* within contexts that have meaning to them. We must provide second-language learners with the same kinds of opportunities so that they can make sense of language by using it for purposes that have relevance to them. Often, the tasks students are given are phony exercises: tracing and copying the letters of the alphabet again and again; learning lists of words simply because they all begin with the same sound or demonstrate a phonics principle; punctuating sentences that someone else has written; listing all the nouns in a paragraph; repeating two sounds until they can hear the difference. These exercises have fractionated learning into little bits and pieces that, while important components of the reading, writing, speaking, and listening processes, of themselves make little sense to the learner. "Whole texts," not just isolated words or sentences, but poems, newspaper articles, novels, textbooks, letters, comic books, grocery lists, and songs all provide meaning in meaningful contexts.

■ The learning situations must also be integrated so that all four skills are used together. Rather than simply discussing a topic—whether it be about what they saw at the zoo yesterday or the legalization of drugs—students can write (or have you write) what they know and think, discuss what they have written, and further their understanding of the event or issue by listening to each other's thoughts and interpretations. Then they can capitalize on what they have learned orally by using their newly learned vocabulary in their reading, writing, and sharing. This means not giving students phony tasks whose only real purpose is that the teacher wants it done or that it is included in the workbook. Figure 4.1 shows an example of such a worksheet.

With the critical rethinking and refinements of what "whole language" has meant, however, and our new knowledge about what reading entails, we have modified our assumptions and their implications for teachers.

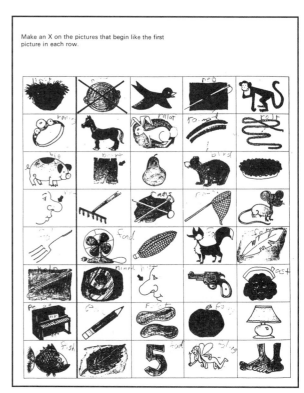

Figure 4.1. This worksheet was given to a second grader. As an exercise, it is just plain bad for several reasons: it does not allow the student to grapple with sound/letter correspondences within a real context; it does not reinforce these concepts because in many cases she does not know the English term for the pictures. The student has attempted to write the word above some of the pictures. Unless the teacher stands over her and helps her with each picture, this student can go far astray.

Orthodoxies Versus Reasonable Choices

Nancie Atwell, in her second edition of *In the Middle* (1998), writes of being caught up in a set of "orthodoxies." She found that "as enlightened and child-centered as [her] new rules were, they had an effect similar to the old ones: they limited what [she] did" as a teacher. We have found, too, that the continual nagging question that Atwell labored under—that very dangerous question: "Am I doing it right?"—limits what we and other teachers do in the classroom. This question keeps many of those who are successful at teaching less able and willing to be innovative. They become less willing to listen to their experiences and trust their instincts about what the students need.

Many teachers truly committed to the philosophy of whole language felt guilty doing things that didn't seem "pure" whole language. Teachers who taught spelling had to defend themselves. Teaching phonics was done behind closed doors. Asking students to copy the alphabet was assigned with guilt. If all activities were not integrated, we somehow felt we were selling our students short. In addition, we believe that teachers with many years of experience rebelled against whole language. They were led to believe that some of the things they were doing, simply because it wasn't "whole" or "integrated," were somehow wrong, and, therefore, they felt themselves to be less able teachers.

In the years since the backlash against whole language in California, we have decided we aren't going to get hung up on whether something is "whole language" or not. Whole language is not, and never was meant to be, an orthodoxy, or a program: it was, and still remains, a philosophy of how language and literacy are learned, and, therefore, how they should be taught. This means that thoughtful teachers can and should teach structures directly, incorporate phonics into their reading programs, and expect students to be responsible for skills that may require memorization.

For instance, when Barb was teaching a very large class of beginning literacy migrant workers and refugees she taught verbs and verb conjugations, but she felt guilty about it.

Her reasoning was sound: students needed some structure upon which to base their writing. It wasn't feasible to expect that they would be able (within the time frame they had and their limited exposure outside the classroom) to figure out the forms for themselves; and last, but not least in importance, students wanted it.

Verb Chart						
Verb	Translation	Past	Progressive	3rd Person Singular	Past Participle	Example in a Sentence
sleep	睡覺	slept	sleeping	sleeps	have slept	I have slept in class before.
eat	吃	ate	eating	eats	have eaten	I eat every morning.
jump	跳	jumped	jumping	jumps	have jumped	I jumped over the wa
run	跑	ran	running	runs	have run	I run to eat lunch. Verey fast,
pat	拍	patted	patting	pats	have patted	I pat the dog.
pet	寵物	pet	petting	pets	have pet	I pet the dog.
be	是	I was we were	being	is	have been	I was little girl.
laugh	大笑	laughed	laughing	laughs	have laughed	I laugh when the wolf ate the pigs.
know	知道	knew	knowing	knows	have known	I know Chinese.

Figure 4.2. An example of a verb chart used, without guilt, with Taiwanese students.

They felt secure in having these forms spelled out to them and to have concrete evidence that they were learning. In retrospect, the decision to teach verbs explicitly was a good one. And, because it was done within the framework of meaningful discussion, it was not a "betrayal" of whole language principles.

Julie, a third grade teacher, teaches spelling. Her rationale is that by the third grade there are certain words that students can and should know how to spell by rote. It is reasonable to expect that they will be accurate on those words, and students are held accountable for them.

Immersion Is Not Enough

We no longer assume that immersing students in literacy is sufficient. Exposure is not enough. Strategies can't be left to chance. Although many children learn to read on their own, many others do not. Fountas and Pinnell (1996) write, "We sometimes mistakenly assume that these needs can be met just by providing good books and encouraging children to explore them. In fact, what most young readers need cannot be found in books alone….It is usually not enough simply to provide children with good reading materials. Teacher guidance is essential." This is especially true when students come from homes where their parents do not read at all, and their experiences with the written word are very limited.

Some students do need direct instruction in reading skills, in structuring their essays, and in learning how to locate information in texts. They may need to be told the meanings of words explicitly so that they can continue reading. The recognition of the necessity to teach skills directly is a welcome one, because, again, it opens the door for teachers to use whatever techniques are available to them to meet the needs of their individual students.

For example, students might need to be shown, many times, what their options are for figuring out an unknown word. Often, beginning or poor readers will automatically turn to the teacher for help when encountering a word they don't know by sight. They might try to sound it out. If that doesn't work, they might simply give up. If they don't learn other methods, such as looking at the context or using the pictures as cues to figure out the meaning, they don't have many options. We can't assume they'll pick up these skills on their own by watching the teacher reading strategically; teaching them explicitly is sometimes a must and is nothing less than good teaching.

A New Understanding of Literacy

In the past several years we have expanded our view of literacy. Literacy is a large category that includes every use of print as a creation of meaning from a text. Literacy, according to Au (1993), is "the ability and the willingness to use reading and writing to construct meaning from printed text, in ways which meet the requirements of a particular social context."

This means reading is not an either/or phenomenon, where one either can read or cannot read. There are many types of literacy events that range from reading stop signs along the way to work, to reading the back of a medicine bottle, to wading through the intricacies of a will or a lease agreement. Each task requires different types of skills and levels of attention; many tasks are group affairs—carried on with a great deal of discussion and often embedded in contexts that carry much social and emotional weight.

Literacy is not simply the skills needed to read and write (as people assume when they believe "illiterate" people are those who cannot read). Rather, literacy is a social phenomenon that exists within a context; it is the ability to use one's reading and writing skills to participate efficiently and effectively in today's complex society.

Literacy Is a Social Phenomenon

This definition expands our view to include many of the complex tasks involved in daily living, such as reading recipes and writing grocery lists. Richie, for example, used to boast quite proudly that he had never read an entire book. And yet, he read the paper, the TV guide, and letters from his nine children. The letters were shared with his family and discussed in great detail. A rich web of emotions and social ties were evoked in the process.

The implication for teachers is that literacy, when viewed as a social event, becomes a setting or an environment through which all other tasks occur.

Second-Language Literacy

Second-language learners are not alike. They come to us with vast differences in their background knowledge and experiences with print. Some come from countries with a high literacy rate where they learned to read in their own language; others are from cultures that have no written language and, therefore, no reading skills to transfer to the task of reading in English. It's not enough to simply label a non-reader "illiterate," because different types of illiteracy demand different strategies.

Of those who cannot read English, Haynes and Haverson (1982) distinguish four types:

Four Types of People Who Cannot Read English

- **Preliterates.** These are learners who speak a language for which there is no written form. They come from places where there are no books, signs, or magazines. They often have no idea that those squiggles on the page (which we call print) have meaning.

Figure 4.3. Hnuku's name and address. She has never held a pencil before coming to school. Her writing shows the beginnings of understanding form.

■ **Nonliterates.** These learners speak a language for which there is a written form, but they have not learned to read. They know that reading and writing have a purpose and that those marks have meaning, but they have simply not learned the skills.

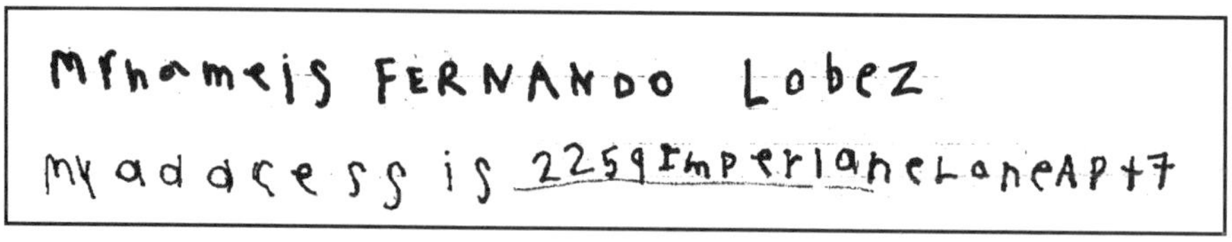

> Mfhameis FERNANDO Lobez
> my address is 2259ImperianeLaneAPt7

Figure 4.4. Fernando copied his name and address. Notice that he does not distinguish between *p* and *b* and does not yet know the concept of word boundaries.

■ **Semiliterates.** These students have very basic skills, such as knowing how to write their names, but not much more than that.

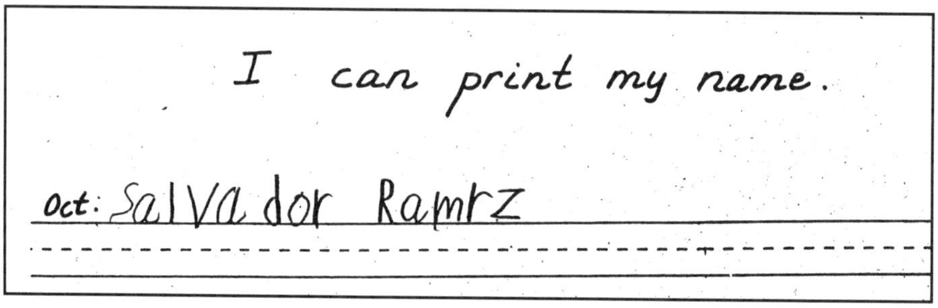

> I can print my name.
>
> Oct: Salvador RamrZ

Figure 4.5. Salvador wrote his name on his own.

■ **Nonalphabetics.** These are literate learners from countries whose languages do not have alphabetic writing systems. Logographic systems, such as Chinese, and syllabic systems, such as Japanese, use characters that represent complete words or syllables instead of individual letters as we have in English. These learners have learned the skills of reading and need to transfer them to the new language, but don't need to start again from the very beginning, "squiggles-are-words" stage.

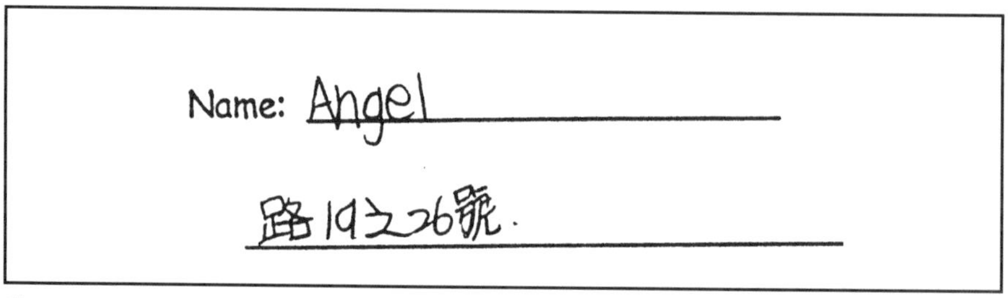

> Name: Angel
>
> 路19726號.

Figure 4.6. Here is Angel's signature in English and part of her address which demonstrates literacy in her first language.

For those ESL students who are literate in their own language, do not delay reading and writing until they have acquired advanced listening skills and oral fluency.

Much of the research in second-language acquisition in the 1980s compared it to first-language acquisition. There are many parallels; thus many teachers, both classroom and ESL, have adhered to the old simplified acquisition model:

Second-Language Acquisition Different From First

LISTENING > SPEAKING > READING > WRITING

First-language learners seem to follow this pattern, spending their first year or so listening to the language around them, then speaking, and only later learning to read and write. And anyone who has tried to learn a second language knows how much easier it is to understand the language than to speak it. However, this listening-speaking-reading-writing model presents some very serious problems that need to be addressed. We know now, due to studies of young children, that this model is inaccurate. Children do not suddenly begin the road to literacy when they reach school. Most children in developed countries have a great deal of prior knowledge about reading and its purposes. During the course of a day, they encounter many types of reading. Many have a host of opportunities to use paper and pencil to communicate messages (Teale and Sulzby 1986; Schickedanz 1986; Newman 1984) long before they come to school for formal learning (figure 4.7).

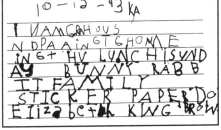

Figure 4.7. Kate's early writing: a mixture of her own composition and words copied from materials she found readily at hand.

Many of our ESL students, such as Andy, Glory, and Beth, studied English in schools in their native countries. They have often been taught by other non-native speakers and have spent a good deal of time learning English grammar. They may know how to read and write in our language, but cannot speak or make themselves understood. The listening-speaking-reading-writing model ignores their strengths by pushing them to learn to speak and listen before they are given reading and writing tasks.

Figure 4.8a-c. Andy, Glory, and Beth exhibit their very "bookish" English. They used pocket dictionaries to find words that represented their meaning. On the scale of literacy and skillful use of strategies, these three rank quite high. The word choice of such learners is often archaic and quite funny. It is sometimes difficult to guess what they are trying to say, as in Glory's case (b).

Name Anby
Date August 7, 1997

DAILY REFLECTION

I (did) Studied english I Go to bichcle I fell off the bichcle I'velvry Enbaged. I might goto see movie

a.

Name Glory
Date August 8, 1997

DAILY REFLECTION

I (did) to munt ; to ride at first in the beginning very quite highly happy behind to take place to munt a person of certain ability or to know mental and physical effors the exercise of.

b.

Name Beth
Date August 6, 1997

DAILY REFLECTION

I liked I liked took a mildly warm water shower.

c.

Much of the literature in the 1990s in bilingual and second-language learning has stated, rather dogmatically, that development in oral language should precede reading. While it is true that in order to read students need to know a certain number of words, this DOES NOT MEAN THAT READING SHOULD BE DELAYED.

The reasons for this are

- Time is passing! If, for instance, Hnuku arrives in the fourth grade, or the eighth grade having had no prior experience with print, spending four months, six months, or a year only on oral vocabulary is time wasted. While learners must have a core vocabulary to start reading, to delay reading and writing until they have oral fluency is to substantially delay their ability to function in the regular classroom.

- Print can be introduced from the first. Compelling research (Hudelson 1983; Edelsky 1986; Ammon 1985) has demonstrated that students who are limited in their speaking ability can still compose texts and learn to read. Learning to read and write should go hand in hand with learning to speak.

- There are so many great books with few words on the market these days; teachers can find myriad resources that help students with minimal reading skills learn content and reading.

- Learning to read can proceed hand in hand with vocabulary development.

This does not mean that a book is plunked in front of the student and he is expected to read it on day one. That would be nonsensical. However, it does mean that the student can and should be a participant in reading events that take place throughout the day. Preliterate and nonliterate students often need a year or more of simple exposure to print before they can actually begin reading independently. Teachers frequently get frustrated because these students don't seem to be learning. But, if we consider that the average Western child has had five years of experience with print before formal instruction begins, there's a lot of catching up to do.

Following are places within the curriculum for you to start making the connections and building on them.

Where to Begin

Connecting the Four Skills to the Curriculum

The first step in learning to read and write in the new language is learning words that are useful to the learners, usually the first words they have learned to speak in their first language. The strategies that follow provide a bridge to the reading and writing tasks required of students, both literate and nonliterate. These strategies are examples of activities that can provide meaningful, quality instruction to groups of students working at widely varying levels of language and reading proficiency: the beauty of the following activities is that they can either be "scaffolded" (Boyd and Peregoy 1997), in the sense that you can initiate them and take complete control of the activity, or they can be turned over to students who are gaining increasing independence.

This is not an exhaustive list, but should help you validate the fact that many of the activities you are already doing with your English-speaking students are also appropriate for your ESL students. This list should also help you develop your own methods and materials. The strategies can be used with the class as a whole or with individual students. These are "rich" activities because students at different levels of ability and competence can profit from them. Many of these strategies help you create a "print rich environment." This is the first priority in any classroom, particularly one that contains ESL students. In order to establish the speech-print connection, students need to see words in action.

Art

This is first on our list because students do not need to know any English or be able to read a word to join in, succeed, and shine. Art is universal. It is something beginners can express themselves with and is often the one avenue they have to communicate what they know and can do. We have found many shy, otherwise unresponsive learners demonstrate creativity and mastery in drawing, weaving, or embroidery. Art is an activity that older, more proficient students can also enjoy. It can be incorporated into any activity, as we will demonstrate throughout the rest of the book. Art is a literacy activity (Dyson 1990; Schirmacher 1998).

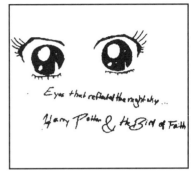

Figure 4.9. Elise drew this picture as an enthusiastic response to the Harry Potter books. She illustrated her own Harry Potter story called *Harry Potter and the Birds of Faith*.

Figure 4.10a-c. Often, second-language learners are gifted artistically. When given the chance, they can render drawings that show their understanding far more than words can. Regina portrays her day at camp (a), Herman shows how he felt walking on the high ropes course (b), and Wade reflects on his sinking boat (c).

Figure 4.11. This wistful drawing shows a student's home in Cambodia. While the other students in the class were learning the rooms of a house, he wanted to show his teacher the home he had to leave.

It allows students to reflect on, organize, and communicate how they represent the real world in symbolic form. Beginners to both reading and speaking English can demonstrate their understandings of stories and concepts through artistic means.

Encourage students to articulate what they have drawn: students can dictate their thoughts to the teacher or write their own words.

Labeling

Surrounding Students With Words—Some Strategies

One of the first ways students learn a second language is by learning the English words for objects they know in their native language. Making lists embeds this task within a meaningful social context. Ventriglia (1982) notes that teachers can facilitate abstracting meaningful concepts and labeling in the second language by

- Presenting words with concrete objects or pictures.
- Organizing vocabulary into units, grouping words by concept.
- Expanding the vocabulary words in a meaningful concept.
- Using all the senses in teaching vocabulary.

Even though students may not make the connection that those squiggles are a graphic representation of the concept, seeing the squiggles every day helps reinforce the connection.

Label items in the classroom. Label such things as the window, cupboard, desk, and so on. Again, put written labels on objects they already know in their first language. If they are already literate, they can also write labels for each item in their first language.

To reinforce visual discrimination and practice sight-word recognition, make labeling into a game. Label classroom items, then make a duplicate set of labels and ask the student to match them to the labels about the room. This activity is appropriate for all age levels and classes, especially in content areas such as science and physical education, which have their own specialized vocabulary and equipment. Labeling is particularly useful when you have new students and must find worthwhile tasks to occupy them while they adjust to their new environment.

After you, an aide, or a buddy have played this with a student a number of times, take the labels off the items and have the student return as many labels as he knows to their proper places.

Lists

Lists are a natural development and extension of the labeling strategy. Readers and writers build vocabulary and learn to interact with the written word from seeing words in print to watching, listening, and helping develop lists that are grouped in some logical way. Display lists of words that the class has brainstormed as a lead-in to a writing exercise, unit of study, or activity.

How do animals protect themselves?		
Use teeth	Quills	Jumping
Use their horns	Some kick	Climbing
By growling	Fly	Use claws
Running	Camouflage	Scare enemies
Fighting	Stink	Run

Figure 4.12. This list was written by a first-grade teacher made from ideas elicited from her students.

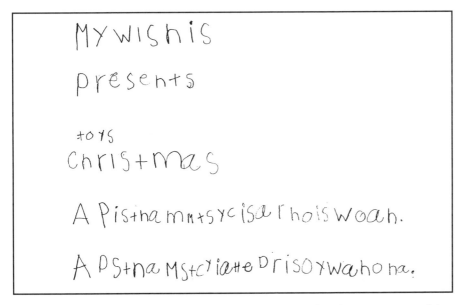

Figure 4.13. This is a first grader's list of what she wants for Christmas. Most of the words were copied. She composed the last two sentences herself.

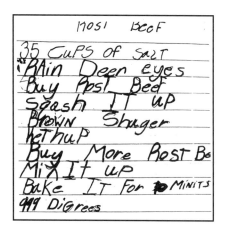

Figure 4.14. A first grader's recipe for roast beef.

Yesterday	I saw six ducks.
	I saw ~~some~~ many dragon flys.
	I saw two lizargs.
	I saw four mosquitos.
	I saw a dog.
	I saw four fishs.
	I saw a squirrel.
	I saw two ravems.
	I saw four birds.
	I saw ~~some~~ many ants.

Figure 4.15. This is a list of animals seen during a walk around the lake made by an older, more proficient learner.

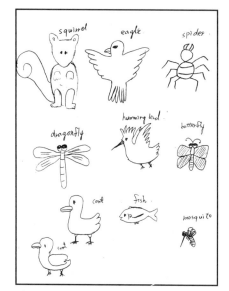

Figure 4.16. Lists can also be accompanied by drawing to aid in rereading.

Limei Li	
Bob Ewell	
1	Mayella's father
2	heavy drinker
3	liar
4	left-handed
5	hulking
6	live in the dump
7	has 8 children
8	can write his name
9	make his children go to school only the first day of the year.
10	shoots animals all the season

Figure 4.17. Limei lists facts she gleaned about the character Bob Ewell from the novel *To Kill a Mockingbird*.

All levels

- Appropriate behavior in the classroom
- Phys. Ed.: the rules of games
- Science: important vocabulary; lab rules and procedures
- Math: technical vocabulary; words with specific math meanings, such as *product* or *square*
- Art: rules for set-up and clean-up
- Social science: vocabulary for current unit of study
- Language arts: color words; emotions; winter words; vivid verbs; story starters such as *firsts, lasts, important people, things I get mad about*

Lists can be used in many ways for many different purposes. Depending on the level of your students, either you or they can do the writing. The following examples show the many kinds of lists students can produce.

Make and Display Charts

Whenever possible, combine a word with a picture. Display charts that combine words and illustrations. Attractive, easy-to-use charts are available ready-made from most teacher supply stores, or ESL students can be given the task of making the charts, thus reinforcing the word meanings as well as allowing them to contribute in nonverbal ways to the class. Here are some suggestions for chart construction:

Elementary level

■ Colors, animals, money, toys, shapes

All levels

■ Science: the human body, food chains, ecosystems
■ Math: symbols such as > < + = % with their verbal meanings. Words for equivalents such as: *sum = add difference = subtract*

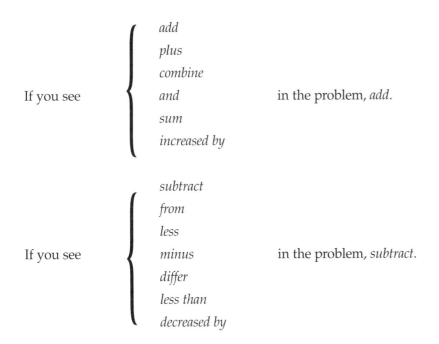

If you see
- *add*
- *plus*
- *combine*
- *and*
- *sum*
- *increased by*

in the problem, *add.*

If you see
- *subtract*
- *from*
- *less*
- *minus*
- *differ*
- *less than*
- *decreased by*

in the problem, *subtract.*

■ Phys. Ed.: equipment; familiar commands or techniques, such as dribbling, passing; common vocabulary
■ Music: time equivalent for notes; words for symbols such as treble and bass clef
■ Social studies: maps; time lines
■ Shop: safety rules; equipment and tools

Design Activities Using Environmental Print

Because these words are relevant to their lives, most English-speaking children know environmental print long before they come to kindergarten. Even the newest ESL students can pick out words they recognize, such as McDonalds, K-Mart, and Citgo. Goodman writes:

> The development of print awareness in environmental contexts is the root of literacy most common to all learners….In the print-rich environment of most present cultures, young children are consciously interacting with, organizing and analyzing the meanings of the visible language….The development of knowledge about print embedded in environmental settings is the beginning of reading development. (qtd. in Teale and Sulzby 1986, 6)

You can invent a host of activities that employ words seen in everyday life, such as McDonalds, Safeway, and Stop. Many of the words are intimately tied to a configuration or logo that gives a decoding clue. McDonalds, for instance, is written with the "golden arches" and Stop is always within the context of a red octagon. As the students develop more skills, they will be able to decode the words without the use of these visual clues, but they are an important first step in equating sign-symbol correspondence.

Elementary level

- Have children bring in empty boxes and cans and put together a class grocery store.

- Have the students brainstorm all the places they see words: labels, billboards, television, packages, traffic signs, and so on.

- With the entire class, take a tour of the school or the neighborhood to scout for words.

All levels

- Have students collect all the words they see and categorize them in different ways.

- Have students keep three-day journals of all the different kinds of reading they do in a day, from street signs to school assignments.

- Have a T-shirt design contest.

- Write a class yearbook.

- Write a classroom telephone directory.

Use I-Can-Read Books and Dictionaries

The variations on this theme are endless at all levels. This is another way to reinforce students' vocabulary and demonstrate what your regular students know; it is also an activity you can implement immediately with your new students.

- Beginning students can cut pictures from magazines or newspapers of all the words they recognize, from *house* to *lion*, then paste one picture onto each page of a blank book. Underneath each picture, you or an aide print "I can read..." and then the word. Usually the students quickly remember that each page starts with "I can read" and, since they chose the pictures, they are able to "read" the book almost immediately and feel a real sense of achievement.

- Preliterate students can cut out pictures of things for which they know the English word, and paste the pictures into their books. In the content areas, you can implement this activity before students are able to do regular class work.

- Students can categorize words—foods, body parts, or furniture, for example—and add new words to each category as they expand their vocabulary.

- Those who are already literate and have learned more English can print the words next to their pictures (figure 4.18). Advanced students can alphabetize and write definitions for their words.

- ESL students can work with an aide or a buddy, using their dictionary for review. They can also practice the words by themselves while the rest of the class is involved in other activities. This is a terrific confidence booster; it demonstrates concretely to students how far they have advanced in their knowledge of English.

Figure 4.18. A third-grader's picture dictionary.

Use Games

Games are not simply time fillers; treat them seriously. Ventriglia (1982) notes that children acquiring a second language "appear to learn language best in conversations or in game-like situations where language is used meaningfully and is associated with some concrete reference at the beginning." Games provide this context for socializing and reinforcing language. Native English-speaking students can become the teachers and can learn valuable lessons in patience and modifying their language to provide input that's comprehensible to the language learner. Learning the rules to games requires careful listening. Games have a clear repetitive structure, in which words are tied closely to actions. They are also strong motivators. Even the shyest, most reluctant, or non-verbal students will get involved in a game and forget their inhibitions. When the focus is on having fun, vocabulary is learned as a by-product and friendships are fostered. You can choose the level of sophistication of rules and vocabulary you want reinforced. The game "Sorry," for instance, uses colors, counting, recognizing numbers, and several important survival words and phrases, such as *sorry, start,* and *It's your turn*. Here are other suggestions:

- Bingo (can be modified for any type of lesson)
- Trivial Pursuit, Jeopardy, Go Fish
- Board games: Sorry, The Last Straw, Candyland, Operation, Hungry Hippo, Yahtzee, Clue
- For older students: Monopoly, Risk, Boggle, Scrabble
- Guessing games: Simon Says; Mother May I?; Win, Lose, or Draw
- Card games: Concentration, War, Old Maid, Go Fish, Cribbage
- Word games: Twenty Questions, Ghost

Many games can be modified, with questions tailored for any content class or lesson. Make your own version of Trivial Pursuit, Jeopardy, or Go Fish.

Use Tapes

Commercially produced tapes have shown to be very effective with both beginning readers having trouble with phonics to older middle, high-school, and adult readers who have found little but failure. Although these tapes are expensive, you may find them worth the money. You can also find better readers to do the recording, and make your own. A word of caution— they are not a "center" activity and demand a great deal of input and reporting to you as the teacher.

You can tape almost anything—stories, songs, rhymes, or chants. Tapes are useful: they reinforce the speech-to-print connection as well as meaningful vocabulary and allow your ESL students to work on reading while you are engaged in another activity. However, tapes should not be used simply as fillers when you have nothing else for these students to do. Taped books used by ESL students should already be familiar to them, having been read and discussed with the class or another student. You should not try to "break new ground" with tapes; they are better used as reinforcement of previously covered material (Carbo 1992). For beginning students, be sure to program in a "beep" at each page-ending so they know when to turn the page. Without this you can sometimes discover a student "reading" three pages behind the text!

- You get double benefits if you allow your regular students to do the taping for you, giving them extra practice in reading.
- Tape songs for pleasure listening. Try to include English-word recordings of songs from students' own cultures.
- If possible, send tapes home with the children. Discussions with parents in their own language will greatly benefit students.
- At the secondary level, tape your lectures so that the students can take them home and listen to them a second time for learning reinforcement.

Songs

Songs can be a delightful way to work on rhythm, pronunciation, and vocabulary. People of all ages love to learn and sing songs. You can ask your native English-speaking students to find pictures or props to teach ESL students the words.

The use of songs doesn't have to be limited to the primary grades, and the songs don't have to be juvenile tunes only a kindergartner would love. Students of all ages listen to the Top 40, whether they understand the words or not, and many second-language learners comment that they learn a great deal of their language from the radio and TV. You can capitalize on this by bringing in songs for discussion, songs to illustrate a theme or even a grammatical point. Use such perennial favorites as Bob Dylan or Peter, Paul, and Mary, or social commentators like Pink Floyd, or language-development songwriters/artists such as Bob Schneider of Toronto. Give students copies of the lyrics so that they can read them as they follow along. If you can't stand to watch MTV or Much Music, get one of your students to tape some of the more interesting songs for class discussion.

- Buy a book of camp songs, or Boy Scout songs. Those songs have been around forever, with good reason. "If You're Happy and You Know It," "The More We Get Together," and so on are great for reading, pronunciation, and just plain fun. Barb makes her summer students sing every day. Even though she has to put up with groans and "We no sing today, Teacher," they really like to try to outdo each other on Valderi Valdera and "There'll be a hot time in the old town tonight, FIRE! FIRE! FIRE!" Hearing a student spontaneously start singing "Oh My Darling," during a walk or an art project is very gratifying.

- History: use folk songs or spirituals such as "Swing Low Sweet Chariot" to enliven an understanding of slavery.

- Social Science: use songs from other lands to give insight into other cultures.

- Government: use social commentary songs such as "Eve of Destruction," "Rain on the Scarecrow," or Neil Sedaka's "The Immigrant."

- English: English classes are the perfect place to study songs. You can look at poetic theme, rhyme, sense of place, as well as natural rhythm and cadence. The early Beatles' and Rolling Stones' ballads are naturals. It may be dangerous to allow students to choose their own, since many rock groups write a wide range of songs that sometimes includes erotic or violent material. You may want to get together with other teachers and compile a list of songs you would like to include and let the students choose from these. Or have the students copy the lyrics and get prior approval for a song to study.

Drama

Drama is one of the most effective ways to develop language. Drama "can be a link between speech and writing. Through drama, children are guided to imagine, explore, enact, communicate, and reflect on ideas, concepts and feelings" (Stewig and Buege 1994).

Moffett (1967) goes so far as to assert that "drama and speech are central to the language curriculum, not peripheral....I see drama as the matrix of all language activities, subsuming speech and engendering the varieties of writing and reading."

The benefits of drama for ESL students cannot be overstated. They gain confidence in English and in themselves. When students are listening and responding to stage directions and hearing the others use the vocabulary, comprehensible input is built in. For instance, during a production of *Goldilocks and the Three Bears*, Mercy (playing Goldilocks) was two beds ahead of Nicola the narrator, who was just getting Goldilocks up the stairs from the living room. When Nicola read, "So she climbed into the first bed," and the chorus chimed, "This bed is too hard" Mercy leapt back onto the first bed.

Understanding dialogue and sequence comes from practice and repetition: necessary skills for language learning, but often tedious and boring. Drama builds all the skills—listening, vocabulary, reading, and writing— within a framework of fun and active participation. For instance, Barb and a group of middle- and high-schoolers, produced their own version of *Lon Po Po*. As this particular group were all Taiwanese, they were familiar with the story. The students wrote their own script. In it, the wolf killed and ate the youngest child, played by Dora. The children, hiding in the dark, were alerted to imminent danger because the wolf ate very loudly, and then, when they asked him to share, threw them a bloody finger. At the end of the play, mother and father came home to find the wolf dead and the children in the tree. The narrator's final lines read: "So, the children explain what happened the night before to mother and father. After that they are very hungry so they BBQ the wolf and have a wonderful meal. The End."

The logic of the family having a wonderful meal when Dora is dead, did not appeal to Barb's sensibilities, and long discussions ensued as to whether they should have the father cut Dora out of the wolf's stomach and find her alive, or whether they should mourn her loss. The group liked their ending as it was, and thus it stayed. Dora's dead. Oh well. Let's BBQ and be happy.

Everyone can participate, even those who have little or no English. A chorus can provide safety in numbers, and the lowest students can be carried along with the rest of the group. For example,

Chorus: Little Pig, Little Pig, Let Me Come In!
          Not by the Hair of My Chinny-Chin-Chin!

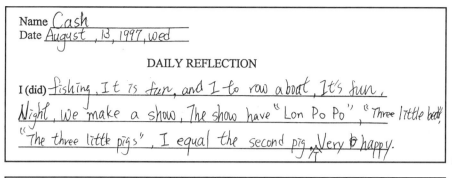

Figure 4.19a-b. Here are Lynne's and Cash's reflections on their roles in *The Three Little Pigs* (a) and *Goldilocks and the Three Bears* (b).

The lowest students do not have to have speaking parts. In many plays parts can be built in for everyone. For example, in *Goldilocks and the Three Bears*, students portrayed a great big bowl, a middle-sized bowl, and a wee, tiny bowl, three chairs, and three beds. The children who were not actually onstage were the chorus.

Using drama doesn't have to entail elaborate plays. It can be as simple as having children enact Mother Goose rhymes such as *The Queen of Hearts* or acting *My Darling Clementine* while the others sing the lines.

- History: Dramatize an important historical event.
- Government: Enact a bill into law; hold a trial; poll the student body on an issue; hold an election.
- Social Sciences: Use socio-dramas—set up a situation in which the students have to make difficult choices and ad-lib their solutions.
- English: Reenact a scene from a play or a piece of literature.

Elementary Level

Use rhymes, fairy tales, and puppet shows. Puppet shows are particularly effective for ESL learners when they manipulate the puppets while you read the script. The students are responsible for understanding the material and responding on cue, but are not required to produce language themselves.

Patterned Language

Patterned language involves texts in which certain language structures are repeated again and again. Patterned language is a particularly important source for beginning readers and beginning language users. The writers of those endless drill-and-practice foreign-language textbooks recognized the importance of patterned language in language learning. Giving readers the strategy of imitating phrases helps them make the transition from labeling to sentence formation. It allows them to hear and repeat chunks of language that are meaningful. Patterned language has many positive features:

- The repetition gives students the practice they need in order to internalize a form.

- Students can use these patterns as building blocks—they make generalizations from the patterns they have learned and can then move on to create their own sentences.

When the forms are practiced consistently, they become instinctive. Students can focus on communication and learning new structures with the security of having a few forms well learned.

Ventriglia (1982) notes that students learning a second language naturally adopt a strategy of following patterns, but they learn patterns that are meaningful and useful to them, ones that can be applied in a social context. Long meaningless drills found in textbooks are easily forgotten. But by selecting topics that interest the learners, using phrases elicited from them, and practicing these phrases in a game-like situation, you can use patterns successfully, not only to reinforce vocabulary, but to introduce new linguistic patterns in a systematic way. The students can easily transfer the patterns they have learned and apply them to new social contexts.

Make a distinction, therefore, between these types of sentences and the traditional "This is a _____." sentences found in many older texts in which students simply fill in blanks. Barb once consulted with a tutor who had been working on such sentences with two twelve-year-old boys. They couldn't remember the difference between *a* and *an* from one day to the next, and the tutor had decided that they were learning disabled. Jumping to this conclusion based upon such insufficient data was damaging. The boys weren't learning disabled, they were simply bored struggling with a very minor grammatical point that had little relevance or significance to them in the face of the huge task of learning the English language.

With the following types of patterned language, you can avoid tedium while retaining the positive aspects of this type of continued practice of forms.

For example, several students of varying levels did their own version of *The Very Hungry Caterpillar* by Eric Carle (figure 4.20). Because they knew the format, they could reproduce in their own words, at their own level of proficiency and skills, a book they could each be proud of.

A chant is

> A group of words that comes alive when given a rhythmical reading.…Any speech exercise based on a strong rhythm contributes to the development of speech and language skills. Language learning is accelerated by having fun with and exploring the rhythm in words. An energetic approach, using oral repetition with rhythmical expression, leads to pleasant, stimulating experiences…Chanting, with its rhythmical repetition of words, transcends language differences. It is useful for children in programs of ESL, ESD and beginning readers (Dunn, *Butterscotch Dreams* 1987).

You can use old favorites such as,

- One Potato, two potato, three potato, four
- Jump rope songs
- Or commercially produced chants such as *Jazz Chants for Children* (Graham 1979) and *Big Chants* (Graham 1994).

What if the elementary curriculum guide mandates that you teach your students such words as *can, run, jump, I, and, the, go,* and *was* by October? Or suppose your tenth grader says things like, "I didn't brought my homework," or "I seed that movie last week." Is there any alternative to relying solely on a basal reader or simple memorization of word lists?

One particularly effective use of patterned language involves frame sentences, developed by Marlene and Robert McCracken, which allow the teacher to plug student ideas into a controlled pattern of words.

All levels

The McCrackens (1995) recommend using a different frame sentence everyday: "Some children will grasp their first learned frame and write with it seemingly forever if we use a single frame for several days." They also stress quantity, and insist that, for proper reinforcement, the teacher elicit thirty to forty (or more) brainstormed responses for each frame. Every day students can chant back the previous day's frames and even brainstorm new responses.

Elementary levels

Use frame sentences to help students understand difficult material or to elicit what they already know about a topic. Ask the question, "What do you know about … ?" For instance, "What do you know about mammals?" Set up the frame sentence, "A mammal is an animal that has…" Any topic or issue can be introduced this way.

Frames can be derived from basal readers, from content-area units being studied, or from virtually any source. Once you get started using frame sentences, the possibilities are endless. With ESL students, this is a particularly effective way to work on a problem once you've diagnosed a need.

Figure 4.20. Examples of *The Very Hungry Camper* patterned on *The Very Hungry Caterpillar* by Eric Carle. Note the freedom a basic structure gives students to express their own ideas, creativity, and humor.

For instance, if the student needs to work on the irregular past tense, you can begin sentences like

> Yesterday I went...
> Yesterday I saw...
> Yesterday I ate...

Or you can teach conjunctions and transition words that ESL students often find difficult:

> A horse can walk and so can an elephant...
> A horse can walk but a fish can't...
> A worm can't walk and neither can a fish....

Beginners can simply copy examples given.

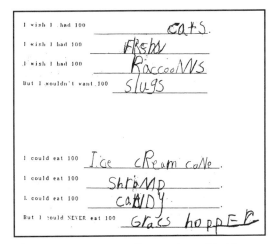

Figure 4.21. Kate as a first grader, added her own ideas to a basic frame.

a.

b.

c.

Figure 4.22a-c. In our summer program, we included several challenge courses that necessitated students doing things they might consider frightening, such as camping under the open sky in an area known to have bears. We decided to tackle the issues head on: we talked about being scared and strategies to think through what to do when one is afraid. We developed frame sentences based on these ideas.

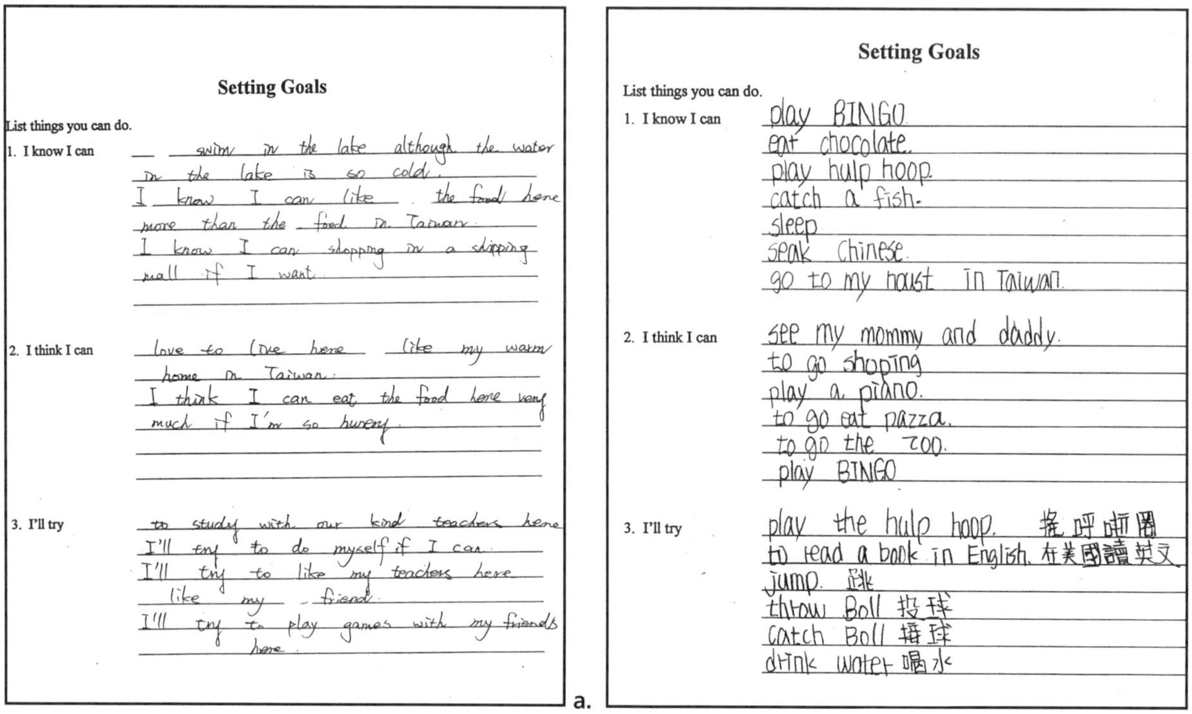

Setting Goals

List things you can do.

1. I know I can — swim in the lake although the water in the lake is so cold.
I know I can like the food here more than the food in Taiwan
I know I can shopping in a shipping mall if I want.

2. I think I can love to live here like my warm home in Taiwan.
I think I can eat the food here very much if I'm so hurry.

3. I'll try to study with our kind teachers here
I'll try to do myself if I can.
I'll try to like my teachers here like my friend.
I'll try to play games with my friends here.

a.

Setting Goals

List things you can do.

1. I know I can play BINGO
eat chocolate.
play hulp hoop.
catch a fish.
sleep
speak Chinese.
go to my houst in Taiwan.

2. I think I can see my mommy and daddy.
to go shoping
play a piano.
to go eat pazza.
to go the zoo.
play BINGO

3. I'll try play the hulp hoop. 搖呼啦圈
to read a book in English. 在美國讀英文
jump. 跳
throw Boll 投球
catch Boll 接球
drink water 喝水

b.

Figure 4.23a-b. More proficient learners can creatively combine words and chunks of language to express their ideas.

Rhymes

Small children enjoy rhymes, often repeating them over and over again to themselves. Non-native-English speakers can pick them up very quickly and derive great pleasure and a sense of achievement from being able to recite them. Rhymes allow ESL students to practice (within the context of a whole text) the forty-four sounds of English. Learners are able to model intonation, stress, and pronunciation in a fun, dynamic, and meaningful way.

Rhymes can also be incorporated into literacy activities at the elementary level.

- Choose a familiar rhyme such as "Humpty Dumpty." Using pictures for each scene, have the students put them in order. When they have learned the words and the sequence of the rhyme, they can begin to match pictures with words.
- Prepare a pocket chart of word cards so that the students can follow the words as they chant them. Make duplicate word cards of the rhymes, and then have the ESL students place them in the correct order as they recite. Beginners can start by matching word cards and placing them on top of the words of the poem that have been written on large paper. This not only reinforces the sound-to-print connection, but builds sight word vocabulary.
- Say a word and have the group find it on the chart. Remove several words and have individuals replace them in the proper sequence, chanting the rhyme to check if the words have been replaced properly.

- Have class members make their own books into which they can copy the rhymes and illustrate them. This reinforces, in an enjoyable way, not only reading, but writing and spelling, too.
- Give a rhymes concert.
- Act the rhymes out.
- Have students tape themselves reciting the rhymes. Include ESL students taping some they have learned well. Have them tape on several different occasions so that they can monitor their own progress when they hear their voices played back.

Sourcebooks for activities based on rhymes are available in most teacher supply stores.

Conclusion

With language learning, the key is authenticity rather than fractionating reading, writing, listening, and speaking into separate skills, then breaking them down even further into meaningless exercises.

The activities we have listed can be incorporated into the themes you are working on. They don't involve a lot of extra planning or extra work, but the benefits you reap in terms of your students' language acquisition are great.

Fortunately, most school boards and administrations recognize that helping students achieve literacy is not solely the job of the elementary teacher or the high school English teacher. It is the job of all teachers, from the art teacher to the phys. ed. instructor, from the band director to the shop teacher. Reading and writing are an integral part of every course within the curriculum from math to driver education. Language instruction is everybody's business. In subsequent chapters, we will show how this can be done.

CHAPTER 5

READING

In this chapter, we discuss the basics for teaching and promoting reading with ESL students. We focus on

- The process of learning to read.
- What all students need to become successful readers.
- Balancing the needs of fluent and nonfluent readers.
- Meeting the particular reading needs of individual students.

Hnuku cannot read. She is classified as preliterate: she comes from a family that has no history of reading and writing and does not know that print carries meaning. When presented with a book, she cannot tell the front from the back. She was observed holding a picture book upside down, and only when she encountered a picture of a person did she turn it right side up.

If Hnuku arrives in kindergarten this does not present an insurmountable problem. She is immersed in print and sees the teachers modeling reading and writing behaviors daily. Hnuku also hears the teacher giving instruction in the many facets of reading and writing.

If Hnuku arrives in the second grade, she is not only three years behind in formal instruction, but about seven years behind in terms of "literate behaviors." Literate behaviors attend most of our mainstream children who have handled books, seen many hours of television, and read the infinite array of signs and displays that surround people in Western countries. By the time Hnuku reaches high school, the problem of her inability to make sense of print presents staggering obstacles to her ability to succeed in school.

In this particular case, Hnuku arrived at the age of sixteen with no previous schooling. In two years, she has learned to speak very well, and can even write a bit, but she still has not learned to read. She is now eighteen and school officials are telling her that they have done all they can and this is her last year; whether she graduates or not, she has to leave. Science, history, and English teachers do not consider it their job to teach reading. The ESL teacher has turned her over to the latest in a string of tutors and told the tutor to work on phonics. It didn't work before, but, as the teacher says, "We've tried everything else."

Fernando is a recent immigrant from a small town in Mexico. The only English he spoke during an initial session with an intake person was the word "teacher." He has never been to school and is not literate in either English or Spanish. He cannot write his own name.

Hnuku and Fernando are not isolated cases. Many students come to our schools and seem to grasp the spoken language immediately, but lag far behind in reading skills. The ways we have traditionally taught North American children to read often do not work with ESL students, and, like Hnuku, these students struggle with the rudiments year after frustrating year. What can be done?

Defining Reading

At the height of the whole language movement, everything seemed clear: many teachers believed, and proceeded under the assumption, that simply by immersing children in good literature, children would learn to read. In the last years of the 1990s, a tremendous tsunami-sized backlash ensued, and a great number of books and articles came out trumpeting "balanced reading programs." But in many of these "balanced" reading texts, the focus is primarily on how to teach phonics; much of what passes for "balanced" is a thinly disguised "back-to-basics" program.

What does this mean? Things have become very muddy, and many teachers are now unclear as to what to teach and what not to teach. It also seems that, once again, there is much confusion about the place of phonics in the curriculum—when, how much, how often, and even just plain how.

One of the keys to addressing these issues is to refocus on what reading *is*, and what children need in order to learn to read. If we define reading as *getting meaning from print*, then it becomes clearer. Reading is not simply decoding to sound. Knowing the alphabet is not necessarily a mandatory prerequisite to learning to read. As Cooper (1997) writes, "No evidence supports the idea that students develop literacy by being taught discrete skills." If we keep this definition in mind, then we can proceed with some degree of confidence.

For all learners, at every age and every level of proficiency, reading must be for meaning; if one is not getting meaning, one is not reading.

Figure 5.1 shows an example of a real text taken from a remote language in Asia. When Barb was looking for it she found an overhead she had made. It took a great deal of thought to figure out which way was right side up, which way was upside down, and which way was backward. Can you "read" this? Even if you can pronounce the words (we can't!), does that constitute reading? Of course not! Just calling the words does not mean you are reading, because you are not getting meaning. If you do somehow manage to get the meaning of this you will be very surprised (and we're not telling).

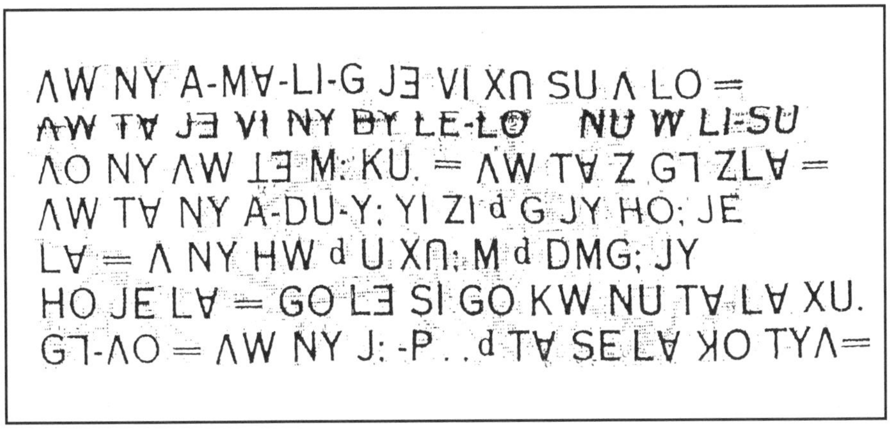

```
ΛW NY A-M∀-LI-G JƎ VI XՈ SU Λ LO =
ʌW T∀ JƎ VI NY ꞐƳ ꞁE-ꞁⵔ   NU W ꞁⵊSU
ΛO NY ΛW ꞱƎ M: KU. = ΛW T∀ Z Gꓶ ZL∀ =
ΛW T∀ NY A-DU-Y: YI ZIᵈ G JY HO: JE
L∀ = Λ NY HW ᵈ U XՈ; M ᵈ DMG; JY
HO JE L∀ = GO LƎ SI GO KW NU T∀ L∀ XU.
Gꓶ-ΛO = ΛW NY J: -P . .ᵈ T∀ SE L∀ ꓘO TYΛ=
```

Figure 5.1. Text of an Asian language. Can you read this?

Students calling out words correctly in English, but not being able to tell you what they understood from the text, aren't reading either. It's called "barking at print." Many teachers assume that because they sound as if they know what they're doing, or they're approximating what's on the page, they're readers. But unless they understand the story, they're not.

According to Frank Smith (1997), two things are necessary for one to learn to read:

1. The availability of interesting material that makes sense to the individual learner.

2. An understanding and more experienced reader as a guide.

Smith unequivocally states that what is important is knowing what reading is and knowing enough about the particular students in your classroom to decide what to do, and how to proceed. In other words, you, as the teacher, know your students best, and, thus, you are the one in the best position to decide which activities will best further your students' competence and proficiency.

If your entire classroom were filled with native English-speaking students who have had multiple experiences, come from literacy-rich homes, and read on grade level, teaching would be relatively easy. But students such as Hnuku make your job more challenging and demand more flexibility. Maintaining a program that meets all of your students' needs is indeed a balancing act on its own.

Creating Balance in Your Reading Program

Balance, writes Cunningham (2000), "is the characteristic of a program that includes multiple methods and is sensitive to the fact that children are at different levels in each area of literacy. Only such a multifaceted program taught well can come close to teaching reading and writing well to all of today's children." Balance is, writes Spiegel (1998), "decision-making by you the teacher, in which you make thoughtful choices every day, every hour about the best way to help every child in your classroom become a reader." Balance does *not* mean (*California Language Arts Framework* 1998) "that all skills and standards receive equal emphasis at a given point in time. Rather, balance implies that the overall emphasis accorded to a skill or standard is determined by its priority or importance relative to students' language and literacy levels and needs." Using rigid, single doctrinaire methods, such as focusing primarily on phonics, always underemphasizes the other essential skills in gaining meaning. In addition, they limit your flexibility in adapting your program to the needs of your students.

The following list includes suggestions to help you create balance in your reading program:

- Always keep meaning as the major focus.

- Keep a balance between teacher-directed and student-initiated reading and writing.

- Remember that skills such as phonemic awareness, letter/sound knowledge, and word knowledge develop in the process of becoming an independent reader. This means embedding the skills within meaningful activities, avoiding phonics first and/or as an isolated activity removed from reading.

- Use both direct instruction and independent practice as means of furthering reading.

- Promote not just the basic skills such as vocabulary and word recognition, but the higher-order reasoning tasks, such as synthesis and analysis from the beginning. Don't limit students to questions such as,

  The names of Jacob's two children are _____ and _____.

  or

  How much of the earth's surface is covered by water?

  These are simply recall questions that limit students' abilities. We must ask questions that promote critical thinking such as,

  Why does pollution in Michigan matter to people in Georgia?

  It goes without saying that students need more help in answering such questions, but it is important to give them the opportunity to grapple with such issues and thoughts.

Reading as a Whole Skill

Many component skills make up the act of reading: recognizing letters and words, predicting, and confirming, to name a few. The temptation for teachers of ESL students, particularly those with illiterate students like Hnuku, is to focus on teaching the alphabet and a large sight vocabulary before attempting whole texts. As important as these are, focusing on each skill in isolation, can be, for ESL learners, not only counterproductive, but can result in poor readers or even in those unable to read at all.

Before anyone can learn to read, the learner must understand that the language we hear and speak can be written down, and that, conversely, what we see in written form can say something to us. Therefore, one of the fundamental things students must learn is what reading is and why we read.

The Commission on Reading stated in *Becoming a Nation of Readers* (1985) that "the most useful form of practice is doing the whole skill of reading—that is, reading meaningful text for the purpose of understanding the message it contains." We can make the analogy to a jigsaw puzzle—no piece is useful on its own, unconnected to the rest. Only together do all the pieces make a comprehensible whole. There is only one way to learn how to read: by reading. Literacy must be introduced through the use of real and whole texts that the students find interesting or entertaining, in an environment where both reading and writing are celebrated and encouraged.

To enable your ESL students to learn to read or to make the transition to reading in English, you must make materials available and consciously direct their acquisition of reading skills: in other words, you must make time for both instruction and independent practice.

All readers need

- To be immersed in real reading for real purposes.
- A wealth of materials they will be capable of reading.
- A helpful guide—someone to guide them in their acquisition of English-language skills and reading.
- A supportive environment.
- Time.

Immersion—Make Reading a Daily Commitment

Any school day should contain frequent opportunities to read. Being immersed in reading involves reading a variety of written materials for a variety of purposes: textbooks, magazines, newspapers, recipes, manuals, comic books, TV guides, Dear Abby, and so on. This means reading whole texts not words in isolation. Sentences are easier to read than words, paragraphs are easier to read than sentences, and whole texts are the easiest to read of all: the text, and the pictures (if there are any), give clues about the meanings of words and concepts that the student might miss on the first try.

Third-grader Robby, reading *George's Marvelous Medicine* by Roald Dahl, could not decode the word *medicine* in the title. He paused and stumbled over it, then went on. Three paragraphs later, he read the word correctly, when mother said, "And don't forget to give Grandma her medicine." Within the context, and the familiar phrase, the meaning was clear.

In the past, readers, including most basals, were often written with the rationale that because stories were shorter and filled with simple words based on a "readability formula," they were easier. In actual fact, they often were not. This is a passage taken from an adult basic reading text:

Jim will fix the mill. Kim, his kid, is big. Kim will fix the rig. Jim will fill the bin. Jim will give Kim the pig. The pig will live in the mill. The pig will dig in the hill. The pig hid. Will the pig yip? Will Kim miss the pig? Jim hit his hip in the mill. Jim is ill. Will Kim give him the pill? The pill is in the tin. The pill is big. Jim bit it. Jim will sit in the mill with Kim. Will Jim quit the mill?

Sentences such as these, even though rigidly controlled for vocabulary, demand that readers have such words in their sight vocabulary. If pictures do not give enough reliable cues that readers can use (in this text there were none), other strategies to get meaning are not available.

Publishing companies responded to the need for simple materials with books that are filled with rich cues so that emergent and beginning readers can successfully make their way through a small text. The wealth of "little books" for emergent and beginning readers make finding good books a much simpler task.

For example, Destiny, in first grade, read the little book *The Ghost* by Joy Cowley (figure 5.2).

She started out, not looking carefully at the words. By the third page, using the predictable text with the pictures as cues for meaning, she was on track. She read "BOO!" with great feeling. She chose to read it again and read it easily and accurately.

I see the door.   I see the window.

2   3

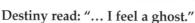

Destiny read: "… I feel a ghost."   **"… I heel a woman."**

Destiny read: "… I see the table."   "… I see the cat."

 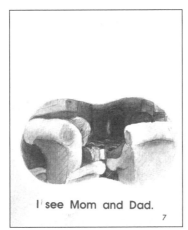 

Destiny read: "… I see a chair." "… I see Mom and Dad."   "… Boo!"

Figure 5.2. Destiny's reading of *The Ghost* by Joy Cowley.

Immersion also means encountering print throughout the day, with time in each period devoted either solely to reading or to a reading-related task, such as following written instructions to make handicrafts, playing games with written rules, and so on.

In chapter 4, "Literacy and the Four Skills," we listed many ways to make your classroom a print-rich environment. Here are some additional ways to help your students learn to read or make the transition to reading in English.

Provide a Wealth of Materials at Your Students' Level

Choosing books need not be a problem. There is a phenomenal array of fiction and nonfiction books available, appropriate for content areas as well as for reading pleasure. A large number of picture books on the market are beautifully illustrated with exceptional language and content. They can easily be incorporated into middle school, high school and adult school classes, because they are not childish, simplistic, or condescending to learners.

For starters, any book on the Newbery and Caldecott awards lists, or from the Children's Book Centre (in Canada) are excellent reading. Browse through your favorite bookstore. Go to book fairs. Find out what kids are reading and enjoying.

Which books to choose? The Primary Language Record (1989) writes that the books that remain perennially popular with young readers share

- A strong story.
- A lively, rhythmical text.
- Powerful, imaginative content.
- Memorable language.
- Interesting illustrations that complement the text.
- Humor.
- Language that is not contrived or unnatural.

Books by favorite authors, such as Dr. Seuss, Tomie dePaola, and Rosemary Wells are good places to start at the elementary level. At the secondary and middle school level, there are also favorites such as S.E. Hinton, Paula Danziger, Robert Newton Peck, and Laura Ingalls Wilder—these authors have remained the top choices over many years.

A Helpful Guide

A helpful guide provides materials and opportunities for students and is familiar enough about reading and the students in the class to know what level of reading each student is at and the particular needs of each at the moment. This is not lock-step instruction (for example, if this is Tuesday, we all should be on page 82, or if this is the 129th day of the school year we should be on page 129). Richard Allington (1998) writes, "What all children need, and some need more of, is models, explanations, and demonstrations of how reading is accomplished. What most do not need are more assignments without strategy instruction."

A helpful guide is someone who

- Knows about reading.
- Knows about literature.
- Knows how to provide different instruction to different individuals.
- Models good reading daily.

Good Practices to Use for All Students

Fountas and Pinnell (1996), as well as other researchers, have pointed out that a balanced program includes a balance of teacher-directed and student-sponsored activities. That means, read *to* and *with* students: read aloud to Hnuku, Salvador, and Franco, as well as to Kate, Ellie, and Rory; allow students to read *by* themselves, whatever their level.

Reading to Students

Reading aloud to students is "…the single most important activity for building the knowledge required for eventual success in reading…There is no substitute for a teacher who reads good stories" (Anderson et al. 1985). Jim Trelease (1985) takes it one step further: "When teachers take time to read to their class they are not neglecting the curriculum. Reading *is* the curriculum [emphasis ours.] The principal ingredient of all learning and teaching is language."

According to Frank Smith, reading aloud, particularly to students such as Hnuku and Salvadore (whether they be first graders or twelfth graders), does three things:

1. It helps them understand the functions and purposes of print.
2. It helps them become familiar with written language.
3. They have the opportunity to learn.

There are other benefits for all students, assert the Commission on Reading (1985) and Allen (1995). Reading aloud

- Provides a model of skillful reading.
- Gets students interested in books and in reading.
- Gives students a purpose for reading.
- Is a key ingredient in creating the risk-free environment so essential for second-language learners and struggling readers.
- Helps build community, in which everyone—good readers and poor readers alike—have equal access to the text.

This is especially important for ESL students who are either not literate or not sufficiently fluent in English to read on their own. If you have a regular reading time every day in your class, you shouldn't feel that you are wasting the ESL students' time just because they are not able to understand every word. At the very least, they see that words have meaning, that writing can be translated into oral speech, and that books are made for knowledge and enjoyment. They are listening to language and listening to others discuss and enjoy what was written. The enjoyment factor should not be dismissed lightly. School can be a stressful place for many students, increasingly so for older students, and especially so for ESL students or struggling readers. Being able to sit and relax and simply listen to a story adds pleasure to their day.

Besides the obvious benefits of giving students a chance to hear words in context, to develop listening skills, and to increase vocabulary, reading to students motivates them to want to read more. They become "hooked on books," which many experts contend is the key to reading success.

Don't stop in elementary school with little ones who are first learning to read or with those whose skills are low. Read to all students at all levels: middle, junior, and senior high. Just because students can read on their own is no reason to stop. Often, students' sophistication in thought and conceptual development far outstrips their reading abilities. When we were at the one-word stage of language, our parents didn't limit the books they read to us to one-word books. We listened to books far beyond our language capacity, which often included many words beyond our understanding. Third graders, for instance, are concerned with and capable of thinking and discussing ethical and moral issues they do not have the skills to read about. Even though upper-level students may gripe at first that reading aloud to them is babyish, they often get caught up in the story and enjoy listening. The same holds true for ESL students; their interests, comprehension, and sophistication may be far above what they are able to read for themselves. Reading to students continues to extend their range and exposure to different types of literature, as well as increases their vocabulary and understanding.

Don't stop with stories. Read textbooks, journal articles, magazines, and technical read-outs. Reading to students in the content areas is particularly useful. In the upper grades, reading demands are different and more difficult. Science, history, and math students in junior and senior high schools are faced with the task of extracting information from texts that presuppose a high level of reading and know-how to find the information they need. In wading through the material to find that information, they may need help. We all know that having someone read poetry to us helps us hear the rhythms and cadences in ways we can't when we approach a poem on a page. Even at the high school and college level, having someone read portions of a text aids comprehension. Barb often does this in her upper-level college classes. When approaching a difficult passage, she can explain difficult concepts as she goes along and direct students' attention to what she feels is important in the text. This does not invite laziness or cheating, it simply helps.

Selecting Books to Read Aloud

Select books that expose your students to literature of a higher quality and reading level than they can read alone. Select books that are stylistically excellent, with pleasing words arranged in pleasing patterns. Storybooks with intense, gripping plots are excellent, as are books with vivid characters and natural dialogue. Select books that reflect the theme you are exploring or books that will enrich students' understanding of themselves and others.

Reading With Students

One-on-One Reading

One of the best strategies to promote reading and further independence is to read and discuss books one-on-one with your ESL students. You can instantly gauge how much they understand, go over unclear parts, and review vocabulary in a personalized way. As you read, move your finger along under the words, synchronizing speech with print. This helps students perceive the speech-sound correspondence within a relaxed, pleasurable atmosphere. Weak readers, and ESL students in particular, can benefit from this type of reading.

One-on-one reading is especially critical for students like Hnuku, Fernando, and Salvador. Wells (1986) asserts that children who have not been read to, who have not had the literate home life that children like Ellie, Kate, Yoshi, and Boris have had (who have been read to since babyhood), need more exposure to books than listening to a story read to the whole class. "They have not yet learned to attend appropriately to written language under such impersonal conditions. For them what is required is one-to-one interaction with an adult centered on a story." Turn this activity over to an older or stronger reader, an aide, a parent, or anyone with free time within the school.

Shared Reading

Shared reading is one of the most significant and critical strategies you can use. Shared reading is reading a book together. For the first couple of times, especially with younger or less proficient students, you will do all the reading. As the students become more proficient they can join in and "share" in the reading.

At the elementary level

- Choose a predictable book, such as *The Great Big Enormous Turnip* by Alexei Tolstoy or *I Went Walking* by Sue Williams. The repeated refrains allow beginners to chime in when they begin to notice the story. Books such as these are important: the print tells a whole, coherent story and the pictures represent the story told by the print. Thus, the reader can use both the language that is, or becomes, familiar on repeated readings and the pictures to supply meaning.

- Focus first on the book itself, advises Cunningham (2000). Introduce the book by reading the title and the author's name. Discuss the story with the students. This builds skill in predicting what will happen next in stories, in using the pictures as cues to meaning, and in connecting spoken language to print. Read it, reread it, talk about it, act it out. We cannot over-emphasize the importance of reading favorite books again and again.

- Read the story aloud, pointing to the words as you read. This builds familiarity with the ideas in the text, the vocabulary, and the overall format. It also allows the students to "hear" the language cadences. This is especially important for beginning language learners. With beginners such as Hnuku, it reinforces concepts we often assume, such as reading from left to right and that words have spaces between them.

- Model strategies for getting meaning: "I wonder what that word is? It starts with a /t/. Let's see. The [blank] has a hard shell. I'll bet that word is *turtle*. Does that make sense?" Discuss the text. Then, with the words available for everybody to see (whether from a big book, a chart, or an overhead) read it again, inviting all the class to read with you. This encourages participation from everyone. As students become familiar with the story, even poor readers can chime in when they know a word or phrase. Within the safety of the group, they do not have to know all the words and aren't put on the spot when they don't.

- Allow students to read the story themselves. Their memory of the language of the story and the pictures in the text will guide their reading.

"I don't know what to read." "I can't find anything." "I'm bored." Sound familiar? Another important benefit of shared reading is that it gives readers a repertoire of known texts from which to choose during independent reading. Often a great deal of time gets wasted during what should be SSR, by students who claim they have nothing to read, which is often a cover-up for their lack of skills, or boredom because they simply don't know what to choose. If they are familiar with certain texts, and enjoy them, they can feel comfortable in choosing them and can experience success when reading on their own. In this way they can move toward independence and autonomy in reading. In the latter half of third grade, Nick, for instance, read and reread *One Fish, Two Fish, Red Fish, Blue Fish* by Dr. Seuss day after day, never losing enjoyment of it. He was a better reader than that and could have been pushed further. Others in his reading group were reading *Bridge to Terabithia* by Katherine Paterson and *Roll of Thunder* by Mildred Taylor. He didn't seem to care. It was familiar, he was consolidating his skills, and developing fluency at his own pace, even though it seemed like lost time to everyone else. He stunned his teacher at the end of the year by reading *The Good, The Bad, and The Goofy* by Jon Scieszka in one day. It appealed to his imagination and his sense of humor. His mother, of course, rushed out and bought him the entire series.

At the secondary level

The shared reading experience looks a little different at this level because you read aloud from a text, and each reader follows along in his own individual copy.

For older students at the junior high or high school level, finding appropriate literature does not have to be the exercise in frustration it used to be. Students who struggle with reading at this age are typically sensitive about being different from their peers; they are often reluctant to read books that they perceive are for "babies." However, there are many beautifully illustrated books with relevant material that will appeal to older beginners. Publishing companies that handle the ESL market have books with collections of stories for beginning readers at the junior high and high school level. Another excellent resource for the busy secondary teacher is the school librarian. This professional will frequently know where to find additional resources if the school does not already have something on hand. If you are comfortable "surfing the net," there are also many resources available on the World Wide Web. In addition, there are computer programs that generate lists of reading materials based on a theme.

The time and preparation required for choosing a book to read aloud necessitates as much energy as any other prep time, otherwise the reading will be a joyless enterprise for both listener and reader (Allen 1995).

Allen offers key questions to ask in choosing appropriate books:

- Is this the right book to meet the needs of these students at this time?

  The interests of the students can play a critical part in your choice. For example, as we discuss below, Melissa Ahlers' choice of *The Outsiders* by Hinton was based on her students' fascination with gangs. These basic readers needed to be hooked before they would sit still and listen to a story, much less try to tackle it on their own.

- Can I read this book in such a way that students won't see it as "boring"?

  Not all books lend themselves to being read aloud. For those who are struggling or turned off reading, the book has to be "long on plot and short on description." Barb has used *Sarah, Plain and Tall* by Patricia MacLachlan with beginning literacy adult students, as well as with more advanced learners. The reading level is fairly low, but the themes of loss, change, and giving up what you know to make a start in a strange place are deeply understood by second-language learners. Therefore, even beginners can connect on many levels and get through the text without being frustrated or giving up.

- Is this a book I enjoy?

  Since reading aloud is a performance, bringing it to life is easier if it's one in which you can connect. Include some personal favorites or some of the children's favorites—those books that have been around for years.

- Does this book meet my instructional purposes?

  You might use a story to introduce a unit or another text, to model a writing style, to demonstrate a genre, and so on. Barb used the hilarious picture book *Officer Buckle and Gloria* by Peggy Rathmann to teach "safety" to a group of middle and high school Taiwanese summer campers. Using the pictures from the story and demonstrations by her son Nick, (thereafter known as "Danger Boy"), students learned key concepts and terminology (such as "safe" and "unsafe"). Both the story and the demonstration alerted them to potentially dangerous activities, such as the high-ropes course, mountain biking, and caving. The lesson was extended by picture drawings (figure 5.3a-c). What started as a read-aloud became a shared reading when the students took the book and the tape back to their cabins to play and replay.

Reading By the Student

Independent Reading

A balanced program includes giving students ample time to read on their own. Because reading is a skill that needs practice, students need extended opportunities and long blocks of uninterrupted time just to read. SSR (or Sustained *Noisy* Reading, where beginning readers simply must be able to hear themselves read because silent reading does not appear until they achieve a certain level of fluency) is a profoundly more effective form of practice than drills in isolated skills. Sustained silent reading should be an integral part of every school day. Devote a certain amount of time to free

Figure 5.3a-c. A lesson on "unsafe" activities was extended by drawings.

reading, ranging from just ten to fifteen minutes with kindergarten children, to as much as an hour or more or an entire class period with older or more experienced students. Allow students to select their own reading material during this time. No book reports, comprehension questions, or records should be required. The only requirement should be that they read silently from one book for a specified amount of time. Non-English speakers can profit from this time even though they might not yet be able to read any words. Steer your ESL students toward books you have read aloud in class or books that others within the class have written. The best books are those that are familiar, having been read and discussed prior to the ESL students' time alone with them.

Besides class time set aside, students should be directed to read on their own whenever they finish work. Reading can be slotted into any spare five or ten minutes of the day.

One key to success, write Forester and Reinhard (2000), is to have a large stock of reading materials available, both new and familiar. Fill your classroom with wordless picture books, catalogs, magazines, trade books, comic books, library books, class-made or individually-made books. The books you have read to the students in read-aloud or shared reading time are natural choices for them.

The other key is for you to read, too. Often SSR fails because the teacher uses this time to grade papers or converse with small groups about other school business. This defeats the entire purpose of SSR. It is important for you to read during that time, to model serious reading, and possibly to share what you have read after the reading time is up. Many students have never seen an adult read—by reading you are conveying the message that reading is important, as well as pleasurable.

Build in time for readers to share what they have read. A classic study of second-language learners by Elley and Mangubhai (1983) found that when teachers flooded the classroom with books and allowed time for sharing, those children made significantly larger gains in reading that children in classrooms that used only basal readers or limited the reading to SSR—without time for sharing. Students get excited about their friends' choices and are eager to read and share in the experience.

Sharing Time

Specific Strategies for the Varying Needs of Your Students

Picture books are a good way to introduce reading to all levels of ESL newcomers. Because these books do not depend on text to tell a story, they can be used to stimulate talk and later, writing. At first, you can allow students to simply page through the books, perhaps during sustained silent reading time. But don't take for granted that they will know even such simple things as holding the book right side up, or starting at the front.

Use Picture Books

The figures on page 122 demonstrate our contention that using picture books is no longer appropriate only for children. This is a fallacy that needs to be expelled. What better way to introduce the theme of alienation than with *Crow Boy* by Taro Yashima or war with *Faithful Elephants* by Yukio Tsuchiya? Even eighth graders, who may groan and sneer when you pick up a children's book, have been moved to tears by the wrenching story of the love the trainers had for their elephants and their anguish over their deaths.

Ask them to identify elements of the illustrations. Then, when the students have acquired more English, you can ask them to tell you the story. You might have them make captions for each page, or you can transcribe their version of the story.

Encourage them to discuss these books in their own language with a peer, an aide, or at home with a parent. In this way they do not have to depend upon their fragmented knowledge of English to talk about what they see in the pictures. Picture books are important because they help students develop thinking skills. They challenge them to think about and articulate what they perceive. Read and Smith (1982) have identified other important skills that picture books can help develop:

- Sequencing—learning how to distinguish a sequence of pictures and develop vocabulary words such as *first, next, then*, and so on.

Narratives in other cultures are often very different from our own; therefore, learning "story grammar" is a fundamental skill that should not be taken for granted.

- Identifying the who, what, when, where of the story.
- Getting the main idea.
- Making inferences.
- Predicting what will happen next.
- Drawing conclusions.
- Establishing cause and effect.

Make Your Own Library If you have a limited selection of good picture books at the junior and senior high school you can—with the help of the librarian, the yearbook editor, and some enterprising photography students—make your own library.

- Start with yearbooks. If the yearbook teacher has leftover pictures you might make your own classroom yearbook.

- Make photo albums. Take Polaroid pictures of students involved in activities, such as building a float or doing an experiment. The content is familiar and can make ESL students feel they are a part of the school while learning vocabulary. Once students have mastered the basic vocabulary, go beyond the school into the community.

- Use magazines. Many how-to magazines, such as *Handyman*, show step-by-step procedures for building things. Pasted on wallboard and laminated, these can be used over and over.

- Use cartoon strips. Cut out frames of a cartoon strip. Blank out the words in the "bubbles" and have students fill them in with their own dialogue.

Use the Language Experience Approach (LEA)

Steps in LEA The Language Experience Approach is one of the most effective reading strategies we have encountered. Simply stated, students dictate stories to the teacher who records them, using the students' own vocabulary, grammar, and life experiences to form the basic reading material.

The experience consists of several discrete steps. You can vary them according to time, size of groups, and purpose.

1. Experience something together. This can be a field trip, a special event such as Valentine's Day, a shared story, a poem, a book, an activity such as baking cookies, a movie, or even something as simple as examining and eating marshmallows.

2. Discuss the event together. This step is critical. Because the emphasis is on discussion as they describe or recall the event, students make gains not only in oral development, but as they analyze the event, in the intellectual growth needed for success in reading.

3. Write the story on chart or butcher paper. Have each student contribute a sentence (unless you are working with a very large group, in which case you can elicit sentences from different children over a successive number of LEA sessions).

> Write each sentence, saying aloud each word that you write. "Mary said, 'I saw a giraffe,'"or "Mohammed thinks that kids' behavior is the hardest thing to adjust to in this country."

> When you have written a number of sentences or completed the story, reread the sentences, moving your finger under each word as you read it to reinforce left to right progression. Answer any questions that might come up.

> Have the students read orally with you?

> Have individuals read the sentence they have dictated?

4. Have the students copy their own sentences or the entire story on paper. If you haven't elicited a sentence from each student, you can now go around the room and encourage each one to generate his own sentence on the topic.

5. Follow up the activity. The experience does not stop with the writing. Other related activities can be included over the next few days.

> Refresh the students' memory by rereading the story, then have individual students read it in its entirety.

> Cut the words apart, and have the students put them in the correct order.

> Reinforce skills and sight words by calling on individual students to, for example, "Show me a word that begins with *m*," or "Where does it say *giraffe*?"

> Ask "What words do you know?" Underline these words and have students place them in their word banks.

> Have students illustrate words or sentences, or even the entire story.

Figure 5.4. First-grader Jeremy drew these characters from *The Nutcracker*, after his class had read the story.

The Language Experience Approach has many features to recommend it:

The Benefits of LEA

- All the language skills are used at once—reading, writing, speaking, and listening.

- Words from the students' own vocabularies are used. Students have no trouble reading words like *hippopotamus* or *Lamborghini* when they come from their personal store of experiences.

- Skill building, such as sight-word vocabulary or letter identification, can be promoted within a meaningful context.

- Oral vocabulary is increased.

- Self-concept is enhanced. A student can look at a page or a book of collected stories with pride and say, "I wrote that."

- The approach is appropriate for all age levels, kindergarten through adult.

- Less proficient students can benefit from seeing text that more proficient students have generated about topics they understand.

- The students' points of view are valued.

- LEA can be done in the students' native language, which is especially useful when the students are illiterate.

- The content is authentic. Because the approach uses the students' own language based on their own experiences, it is immediately relevant; therefore, their interest and motivation will be high.

- The approach can be used in large groups, small groups, or with individuals, either as chart stories with the entire class, or as dictated stories written individually onto sheets of paper.

Do's and Don'ts with LEA

When using LEA with ESL students, there are several things to remember:

- Do *not* use LEA to teach new concepts. Here you are building and reinforcing language already learned. The students' first stories might only be a few sentences, or even a few words long, such as *Hmong house*. That's fine; it is still reading and is meaningful to your students.

- Write exactly what students say. Do *not* reproduce their accent. If someone says, "I lost my chooz" when he means "shoes," write *shoes*.

- Do not make corrections to grammar, word choice, or organization. Zing and Ha, for instance, after several rousing enactments of *Caps for Sale* (in which Barb always had to play the monkey), wrote the following summary, partly reproduced below:

  He wore them on his head. No one buy some hats. And he sat down on a tree, because no one buy her cap. Her leg were tired. He went to sleep. He wake up. He see no cap on her head. The monkeys had the hats. He looked up high and saw the monkey.

  While you are transcribing their story, it is very tempting to write in *the*, correct the pronoun to the masculine gender, and add the plural *s* to *cap* and *leg*. There are several important reasons not to make corrections:

- The goal of LEA is to make print meaningful for the students so that they can acquire reading skills. If you have made changes, and students attempt to read back their work as they originally stated it, they might become confused. In the writing example above, the teacher actually changed *buy* to *bought*; the students could not read the word because they did not know it.

- Your goal is to write a story that reflects the learners' thoughts and language, not to develop a perfectly stated essay. If you focus on surface errors rather than the meaning, you are not only missing the point of the lesson, you are giving the students the impression that correctness is the most important thing and that you are more concerned with form than with content.

- To change students' thoughts is to reject the legitimacy of those thoughts. It isn't their writing anymore, it's yours. Accepting what they say in English during these sessions does much to bolster their self-confidence.

Many teachers feel that if we don't correct students we reinforce their errors. However, put in their proper perspective, errors can be considered as a reflection of a stage of language development—a transitional state that will eventually disappear. These errors are important for you as a teacher, because they give you a written record of what each student knows—and does *not* know—in English. The errors in the example (*buy, her, leg*) show you what Zing and Ha need to learn in the future.

Once it has been written, you can go back over the story and ask students if they want to make any changes. At that point they might very well see the errors they have made and change them themselves. If not, you can point out the errors and give them the correct form—a much more valuable learning experience than making changes yourself during the writing process, and one that does not disrupt the students' train of thought while they are composing.

Figure 5.5. A student's illustration of *Caps for Sale.*

During the course of the school year you can return to these stories with the students to demonstrate just how much progress they have made in English.

- Be extremely sensitive when including ESL students in large-group language experience activities. Many ESL students are shy, feel hesitant about speaking (particularly in a group situation), and generally hover on the fringe of activities. LEA can be a great confidence booster if what the students have to say is important both to you as their teacher and to their fellow classmates. If each is listened to attentively, the importance given to what they have to say can cause great gains in their self-image. Sadly, though, students often will laugh at newcomers for their poor pronunciation or sentence structure. More advanced students might say something like, "Don't call on Lagi, she doesn't know anything." Educate your students to understand that ESL does not equal STUPID, and allow the newcomers the time and the opportunity to contribute to the best of their abilities.

At more advanced levels, or in the content areas, use LEA as a tool to elicit thoughts and brainstorm ideas. You are not looking for perfection, merely ideas, and all students can participate.

Use Literature

The jury is in on the benefits of reading aloud and the need for good literature. Even Jeanne Chall, one of the foremost proponents of phonics and author of *Learning to Read: The Great Debate* (1996) has noted that "few in the literacy community disagree with the need for high quality literature and writing experiences as the nucleus of literacy instruction."

Routman (1996) discusses what literature does for readers:

- Literature allows meaning to dominate.
- Literature concentrates on the development of readers rather than the development of skills.
- Literature promotes positive self-concepts in beginning readers.
- Literature promotes language development.
- Literature promotes fluent reading.
- Literature deals with human emotions.
- Literature exposes students to a variety of story structures, themes, and authors' styles.

Hnuku, Fernando, and Salvador, for example, do not need to be excluded from literature studies, even though their proficiency and reading skills may be weak. Young children do not need to wade through basal readers before being introduced to literature. Older students need not be consigned to the high-interest, low-vocabulary books that were traditionally staples of the reading lab. Good fiction is available for all ages. Young adult fiction for middle-schoolers and high-schoolers can motivate poor readers and help bridge the gap between their current level of proficiency and the language competence they need for success in academic English.

Literature Circles   Talking about books with other readers gives students a chance to explore and refine their impressions and ideas, to increase their understanding of literature by hearing others talk about it, and to become critical thinkers. Literature circles encourage readers to give personal meaning to ideas presented in books.

Literature circles are particularly beneficial for ESL readers because they capitalize on the social nature of learning. They provide structured opportunities for students to read, talk through the ideas they have, listen to others, and gain more insight into passages. Less proficient readers can learn from their peers and reread what they didn't understand the first time.

Historically, and, in today's classrooms, many teachers still group children on the basis of reading ability. It is tempting to do this with ESL students. However, "Putting students into a group where instruction is slow paced is counter to what we know about effective teaching" (Rosenshine 1983). Gunderson (1985) asserts, "Placing ESL students in a group to hear and emulate poor oral reading is questionable at best." Guided reading (Fountas and Pinnell 1996) is one way of providing direct instruction in necessary skills. Literature circles are a way of including ESL students in groups that are not based on their reading levels.

Daniels (1994) defines literature circles as "Small temporary discussion groups [that] have chosen to read the same story, poem, article, or book. While reading each group-determined portion of the text (either in or outside of class), each member prepares to take specific responsibilities in the upcoming discussion, and everyone comes to the group with the notes needed to help perform that job. The circles have regular meetings, with discussion roles rotating each session."

The roles that are considered standard for literature circles are

■ Discussion Director: This person has the official responsibility to come up with good discussion questions and to lead the discussion, soliciting contributions from other members.

■ Literary Luminary Passage Master: This person selects memorable, funny, powerful or important passages for the others to ponder or read aloud.

■ Connector: This person finds connections between the material and the world outside the text.

■ Illustrator: This person has the job of drawing a picture related to the reading.

Teachers who use this method successfully report that they add one job at a time and give all students instruction in how to handle the job. Students need to learn how to take on the responsibility of thinking for themselves, of contributing their thoughts, and leading discussions. Students, especially those learning English, need to become familiar with the structure and the routines before they can become productive members of literature circles.

The book selections must be judicious and take into account the needs, the interests, and the ability levels of the students. Although choice is an important part of literature circles, let's face it—ultimately, the choice is up to you. McMahon (1997) notes that choice of books should be guided by four criteria:

1. The quality of the literature.

2. The interests of the students and the teacher. Find books that appeal to your students. If you or your students are not interested in the genre, the characters, or the story itself, then you'll have a hard time engaging them.

3. Characters that reflect diversity in terms of gender, race, class, and ethnicity.

4. Curricular needs. Sometimes teachers use themes to shape their choices. For one upper-level class working on the theme of

"Immigration," Barb chose *Journey of the Sparrows, 1000 Pieces of Gold, Farewell to Manzanar,* and *The House on Mango Street.* Another teacher chose the theme of "Survival" and selected books such as *The Outsiders, Shiloh, Anne Frank: The Diary of a Young Girl, Hiroshima, The Cay,* as well as others.

Following, is one way to conduct a literature circle. It is an approach that focuses on enjoying literature as literature, rather than on reading literature solely to learn reading skills. Reading becomes the end rather than a means to an end; the readers become better readers as a consequence of being engaged in reading and discussing a good book. In this approach, the teacher is a participant and a member of the readers' club rather than the source of knowledge and the inquisitor who asks questions to check up and test knowledge.

With this strategy there are multiple readings (at least two) of each book. The first is simply for pleasure and comprehension, to become familiar with the storyline and to get a feeling for character and setting. The readers respond as readers, both to the story and to the enjoyment it brings them. The discussions and activities you set up after the reading are designed to help the students understand the story in more depth.

At least two readings are important for ESL readers. The first time they may struggle through the story with only partial understanding. This may be for a variety of reasons: insufficient background knowledge, the difficulty of the reading level, and/or because they are unaccustomed to the style of English language literature. On the second reading, the discussion and responses of other group members will help to increase understanding, and readers can go over the now-familiar material with added comprehension and enjoyment.

It is not necessary to require ESL students to read entire books or understand every word and every concept. You are simply working toward competency and skill. No high school student will be able to understand a book as well as you if you have read it six times and studied it in three college courses. We cannot expect depth and perception from beginners. We can, however, expect progress.

Here's one way of proceeding.

1. Choose a book, or several different books, and obtain enough copies for each student to have one.

2. Do a "sales job" on each one to get the students interested. Show a clip of a movie tie-in or the movie version of the story. Don't show the whole thing. Read the first page. Tell them snippets to pique their interest.

3. Build background knowledge. Tell them what the story is about. For example, when Barb used *Sarah, Plain and Tall* with her class, she brought in "Want Ads" and "Personals" from the newspaper. In the story, Sarah is a "mail order bride," a concept unfamiliar to many students. The class wrote their own versions of the ad the character Jacob might have placed. The students also talked about why they left their

birth countries, what happened, what was different from their home, and how they reacted to this new country. They could connect with Sarah's loneliness and homesickness. When Barb taught *To Kill a Mockingbird*, she talked about students' perceptions of race relations in the United States, stereotypes and prejudices that exist in their own culture, and derogatory words that exist in languages to put others down.

4. If you're using multiple books, have students choose which one they want to read. The selection is based upon their interest, not your judgment of what is appropriate. In this way "reading groups" are determined by students' interest, not by the built-in reading levels we were used to in the past.

5. Meet with each group and set goals, such as how long it will take them to read to a certain point or to finish the book. Samway and Whang (1996) counsel that it is important to set goals and time limits for each section of reading, so that students don't get too far ahead or too far behind.

6. Have students read independently. You may have to read a chapter or two to them so that they get used to the style and have a sense of the storyline. Complex novels such as *To Kill a Mockingbird,* written in a distinctive dialect with many words used in ways not easily explainable, need a great deal of building "into." The parameters of this reading are for understanding the text only. There will be no quizzes or chapter tests. You can have them respond to specific questions at the end, such as "Who did you relate to in the story?" "Tell me about one time in your life when you felt like this character did." Have students keep running journals of their reading. "Stickies" (such as Post-it Notes) are especially useful for keeping track of interesting or important parts.

7. Peterson and Eeds (1990) call this next stage "The Grand Conversation" while Atwell (1998) calls it "dining room table" discussions. Engage in the conversation, contribute your thoughts and opinions, and point out your favorite parts, but don't let the class discussion follow the traditional teacher-led format. The object is for you to be a participant, not the ringmaster.

Grand Conversations are not necessarily "grand" with ESL learners, at least at first. They often don't understand the story; they often don't have the vocabulary or the cultural background to get through the text; and they have no practice in articulating their own ideas.

But this stage is the most important, not only for the ESL students, but for poor, or less-proficient readers. Samway and Whang (1996) assert that "all children should have the opportunity to join an LSC, not just more fluent readers...they all prize these discussions. To deny a student access to these rich times of sharing because of a lack of fluency as a reader [or as an English speaker] is counterproductive. Therefore, struggling readers should be given help." The discussion will clarify for students what they read, what they didn't understand, and the points they missed. They will be swept along by the discussion. They may not

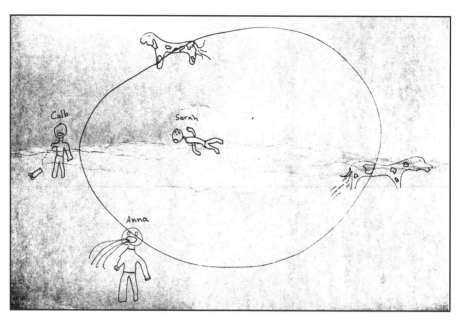

Figure 5.6. A student's illustration of the cow pond, from *Sarah, Plain and Tall.*

get much out of the book on the first reading, but, after the discussion, will return to the text for the second time with much more comprehension and enjoyment. When left open, these discussions are often lively and fun, with students bringing their own background experiences or interpretations to the text. Immigrant students often have different perspectives on experiences we take for granted and can offer interesting comments that enhance the discussion.

Dennis, for instance, who had grown up on a farm, took issue with one episode in *Sarah, Plain and Tall* that other readers enjoyed: Sarah and the children go swimming in the cow pond. He insisted that cow ponds were dirty, germ-filled cesspools and drew his representation of this part of the story (figure 5.6).

You may have to set up activities that give students the opportunity to deepen their understanding of the story. For example, Barb's class nearly gave up on *To Kill a Mockingbird*, declaring it too hard. To help them understand the story, as well as to increase their confidence, she had her students draw maps of Maycomb (the town in which most of the action occurs) (figure 5.7). In order for them to complete this assignment, they had to return to the text to find out where Scout lived in relationship to Miss Maudie, to downtown, to Boo, to the schoolhouse. By talking together, reading for understanding, and graphically representing the town, they had a better sense of what the story was about.

Barb gave periodic check-ups, not for grading purposes, but to see what they understood and to give herself an idea of how much explaining or rereading was necessary. Randomly assigning characters, she had each student list facts about the character and then make inferences (figure 5.8). Then, each student, in character was interviewed using questions posed by other students in the class (figure 5.9).

8. Proceed to the second (analytical) reading using the students' comments you have written down such as, "The lady who spent all that man's money was awful. I just wanted to strangle her." There are always some students who are confident, outspoken, and more fluent than others. Barb remembers spending most of her high school and college years sitting in the back row waiting to be told what the story was about because she didn't trust her own interpretation or was afraid it was different from the teacher's. Sometimes, and this is very true of many of our readers not just second-language learners, she just didn't "get" what the story was about. The second reading, after the discussion, was always much more informed, and, in many cases, more enjoyable. This is an important step and should not be eliminated simply in the interest of time.

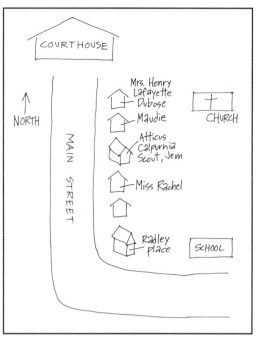

Figure 5.7. Map of the town Maycomb from the novel *To Kill a Mockingbird*.

my character's name: Boo Radley
10 facts.

(WRONG)

1. 33 years old man.
2. white
3. Tall: 6 ½ feet.
4. He dined on raw squirrels and any cats he could catch.
5. a long jagged scar ran across his face.
6. his teeth are yellow and rotten.
7. his eyes popped.
8. He drooled most of the time.

Inferences:
- I guess the one who was laughing at Scout when she shook her head after she's being rolled by Jem.
- he ate cats raw for dinner.
- he is pretty strange person.

Figure 5.8. It was clear from this student's list that he was misunderstanding what he had read. He mistook the children's tale of Boo for a description of what he was actually like.

Dolphus Raymond
- Do you like coca-cola? (It's kidding.)
- Why do you trust Jem, Scout and Dill?
- When you decided your marriage, do you feel guilty to your fiance? Before her suicide, what might she think about that you had black American mistress?
- What do you think about his children? Because they might feel sad if you pretend a crazy man.

Figure 5.9. Questions posed to a student, in character, by "reporters" from the class. Note the depth of understanding it took to compose these questions.

Balancing the Needs of your Fluent and Nonfluent Readers

The perfect class would have all students achieving at the expected level at the same point in time. It never happens. Every class has its Ellies, its Spencers, and its Robbys. If you have second-language learners, you probably have your own Floriens, Francos, and Hnukus. How you modify your assignments and your expectations for them increases their chances for success.

Here are ways to do it:

- Buddy reading. Having two students read aloud together is one way to improve the reading and language skills of both. They can alternate paragraphs or pages. Christina and Gloria, lively second graders, enjoy the challenge of reading aloud together, helping each other get through the "big" words. The simultaneous competition and cooperativeness motivate them to pick books that are at their level and to complete them with enthusiasm. Peterson and Eeds (1990) write, "The sharing of literature aloud anchors the sounds of the language of literature in the minds of the students."

- Books on tape. Many good books are now available on tape. Students can take them home, or use a listening center or a corner of the room during the reading time. Don't think this is a cop-out or that it encourages laziness. Like read-aloud time, it increases students' chances of success, because it sidesteps the problem of struggling through a book that's too hard, it gives them a model of good reading, and it builds their vocabulary (their "story grammar" and their fluency).

- Books of different levels and reading complexity. It doesn't hurt fluent readers to read easy books once in a while, especially if they're well written and appeal to the reader's interest. Many of Barb's students were put off at first by the simplicity of *Sarah, Plain and Tall*, but enjoyed it once they got into it. Offering books that are simpler gives better readers a "breather" and less proficient readers a chance to get through a book on their own.

Working With Different Levels of Readers

Most of all, students need someone to guide them in their acquisition of English and reading skills. Following are strategies you can use for different levels of readers.

With Illiterate Students

What do I do with the Hnukus in my class who are illiterate in their own language?

With illiterate students like Hnuku, you must start from scratch. She might not know things that are so basic to reading that we take them for granted:

How to hold a book and turn pages.
That the markings on the page communicate meaning.
What a word is.
That in English, print moves from left to right.

Unless she interacts with print, Hnuku won't learn any of these things; therefore, you need to involve her in as many activities as possible that include print. The foundation for students' readiness to read and write is their understanding that the language they hear and speak can be represented in print.

As noted in chapter 4, we strongly advocate an integrated approach. Instead of teaching word-attack skills and sight vocabularies, comprehension should be the priority. However, we recognize that there are certain things that your preliterate students need to know. As Bell and Burnaby, in *A Handbook for ESL Literacy* (1984), point out, people who know that a cow is a cow whether it is facing left or right do not automatically recognize that the differences between *p, b, d,* and *q* are significant. They need some training in prereading skills that involve shape recognition.

George Rathmell, in *Bench Marks in Reading* (1984), has listed the necessary prereading skills:

- Ability to recognize similarities and differences in shapes, letters, numbers, and words.
- Ability to arrange items in a sequence, such as smallest to largest, beginning to end, left to right, including classifying items into categories and arranging pictures into a logical narrative order.
- Ability to recognize letters and numbers.

However, the teaching of prereading skills needs to be put in proper perspective and not be allowed to take priority or become focused upon to the exclusion of all else. A balanced program of interaction with real texts, supplemented by practice in visual discrimination, is essential.

Use real manipulables rather than dittoed exercises. For example, you can make a collection of articles such as

- Buttons, rocks, shells, leaves, flowers.
- Stones, nuts, beans, marbles, metal objects.
- Cloth, feathers, corks, bottle caps.
- Ice cream sticks, straws, toothpicks, blocks.

Possible activities include

- Sorting according to properties: size, color, shape, texture, flexibility, order, number of holes.
- Math: weighing, measuring, graphing, adding, subtracting, counting, comparing, estimating, collecting, categorizing.
- Language arts: describing, defining, sharing discoveries.

These activities can be done individually or in small groups. Create a special corner in which collections of various manipulables are always available.

Where should I start?

First encounters with reading must be interesting and of practical value. Help students learn the most useful vocabulary.

■ Start with their names. Children—and adults—derive intense satisfaction from seeing their own names in print, and will copy them many times, learning the names of the letter as a matter of course. A Mexican woman once came into Barb's ESL night class. She was an illiterate migrant worker who wanted to know how to write her name. Barb wrote *Maria* on a piece of paper, whereupon Maria spent the next forty-five minutes practicing. When she was satisfied, she left. She never returned; she had learned the one thing she had come for.

■ Go on from the students' names to the survival words they have learned. They can then make word cards for their desks, chairs, and so on, advancing to other items in the room.

First Encounters With Reading

At the elementary level

■ Raid the preschool and kindergarten for shapes, colors, numbers, and so on. Begin with very simple exercises, such as recognizing triangles versus circles, then move on to more difficult tasks, such as matching letters or words.

■ Stock your room with wordless picture books. During free-reading allow students to browse through these, or have a buddy or aide discuss the pictures.

■ Have students make their own books to read.

At the secondary level, vocabulary should include

■ Names of teachers.

■ Students' own addresses, telephone numbers, and other words they need to know to fill out forms.

■ Common signs (*Men, Women, Help, Exit*).

■ High frequency words (classroom objects, home objects, public transportation, names of businesses and public buildings, facilities in the community, and so on).

■ Basic subject-matter vocabulary, equipment, common instructions and procedures.

■ Days, months, expressions of time.

Figure 5.10. This picture is from a "storybook" a student made of her favorite story, *101 Dalmations*. She "read" this book for days to herself and to anyone else who would listen.

What do I do when students don't know their alphabet?

Perhaps your students are preliterate. Or maybe they can read, but in languages that use a written system other than the Roman alphabet. They might read characters such as Chinese, or non-Roman alphabets such as Arabic, Hebrew, or Thai. What do you do to teach them our system?

Students need to know the alphabet and the words and shapes associated with each letter. The sequence, useful for dictionary work, can be learned much later when this skill has some purpose. At the very least, students must be able to look at the written forms of letters, be able to trace, complete, and copy letters. This raises another question of priorities.

Anyone who has already learned to read has the skills needed to understand print. Learning the alphabet before meaningful reading is pointless. Don't spend large amounts of time teaching the alphabet while holding off on other learning. Students can learn the letters within the context of meaningful vocabulary.

For all levels

- Begin with the suggestions for illiterate students.
- Use the language experience approach (LEA).

At the elementary level

- Practice one letter a day. For example, give each of the students cards with the letter *r* on it, and have them find all the words that begin with *r* in the room or on the chart-stories they have elicited.
- If you don't already have one, find a large chart of the alphabet and display prominently. You can also buy or make individual strips to tape to each student's desk for easy reference.
- Have "name banners" with the names of your students displayed around the room for the ESL students to refer to when practicing letter writing and letter recognition.

At the secondary level

- Begin using the suggestions noted for elementary children.
- Use high-interest, low-level reading books.
- Use picture dictionaries.
- Find books that the students are familiar with in their own languages. If you can find stories translated from the students' languages, the familiar content will guide their comprehension in the new language. Find a copy of a story Bible, or perhaps the Koran, or fairy and folk tales from their countries.

Accommodate the needs of your students. To illuminate the varying levels and needs of the students we have highlighted in this book, we have designed charts. The charts focus on what each level of literacy looks like, what your primary objective(s) for that student should be, and strategies you can use to achieve that goal (figure 5.11-20).

Hnuku, Fernando: Preawareness, no English skills—Elementary

Characteristics:

- Does not know that print has meaning
- Does not know what books are
- Has not held a pencil or pen
- Cannot look at pictures and see more than simple shades of color
- Cannot see drawings and identify them for what they are
- Does not know how to handle a book or turn pages
- May or may not be able to copy words
- Can demonstrate understanding of a story by drawing a picture
- Cannot write their names

Objective:

- Help them make the connection between print and meaning

Strategies:

- Read to them
- Label items in the classroom
- Use environmental print, picture books
- Use the English they have to create language experience stories
- Sing songs, rhymes, chants
- Provide opportunities to draw, copy, and practice writing
- If possible, get one-on-one help to:
  - Read to them
  - Assist during content learning
  - Learn basic vocabulary and sight words within real stories
  - Build background knowledge prior to lessons

When to include them:

- Hnuku and Fernando can be included in most activities. They can "write" journals, sing songs, and listen to stories with the rest of the class
- *Transition years:* Hnuku and Fernando can be included in most activities. During SSR they can read at their own level (picture books, little books). During literature circles they can either read on their own, or have someone read a story to them so that they can be included in the discussions. Coordinate with the ESL teacher, aid, or other volunteer to dovetail tasks

Figure 5.11

Hnuku, Fernando: Preawareness, no English skills—Secondary

Characteristics:

As Hnuku and Fernando have few literacy and oral skills, it would be an exercise in frustration to place them in the regular classroom. They are unable to do the work productively.

Objective:

- Help them make the connection between print and meaning

Strategies:

- Read to them
- Label items in the classroom
- Use environmental print, picture books
- Use the English they have to create language experience stories
- Sing songs, rhymes, chants
- Provide opportunities to draw, copy, and practice writing
- If possible, get one-on-one help to:
  - Read to them
  - Assist during content learning
  - Learn basic vocabulary and sight words within real stories
  - Build background knowledge prior to lessons

Where do they go?

- A Level I program if available
- Phys. ed.
- Keyboarding

Who supports them?

- The ESL teachers

When to include them:

- In activities that can be presented visually.

Expectations:

- Hnuku and Fernando will follow along with what has been modeled.

As they get older, Hnuku and Fernando's lack of knowledge about print and lack of experience become more and more serious. In fact, they increase exponentially at the secondary level. The lag is cumulative. The strategies listed continue to be useful for them; however, it becomes more a matter of *who* is going to deliver these services, than *what* is to be delivered.

Figure 5.12

Salvador: Emerging Awareness—Elementary

Characteristics:

- Understands that print carries meaning
- Can demonstrate understanding of general terms like *read, page, storybook*
- Engages in "pretend" reading
- Can tell a story from pictures
- Can read and write name
- Beginning to read environmental print
- Beginning to track from left to right
- Can repeat all or parts of predictable texts
- Beginning familiarity with "story grammar" of English language stories, such as "once upon a time"
- Is beginning to write words
- Can copy with relative ease

- Is not fully aware of word boundaries
- Does not understand the concepts of letter, words, numbers

Objectives:

- Reinforce the print to meaning connection
- Build sight word vocabulary
- Build background knowledge
- Reinforce sound/letter correspondences

Strategies:

- Follow strategies developed for Hnuku and Fernando
- Read, read, read to him and with him
- Use familiar patterned books for modeling and reading
- Use frame sentences

When to include him:

- Salvador can be included in all activities, especially all-class reading and teacher-initiated activities
- He can read at his own level
- Put him in a literature group he chooses by interest, or use the literature circle time to work with him individually on reading. Find ways for him to read the book, such as have someone read it to him, or listen to it on tape. Tailor the assignments you give him. Assess him orally for comprehension. Allow him to express his understanding through art or another medium.

Figure 5.13

Salvador: Little Experience With Reading—Secondary

Characteristics:

- Very little experience with reading
- Understands print carries meaning
- Can read and write name
- Beginning to read environmental print
- Beginning familiarity with story grammar
- Beginning to write words
- Relies on another person to read the text
- Needs a great deal of support for guidance and strategies
- Ability to think and reason far outstrip his reading and writing capabilities

Objectives:

- Reinforce the print to meaning connection
- Build sight word vocabulary
- Build background knowledge
- Reinforce sound/letter correspondences

Strategies:

- Follow strategies developed for Hnuku and Fernando
- Read, read, read to him and with him
- Use familiar patterned books for modeling and reading
- Use books on tape
- Use frame sentences
- Capitalize on his ability to think and talk by using verbal strategies to support written ones

Where does he go?

- ESL
- Bilingual classroom
- Content classes
- Resource room

Who supports him?

- If you don't have enough students to build a program, you must hire someone to help him. One-on-one is critical to make sure he knows what the assignments are and what he needs to do.

When to include him:

- Group and pair him with supportive kids in English, social studies, and science.

Expectations:

- Expect input and participation
- Verbal assessments

Figure 5.14

Angel, Beverly, Newton, Spencer, Destiny, Andre: Emerging Readers—Elementary

Characteristics:

- Knows that print records the story
- Can recognize words within a text
- Looks at the text and words when reading
- Can spell a few words
- Understands that the sentence and pictures go together
- Are familiar with "story grammar"
- Are developing strategies to predict meaning
- Takes information from a variety of sources
- Still reads aloud
- Are aware of word boundaries when writing
- Are beginning to understand the conventions of punctuation

Objectives:

- Learning strategies in reading: using pictures, graphophonic cues, meaning
- Move reader along from dependence to independence

Strategies:

- Follow strategies developed for Salvador
- Encourage independent reading
- Books on tape
- Stories in their first language
- As their skills and oral proficiency develop, add:
  - Frame Sentences
  - Content at a simpler level
  - Easy readers
  - Stories translated from their first language
- Guided reading for specific strategies

When to include them:

- With support, include these students in all activities.

Figure 5.15

Angel, Beverly, Newton, Spencer, Destiny, Andre: Inexperienced Readers—Secondary

Characteristics:

- Have limited experience with texts
- Can recognize some words within easy books, mostly stories
- Choose to read very simple, familiar texts, if at all
- Very rarely read for pleasure
- Can spell a little
- Are familiar with story grammar
- Are developing strategies to predict meaning, but usually very dependent on just one
- Still read aloud or sub-vocally

Objectives:

- Learning more strategies in reading
- Move reader along from dependence to independence
- Develop background knowledge in content areas

Strategies:

- Teach strategies for getting information from reference and nonfiction texts
- Build background information
- Expand vocabulary

Where do they go?

- In-class support
- If ESL program, parallel program with SDAIE or sheltered
- ESL Resource room

Who supports them?

- Peers
- ESL/bilingual
- The reading teacher

When to include them:

- In group work

Expectations:

- Class work with modifications in *time* allowed for completion, in length of work turned in, and in the amount of ground covered.

At this level, native speakers who don't read well have a high frustration level. Their spirits are flagging. The work they do can be the same as the work given ESL students. Don't make it too simple! They have to understand the concepts, whatever their reading level. Make no assumptions.

Figure 5.16

Abir, Nick, Robbie, Franco: Advanced Beginners, Gaining Fluency—Elementary

Characteristics:

- At the lower grades, many of our literate second-language learners are at a similar level to readers gaining proficiency in their native language.
- Reading is becoming more automatic
- Are confident when reading familiar texts
- Pay attention to the words on the page
- Are growing in their independence
- Begin to read silently as they mature
- May use invented spelling
- Can read for a variety of purposes
- Select books that interest them
- Can retell stories they read in their own words

- Can extract the main idea
- Use punctuation appropriate to the text and the difficulty of the purpose they are trying to achieve

Objectives:

- Wider parameters to experiment with and experience language
- Encourage increasing fluency

Strategies:

- Read, read, read
- Read in the first language
- Provide structures and models to base writing on
- Have students write responses to reading
- Concentrate more on revision and editing in writing
- Work on using the background knowledge they have

- Encourage inferential thinking skills, such as prediction and sense of story structure to comprehend stories and new material

When to include them:

- All activities, with some modification for reading and writing levels

Figure 5.17

Abir, Nick, Robbie, Franco: Increasing Experience—Secondary

Characteristics:

- Reading is becoming more automatic
- Are confident when reading familiar texts
- Are growing in their independence and stamina
- Still need support in content area texts

Objectives:

- Wider parameters to experiment with and experience language
- Encourage increasing fluency

Strategies:

- Help them with unfamiliar material
- Teach skimming/scanning skills
- Encourage variety in length and difficulty of texts
- Encourage

Where do they go?

- Content classes

Who supports them?

- Teacher, ESL, resource

When to include them:

- All the time

Expectations:

- Content work with some modifications in activities, tests, and pace

The challenge for these students is finding appropriate material for the level at which they are reading. Walk them through the texts; it is counterproductive to ask them to read the passages and expect them to understand.

Figure 5.18

Rory, Jeremy, Ashley, Boris, Yoshi: Increasing Fluency—Elementary

Characteristics:

- Can approach unfamiliar texts with more confidence
- Have good control of basic word analysis and self-monitoring strategies
- Can apply their strategies in a wide variety of situations
- Begin to draw inferences from books
- Can use directories such as a telephone book and table of contents
- Need support with cultural aspects of texts
- Can write quite sophisticated stories
- Pay attention to organization when writing
- Use context to predict meanings of unknown words

- Develop personal voice in writing
- Can self-monitor comprehension and strategies available when comprehension breaks down

Objectives:

- Gain experience in tackling a variety of texts
- Increase speed and fluency
- Increase confidence

Strategies:

- Encourage self-selection
- Shared reading
- Use books on tape
- Read to them, with them

When to include them:

- All the time

Some of these students, such as Yoshi, might be very good readers in their own language, but struggle through many types of text in the second. It is important to give them opportunities to read in the first language, but also to balance their skills by giving them easier tasks and texts from time to time, as well as challenging them with tougher tasks.

Figure 5.19

Rory, Jeremy, Ashley, Boris, Yoshi: Increasing Fluency—Secondary

Characteristics:

- They read very well in their own language
- They need vocabulary
- They need background knowledge

Objective:

- To keep up with the rest of the class

Strategy:

- Content in their native language, if possible

Where do they go?

- Mainstream all the time

Who supports them?

- You do

When to include them:

- All activities

Expectations:

- Same as others in the class, with some extra time allotted to keep up

The advantage Yoshi and Boris have is their strong academic skills in their own language. The solid schooling they have had in their home country, gives them the background knowledge needed. They can look up vocabulary up in their own language.
You don't have to spend a great deal of time figuring out the steps to get them to understanding.

Figure 5.20

Grouping

The question of grouping students is an issue that teachers have struggled with for many decades. Many of us remember when reading time consisted of sitting in small groups around a teacher doing round-robin reading while the rest of the class sat at desks doing worksheets. Fortunately, this is a dwindling practice. However, with the range of needs and levels you will find in a classroom (such as our hypothetical one) grouping is a necessity. Hnuku needs a great deal of attention, as do Salvador and Fernando. Again, flexibility is key. There are times when you want to do whole-group activities, times when you want to do small groups, and other times when you want to work with individuals.

This is what one second-grade teacher has done to accommodate the different levels of students in her classroom. Katrina believes that reading should occur throughout the entire day. The students read during their content period. She reads to the entire group every morning and reads with them when they work in math and science. She gives them time for self-selected reading, and she has set aside a time specifically devoted to reading instruction. She uses a variety of methods to teach reading and takes advantage of ESL, Title I, and bilingual help to assist her students. She does a variety of activities during reading time. Students go to various centers, such as the computer center, the make-a-word center (playing with magnetic letters and making words from larger words (Cunningham 1992)) or read independently, while Katrina works with other groups.

- Low-level language learners. During reading instruction time, Hnuku, Salvador, and Fernando go to the ESL room to work on reading. There is no one good time for students to be pulled out of the classroom, but if this is an option, here is a time when the ESL teacher can work on reading and language skills in small groups with students of the same level.

- Intermediate language learners and emerging readers. This group includes Angel, Beverly, Newton, Spencer, and Destiny. The Title I teacher comes into the classroom to work with these students. She works on building vocabulary and reading skills and strategies at a level and with books they can succeed with.

- Moderately experienced readers: Rory, Tony, Nick, Jeremy, Robby, and Bounkham. These are students who are catching on to reading, or, in the case of the second-language learners, have learned some skills in their first language.

- Strong, experienced readers: Yoshi, Ellie, Kate, Ashley, Molly, Austin, and David. Even though they are good readers, solidly launched in reading and capable of working ahead on their own, these students still need individual attention and focused interaction several times a week so that they don't get lost in the shuffle of needs. They are beginning to get going in literature circles.

Katrina also consults with the Title I teacher when she notices particular strategies that students need to work on. It doesn't happen as often as she likes, because it seems that the best readers need little help and the least fluent readers need help in everything.

During this hour of "reading time," while the lowest students are away working with the ESL teacher, she reads aloud from a chapter book. She chooses books that are at a much higher level than the students can read on their own, but she believes that she needs to push and challenge all of them, including the best readers. They gather on the carpet to listen to and discuss a book chosen with the interests and personalities of the students in mind. The less-proficient students benefit from the conversations (which are very lively) and from the rich vocabulary of the literature selections.

Katrina also groups students during writing and during content. The ESL teacher comes in during content, and twice a week a volunteer also works in the classroom. At first, the less-proficient students were grouped together, but over time the students were divided in terms of personalities and level of proficiency, so that the lower ones could benefit from the example and the language of the students at a higher level. During writing, a bilingual interpreter comes in to work with the Spanish-speaking students, reading to them, translating, and writing with them.

Brenda, a fourth-grade teacher, works in a similar fashion. Her better students are launched more solidly into literature circles, but she does not have these working every day. She reads aloud to the students every day during the large reading/literature/language arts block she has set aside for the morning. During part of the week, she guides the class through the literature anthology. Hnuku, Salvador, and Fernando continue to work with the ESL teacher at this time. Right after lunch, the students do self-selected reading for twenty minutes. She has brought in many books that are high-interest, low-vocabulary and picture books of all genres and reading levels that all students have access to. Brenda does not use literature circles all the time. She works through one round of circles, then returns to a more traditional format so that she can work with different levels on different skills. This adaptation seems to help the lower-level students.

The Role of Phonics

Do I need to teach phonics?

The issue of phonics has again sprung to the forefront of the debate over how best to teach reading. No one will dispute that using the graphic configuration of words is one way to figure out what a word is. And, just as they need to know the alphabet, children need to know some basic sound-letter correspondences. They need to be familiar with the various sounds each letter can represent. Many of our words do follow consistent patterns. How *much* phonics is the issue.

There *is* a place for explicit direct help in developing a command of phonics. But this teaching must be strategic, selective, and based on the learning needs of your students.

Polly, for instance, had several fifth and sixth graders who had very weak phonemic awareness. It would have been pointless to start with *A*, learn *B*, and so on. She pinpointed the letters they had difficulty with and, using the "Make a Word" strategy devised by Cunningham and Cunningham (1992), she targeted these letters for students to practice within the context of real words.

Phonics instruction, writes Galda et al. (1997), "should never sacrifice comprehension nor should it replace independent reading activities." Teaching phonics exclusively ignores meaning. When introducing phonics, use only known words, not isolated sounds. Reading, writes Sarah Gudschinsky, author of *A Manual for Preliterate Peoples* (1973) should not begin with anything smaller than a word. Sound-letter correspondences can be learned and reinforced within the context of "real" reading. The U.S. National Commission on Reading (1985) states: "Phonics instruction should aim to teach only the most important and regular of letter-to-sound relationships, because this is the sort of instruction that will most directly lay bare the alphabetic principle." This means teaching consonants that have only one sound, such as /m/. The Commission goes on to state : "Once the basic relationships have been taught, the best way to get children to refine and extend their knowledge of letter-sound correspondences is through *repeated opportunities to read*" [emphasis ours].

Of course, in the primary grades children can learn basic sound-letter correspondences along with their classmates, but with older students, the more time spent learning these in isolation, the more time is taken away from reading itself—and constant drilling is tedious. Before they realize that the skills they are learning will eventually lead to reading, the students may become discouraged. Insistence on mastery of phonics may lead to more and more discouragement. The time allotted for phonics drill should be minimal in relation to activities spent encountering meaningful print.

While it is true that sounding out words is an important word-attack skill, it is not necessarily true that a word will be meaningful once it has been sounded out. For example, an English speaker might be able to "read" a Spanish text so that a Spanish speaker could understand what he's saying. However, if the reader's Spanish is so limited he cannot understand more than the occasional word, he is only barking at print. The same principle applies to English words. Anyone with reasonable word-attack skills can sound out the word *calumniate*. However, knowing how it should be pronounced doesn't give one any clue as to what it means. The meaning must either come from the context of the sentence or from a dictionary.

Good readers read for meaning. Poor readers are so busy decoding words they cannot concentrate on meaning and often lose the thread before they reach the end. Second-language readers, even though they may be fluent readers in their first language, tend to resort to poor strategies, such as reading word-for-word, working out every word laboriously. Thus, too much stress on sounding out words limits readers' strategies for getting meaning and also stresses correctness over understanding. Yoshi, for instance believed he had to translate each and every unfamiliar word in a sentence, before he would even attempt to read it through. His skills were bogged down because he was anchored to that dictionary. Mary knew he could read the material, but he was afraid to attempt it. Students must learn to focus on context and use syntax as a way of predicting meaning, rather than learning only to sound out words.

The problem of learning the sound-letter correspondences is particularly difficult for children whose first languages don't discriminate between sounds that are distinctive in English. We have all heard jokes about "flied lice" and "rotsa ruck." This is because Japanese and Chinese speakers hear one sound where English speakers hear two. Cree speakers don't have /sh/ in their language and will say *sip* for *ship*. Arabic speakers do not distinguish between /p/ and /b/. Concentrating upon these individual sounds when the student cannot distinguish between them is pointless. Even if Li can't say *rice* the way we might wish it or distinguish the /l/ and /r/ sounds, if he knows the difference between *lice* and *rice*, he will never make an error in the context of a story. Eventually he will be able to hear the difference, but until then you have better things to do than drills between minimal pairs.

There are many ways to embed phonics instruction within a meaningful context. Research has demonstrated that in classrooms where phonics are taught *in the context* of rereading favorite stories and songs and poems, children develop and use phonics knowledge better than in classrooms where skills are taught in isolation (Routman 1996; Moustafa 1998; Cunningham 2000).

Here are a few ways to embed phonics instruction:

- Work on sound-letter correspondences using words elicited in a language experience activity (LEA).

- Teach rhymes that focus on one particular sound. There are many books on the market that focus on particular sounds.

- Mary used tongue twisters with her beginners: *She sells seashells by the seashore*? It sounds corny, but her adult students loved it!

- Pick out known words that begin with the same letter and have the students put them in their word dictionaries or on word cards with illustrations.

- Use your name banners to illustrate beginning and ending sounds.

- Use the student-made dictionaries to illustrate words that begin with certain sounds.

- Make alphabet books together.

- Make word lists and word banks.
- Emphasize certain sound/letter relationships during writing workshops.
- Give students plenty of opportunities to write, helping them write the sounds they hear in the words.

Working With Students Who Are Literate in Their First Language

What if the language students have first learned to read moves from right to left, or bottom to top?

Although languages such as Arabic, Persian, and Hebrew use an alphabetic system, they are read from right to left. The problem of switching ESL students to left-to-right reading is resolved primarily through modeling. Students who are already literate will have learned proper eye-movement; now it needs to be reinforced in the proper direction.

Reading / Writing in the Correct Direction

Several methods can ensure that students move from left to right when they read or write:

- Monitor their initial reading experiences, making sure that they are reading correctly.
- When reading aloud, move your finger under the words you are reading.
- Provide a guide for the first few reading and writing experiences, such as arrows on the top of the page, or traffic lights showing green on the left and red on the right.

My students are literate in their first language. Where do I go from here?

We used to believe that a person only learns to read once. It's not as simple as that. The skills of reading, true, are only learned once, but the cognitive demands that are placed on second-language learners are greater and more complex than those placed on first-language readers.

Developing Second-Language Literacy

While many educators insist that it is essential to learn to read in the first language and to continue to read increasingly challenging texts in the first language, this is practical and possible in only a few languages. More book publishers have responded with texts in a number of languages, and there are more options available by searching the Internet. An ESL site will often have links to publishers, texts, materials, catalogs, and so on. If you do not have access to the Internet at your school, many local libraries have stations for pubic use.

- Start with material students already know.

    The school district in which Barb worked had a large number of Hmong students. For many years there was very little written in Hmong because it had been, until recently, an oral language. Finally, they were able to obtain the written versions of some of the favorite

Hmong folktales, such as *The Plain of Jars* and *The Lady and the Tiger*. Even beginning students, because they knew the stories beforehand, were able to read them with comprehension.

- If at all possible, allow students to continue reading in their own language. This will help them master the skills and fluency needed to be efficient readers. The Internet provides newspapers in many languages.

- Encourage literate parents to read to the children in their own language; this is one of the best ways to support their child's intellectual development. Parents are often under the erroneous impression that they cannot help their child because they cannot speak or read in the new language.

- Augment use of translated materials (if available) with LEA—the language experience approach.

- Have aides, peers, or older students read to them as often as possible, identifying known words and discussing content.

- Allow time for reading assisted by tapes.

Aiding Comprehension in Both Language Arts and the Content Areas

What if the students have a reasonable sight-word vocabulary, but still cannot comprehend simple materials?

Filling in the Gaps   ESL learners face many difficulties in reading a second language: vocabulary, differences in style between written and spoken language, poor study skills, and lack of background knowledge.

Vocabulary: Lack of vocabulary can severely inhibit reading progress, as evidenced by this scavenger hunt form, which was simple enough for English-speaking campers (figure 5.21).

Some vocabulary, such as essential vocabulary for content areas, simply must be taught directly, so that the students can understand the reading.

Differences in style: Narrative fiction is much different from content area textbooks, and students who do not know how to vary their strategies to suit the particular text often stumble and give up or gain nothing.

Study skills: Mary had two students who had weak educational backgrounds. One could speak English fluently, and while the other could understand a great deal and communicate his thoughts, his vocabulary still had many gaps. Reading was a problem for both and they struggled with their history and English assignments. Mary showed them how to skim for the necessary concepts by helping them determine which paragraphs contained the important ideas and which material they could disregard. This took time, but by the end of the year, they could work independently.

Lack of background knowledge: Gunderson (1985) writes unequivocally that "a system that fails to give adequate attention to background and vocabulary teaching is destined to be unsuccessful with ESL students." Barb discovered in one of her upper-level linguistics classes that even though she stressed reading the assignments before the lecture, students were not doing so. Frustrated, she asked why. One of them explained that reading it after was easier, since they now had the background knowledge to understand what the text was saying. She realized, to her chagrin, that she was not practicing what she preached in other classes. How much more so is this true of our work with ESL students?

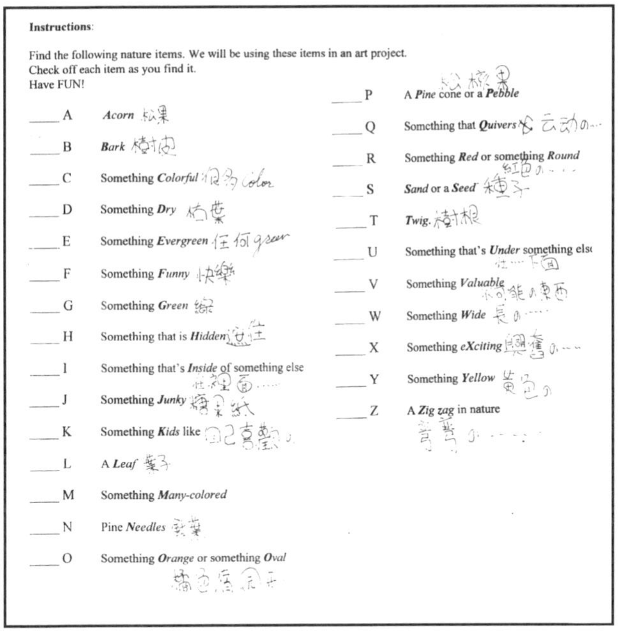
Instructions:

Find the following nature items. We will be using these items in an art project.
Check off each item as you find it.
Have FUN!

___ A *Acorn*
___ B *Bark*
___ C Something *Colorful*
___ D Something *Dry*
___ E Something *Evergreen*
___ F Something *Funny*
___ G Something *Green*
___ H Something that is *Hidden*
___ I Something that's *Inside* of something else
___ J Something *Junky*
___ K Something *Kids* like
___ L A *Leaf*
___ M Something *Many-colored*
___ N Pine *Needles*
___ O Something *Orange* or something *Oval*
___ P A *Pine* cone or a *Pebble*
___ Q Something that *Quivers*
___ R Something *Red* or something *Round*
___ S *Sand* or a *Seed*
___ T *Twig*.
___ U Something that's *Under* something else
___ V Something *Valuable*
___ W Something *Wide*
___ X Something *eXciting*
___ Y Something *Yellow*
___ Z A *Zig zag* in nature

Figure 5.21. This student's translation of items on a scavenger hunt form reveals his lack of English vocabulary.

Cathy Hsung was assigned to read *Pilgrim's Progress* in her high school English class. She could read all the words out loud correctly, but with little comprehension because the vocabulary, some of it archaic, was beyond her language experience and her background information was weak. As a Buddhist, she did not understand the concepts of sin, guilt, and redemption. Mary had to go to great lengths to fill in the basic information about Christianity (that we, in Western cultures, take for granted) before Cathy could begin to make sense of the text.

Getting Them *Into* the Text

Reading depends on knowledge—not just about words and sound-letter correspondences, but also about the world. The reader brings the sum total of his personal experiences to reading. Refugee or immigrant students, or those from remote reservations, may have either a very limited range of experience in terms of the school environment, or their life experiences may have been totally different from those in the stories they encounter. Those students who have spent most of their lives in refugee camps will not have the background knowledge to understand what we might consider a simple story about shopping in the big city. We cannot take for granted that just because the vocabulary is limited the story will be easy to understand. There must be a contact point—some core of knowledge to begin with, or they will not understand.

For instance, Miguel was struggling to read a story about pancakes. He was making many errors, and obviously getting very little from the reading. His teacher asked him, "Miguel, do you know what pancakes are?" With companions all around who had been remarking on how they loved pancakes, Miguel assured her that he did.

"Do you eat them very often?"
"Every day."
"What do you like on your pancakes?"
He rubbed his tummy. "Salt. Yummy."

Prepare for the Reading Assignment

Preparation for reading is a crucial part of the whole act of reading, whether at the elementary or secondary level, in language arts, or in the content areas. It should not be slighted or skipped because it often determines whether that day's lesson will be a success or a failure for the student.

Emphasize the prereading segment of any reading task. The U.S. National Commission on Reading notes that although prereading is the most important part of any reading lesson, it is certainly the most neglected. Prereading involves more than simply deciding which words will be difficult and discussing them beforehand. The prereading process can include

- Discussing the content first.
- Reading the selection aloud to your students before they read it themselves, helping them with difficult concepts and words.
- Showing a related filmstrip or a movie.
- Going on a field trip related to the subject.
- Having students brainstorm and share what they know about a topic before introducing the text.
- Predicting what will happen by looking at the pictures that accompany the text.

For example, Melissa Ahlers was faced with a difficult class of limited English-speaking eighth graders. These students were a notorious bunch—poor readers with the attendant behavior problems. Many of the boys, if not already in gangs, were deeply attracted to the idea. They were becoming increasingly disenfranchised from what was happening in school. In thinking over what book to choose, Melissa decided on *The Outsiders* by Hinton, because its plot centered around the theme of gangs. The two overarching questions she chose for the unit were:

1. Why do people join gangs?
2. What are the consequences of being in a gang?

She rented the movie, ran the tape forward to the scene where Johnny and Pony Boy are confronted by the Soc and Johnny knifes the Soc. The class watched, enthralled. Then she abruptly turned the tape off, just as Pony Boy, his head held underwater, loses consciousness. The class protested shrilly.

She began a discussion and, as a whole class, they brainstormed about gangs. Melissa, using a modified LEA, wrote their thoughts on the board. They made comparison lists on the following ideas:

1. What's the difference between a gang and a club?
2. Are gangs good or bad? First the students voted. Then they listed both good and bad qualities.
3. They listed the gangs in the area.
4. They discussed how you can tell someone's in a gang.
5. They discussed what you need to do to become a member of a gang.

Very lively discussions about gangs ensued. The students were interested and engaged and had many thoughts to offer. Melissa took the chore of writing away by doing it for them, to keep the enthusiasm up and the conversation flowing. The following day, she showed a little more of the movie. Some had seen the movie already and, with typical eighth grade abandon, shouted out what was going to happen. Then she read the first chapter of the story to the students, and for an entire class period the students listened quietly. Over the course of the next several weeks, they continued to read the book, on their own, in small groups, as well as listening to Melissa read to them. Because she had chosen a topic that the students were intensely interested in and knew a great deal about, the students read with more attention and depth than at any other time she had that particular group of students. Although she taught this book to only ESL students, what she did would have carried over easily into a mixed class.

Making it *Through* the Reading With Comprehension

ESL readers often arrive at school with poor study skills. They do not know how to extract information from a text or how to read for the purposes demanded. They need extensive practice with the varied tasks of reading in the content areas. Here again, the prereading segment of any reading task is critical. In addition to the suggestions above, we recommend that you

- Ensure that students know what they are expected to get out of the reading selection: the main idea, a general understanding, or specific facts to be recalled later.

- Ensure that students know what is required when answering any comprehension questions. If presented with a choice, do they need to pick out which statements are true or must they put the sentences in order? Is there more than one correct answer?

- Walk the students through the reading selection, pointing out clues that aid comprehension, such as pictures, maps, italics, boldface print, and so on.

- Help them look at print configurations, such as the sizes and shapes of words, italics and boldface print, for clues to the relative importance of the information.

- Help them recognize what to look for. Often readers get hung up feeling they need to know each word before they can go on to the next, thus spending an inordinate amount of time looking up words in the dictionary. Help them look for key words in a selection, such as the nouns and the verbs, then predict the meaning of the entire sentence based on these key words.

Strategies

Apply Skills Learned *Beyond*, to Other Reading Tasks

Encourage Extensive Reading

Encourage extensive reading at a similar or easier level than regular class members. Find selections that will help promote competency in the strategies students have learned.

- Have a classroom discussion about students' outside reading.
- Have students keep journals that record what they've read.
- Allocate time to talk with each student individually about his current reading. Get to know individual likes and dislikes so that you can steer students toward books that interest them.
- Read other works by the same author, books of the same genre or on the same topic.
- Retell the story through another medium, such as film, drama, radio drama, or through another literary form such as poetry, drama, or song.
- Write class (or school) newspapers, and/or magazines, relating to the topic.
- After they've completed reading something, have a discussion to see if students' attitudes, ideas, and interpretations have changed.

A Supportive Environment

A supportive environment is one that is sensitive to the various needs of the members of the class. Franco needs different instruction than Kate. Pete likes to read adventure stories, Ellie is into high fantasy—what Nick distastefully calls "girl stories." Hnuku needs high-interest, low-vocabulary books, picture books, and books on tape.

Ways to support reading include the following:

- Flexibility: This means that the class is open to change. Reading groups, the mainstay of much of reading instruction in the past, were often fixed. A redbird was always a redbird and an eagle was always an eagle, and the kids knew it. But Beverly can make gains in an astonishing amount of time, or she can plateau. Because learning spurts and coasting occur in every child, flexibility is a key strategy for adapting to the changes.
- Student-centered: This means that the class is not a "one size fits all" classroom, in which every student reads what the teacher assigns, takes the same tests and gives only the right answer to teacher-initiated questions. Zemelman et al. (1998) write: "Making school student-centered involves building on the natural curiosity children bring to school and asking kids what they want to learn." It means active teachers who meet the students' needs by designing experiences based on their knowledge of the curriculum, of developmentally appropriate tasks, and of the students themselves.
- Build on the background knowledge that students DO bring from their various cultures and experiences.

- Supportive: Accept and celebrate a variety of individual strengths.
- Recognize and acknowledge the place for errors: We often get hung up on correcting mistakes, particularly in reading. Some teachers have students read aloud as a way of checking their comprehension. When students are reading along and stumble over a word, it seems intuitively right to jump in and correct them, but this must be done only with caution. We believe that asking individual students to read aloud without having a chance to rehearse, is often not a good indicator of how well or how much a reader is comprehending. Reading aloud TO someone is excellent practice, but not until readers achieve a certain level of fluency.

Some readers can read aloud perfectly—they sound wonderfully fluent, but comprehend little or nothing. Sixth-grader Jose, for instance, was turned over to tutors and classroom aides for two or three hours each day. The tutors were told that he needed practice in reading, and so he spent most of that time reading to them. He sounded good; he made few mistakes. However, when asked what he had read, he couldn't tell them.

The enormous amount of time and effort spent was not furthering his comprehension at all. This time could have been better spent reading to him, with him, building strategies and background knowledge.

Other readers seem to stumble over every other word, making the task of listening to them particularly discomfiting. The temptation is to jump in and help. However, errors in reading aloud do not necessarily mean that the reader is not able to understand the text. Ken and Yetta Goodman, early on in their original research of reading, report that some errors are "better" than others.

For instance, in the fifth grade Maia read a short passage about elephants.

Her reading:

> *The elephant is the largest animal in the world that lives on land a full-found. Elephant may have a weight of about four tons and may be nine feet tall. Because elephants are so large, they have no natural enies other than man. Science elephants have so few enies, they are sually easy to get along with and almost always act friendly. Elephants usually live in heards(?)...A femaly, or laddy elephant is called a cow...During the hottest part of the day the herd will? Huddle?*

Readers are often tempted to jump in, correct her immediately, or disrupt her thought processes by telling her to go back and sound out the words so she can get them right. She might be labeled as a disabled reader, and on the face of it, it seems she didn't get much out of it. In talking over the story, however, she didn't understand the key words *full-grown*, *herd*, and *huddle*, but she was able to pick up most of the story, and even though she mispronounced *enemies* she used the word accurately in her retelling:

"The elephant don't got enemies. It's the largest animal. It usually herds with usually members of 30. They go a lake for drink water."

Most of her miscues were not reading problems per se, but background knowledge. She could find the right information from the text when asked questions such as, "Why don't elephants have any natural enemies?"

Time

The most important element we want to emphasize in terms of a supportive environment is the time and the opportunity to read, read, read. Peterson and Eeds (1990) stress that an essential component of a literature study program is "the provision of time for extensive reading on one's own. Children need time to read in peace, to just read without worrying about having to do things afterwards...Learning to read is a continuous, cumulative accomplishment."

This means time to

> Be read to.
> Read on their own.
> Respond to the books read.
> Discuss the books.
> Conference about interpretations.

And time to grow in reading. With students who are non-native English speakers, particularly Hnuku, it takes a lot of time. Most preliterate students have a different learning curve. Sometimes it appears they learn very little for the first year. They can be very quiet, indicate little comprehension, and so on. Don't be fooled. They are internalizing much and will respond quickly the following year. Time is important for these students.

The lack of opportunity to read and be included in "real" reading and authentic literacy tasks limits students' chances to learn to function in a literate world.

Conclusion

When we teach reading, these are our underlying assumptions:

- Reading must be for meaning.
- We learn to read by reading.

Reading does not happen in a vacuum. Readers need repeated opportunities to practice. They need a guide to help them over the rough spots and teach them strategies to get *into, through,* and *beyond* a text. And they need a comfortable environment in which they can attempt to read without fear of being jumped on for their mistakes. By providing these, we can move our learners from confused nonreaders, to competent readers able to tackle any reading text or task.

CHAPTER 6

WRITING

In this chapter, we look at acquiring the skill of writing. We focus on

- Using a process approach to writing with ESL students.
- What students need to become successful writers.
- Commenting on student papers and assisting with revision.
- How and when to correct errors.

The Process Approach to Writing

Yesterday last night of the teacher Mary Eckes would one to student all student in class-person doesn't get to have to know. This when student dd to get befor big one the squash all way came back to school at reach home family and neighbour. that right your are want to see becouse youre are doesn't have. doesn't know.

In the past several decades, the emphasis in teaching writing has shifted from "product" to "process." Gone are the days when the only audience was the teacher who was judge, jury, and executioner. But in many classrooms, particularly high school classrooms, a piece like the one above often comes back bloodied with ink marks, graphically demonstrating just how far Cham falls short of the mark in approximating standard English. Although she may be given a chance to change her ideas or fix what is wrong, deciding what to fix and whether the final product will achieve a passing grade are other issues.

It is useful to use the writing process as a starting point for a discussion on writing with ESL students. Research has revealed that writing is not a linear process in which writers start at the beginning and work though error-free to the end; it is a cyclical process in which the writer continually circles back, reviewing and revising. Some start with outlines, others just start, discovering as they go where they're headed. Most writers plan, compose, then read what they've written, edit as they go, write some more, revise a little, and so on.

Genuine learning takes place during the process of putting thoughts down on paper. Writers, whether children or adults, do not become writers by simulating writing—filling in blanks on dittoed sheets, learning grammar rules, memorizing vocabulary, or practicing lists of spelling words.

Writing authentic texts involves orchestrating all facets of language at once; a writer must consider the "social, situational aspects of creating a piece of writing at the same time as she deals with decisions about meaning, spelling, grammar and punctuation" (Newman 1984). With ESL learners, it is tempting to focus first on vocabulary development, spelling, and grammar. However, this bottom-up approach returns to the use of such strategies as word drills that have limited instructional value. It also neglects the main goal of writing: to create a meaningful text for a reader.

Who Is the ESL Writer?

It is impossible to come up with a simple profile of an ESL writer. There are many variables operating, as the following student examples show (students are roughly the same age):

Boris, in a journal response writes,

> *Most people do not listen with the intent to understand, they listen with the intent to reply.*

Although he just arrived in the U.S., Boris's English is nearly flawless, and his writing better than many college students.

Yoshi, writing on the same topic, says,

> *The person who talks neither so important not interesting things, I've neve listens so hard. I've reacted at random. But it is a problem, even it is not important things for me. I have to tend to heare as much as I could. Becaseu even his/her story is not important for me, it may so important for him/her. And I have to resonse sparsely. And we I don't have to wast of the time to hear ever which is not important or curious for me.*

Yoshi has understood the reading and has good ideas, but he can't yet express them fluently. There are many grammatical errors that slow the reader considerably.

Andre, after viewing the movie *Charlotte's Web* writes,

> *PIG*

> *Thes store abayt a pig. He don't want to pepele eat him and he don't want to die. Spider halp him and safe his life. Spider tiche him howe to dans. And he wini the first plase on a scow. And hese ownar sad I will liwe hime a lifi.*

Andre has had limited schooling in both his language and in English. His writing has many grammatical errors and is very simple.

The name below was signed by a student with no prior schooling.

Figure 6.1. This signature shows the student's inexperience with print.

But writers are writers and all writers face two challenges:

■ What to say.

■ How to say it.

And all writers

■ Have a purpose or intent when they write.

■ Make mistakes.

■ Have crummy first drafts (Lamott 1995).

■ Must orchestrate many things when they write, making complex decisions about such things as audience, form, organization, as well as punctuation, word choice, spelling, and so on (Newman 1984).

■ Must operate simultaneously on two levels: composing (creating ideas, putting their thoughts in logical, articulate form), and transcribing (physically writing a text) (Barr et al. 1989).

ESL writers, some of whom are learning to write for the first time and others who are accomplished writers in their own native language, must cope with the challenge of formulating thoughts using words, grammar, and structures that are unfamiliar to them.

Helping Students Become Successful Writers

To learn to write well, every beginning writer needs

■ To be immersed in writing.

■ A supportive environment.

■ Feedback and guidance from interested readers.

■ Time.

Immerse Students in Writing

Being immersed in writing means not only frequent opportunities to write, but frequent opportunities to read, both finished products and the ongoing work of other writers:

■ Allow your students to write. Allow? Does that sound like a strange concept? We have seen many teachers who do not believe that children should be allowed to write on their own until they have control over forms, have what the teacher deems is sufficient vocabulary, or sufficient command of the English language. We vehemently disagree with this viewpoint. Zemelman et al. (1998) concur. They state that "All children can and should write…writing should not be delayed while reading or grammar is developed first; rather, experimenting with the ingredients of written language is one of the prime ways of advancing reading achievement and mastering the conventions of language."

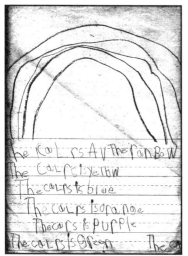

Figure 6.2. This student's writing displays a good deal of knowledge about words, sound-letter correspondences, and English grammar. In addition, he had something he wanted to communicate.

Cathy Tegen was team-teaching a summer program with a teacher who believed that the limited-English-speaking children in the class should not be allowed to write. Cathy persuaded her to give them a chance. Figure 6.2 shows what one student, who had hitherto never been allowed to write, produced.

Encourage the Writing Process

Allow students time to work through the stages of the writing process. The writing process has been researched in detail over the past few decades (Emig 1971; Graves 1975; Flower and Hayes 1977; 1986) and has helped us align what we do in the classroom with what real writers do.

The process can be divided into the following major steps:

1. Prewriting: This is the thinking stage, also called the "percolating" stage, the "get-ready-to-write" stage, the stage in which students pull their thoughts together and make the initial decisions about where to start, points of view, characters, as well as the information they want to include.

2. Drafting: In this step, students put their thoughts on paper. This tentative, exploratory stage can often be the hardest part; articulating what one is thinking can be a long and sometimes arduous process. Putting pencil to blank page is a major step.

3. Revising: Revision means "seeing again." At this stage writers clarify and refine their ideas, adding, subtracting, and moving text around.

4. Editing: Editing is putting a piece into its final form. The focus changes from content to mechanics. Writers polish their writing by correcting spelling, punctuation, sentence structure, and so on.

5. Publishing: In this final stage, writers share their writing with an appropriate audience.

Working with limited-English writers presents special challenges, particularly at the earlier stages. Not only are many older students at very low proficiency levels and beginners to the entire schooling process, but ESL writers are often what Tompkins (2000) refers to as "novice writers," that is, unaware of audience, purpose, and form. They have few strategies at their disposal, they are more concerned with mechanics than ideas, and they view writing simply as putting words on paper. Thus, for them, revising means "fixing," or making their piece longer, not better.

For instance, Joaquin wrote a paper on the Titanic (figure 6.3a). Although this paper has many grammatical errors, it is lively and filled with strong details. It demonstrates Joaquin's understanding of what happened when the Titanic sank, and it shows his sense of humor (a whale ate him). There is much good in this paper.

Yet, note Joaquin's revisions: he simply made it neater and made a few grammatical changes (figure 6.3b). He did not seem to know what needed

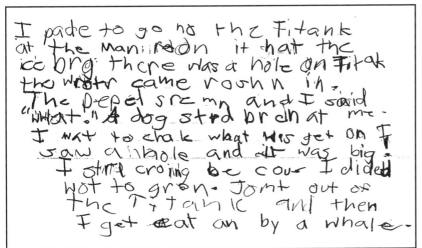

Figure 6.3a-b. There is little difference between Joaquin's first draft (a) and his second draft (b).

to be added or how to improve his writing. In helping him, his teacher focused on correcting the many errors in spelling. This is understandable because these are the most obvious mistakes and obscure much of the meaning.

Six-trait writing* helps both mainstream students and writers like Joaquin improve their writing. Rather than overwhelming students with too many tasks on too many fronts, selecting one trait to work on helps students focus. For example, Joaquin has good ideas. He could make this story more vivid by adding details about what he saw and how he felt when the water came rushing in. He might choose to work on word choice. Setting reasonable goals for him puts success within his grasp and takes much of the burden of improving the writing off your shoulders.

Working with beginners such as Joaquin is not a quick-fix operation. It's a long involved process of working on many fronts: teaching writing skills and problem-solving strategies, allowing students to write freely and frequently so that, over time, the writing becomes more fluent, less error-ridden, and less problematic. Working with such writers is very labor-intensive: simply put, you have to do a lot of the work for them because they can't do it themselves. But we have to be judicious about doing things for students all the time, because this can lead to reluctant or disabled writers. We need to encourage risk-taking and push students beyond what is safe and easy.

---

* Six-trait writing is a model that originated in Beaverton, Oregon in 1984. Traits "are simply qualities that are noticeable to others and that help us define whether performance— any performance—is strong or not." The six-traits of writing are ideas (mainpoint or storyline), organization (structure), voice (the writer behind the message), word choice (vocabulary), sentence fluency (how the writing sounds), and conventions (mechanics). See <www.nrel.org/eval/writing/> and Spandel (1997) for further discussion.

At this point, we'll describe ways to support the writing process and give examples of what students produced. At the end of the chapter, we will describe in more detail how to help students become competent at the revising process.

1. Prewriting

Prewriting is perhaps the most important step for novice writers in both the first and subsequent languages. Yet it is often the most neglected step. Prewriting is a time for students not only to generate ideas, but to pool their collective knowledge of vocabulary and grammatical structure appropriate to the lesson. All students, and ESL students in particular, need to have a great deal of stimuli before they write. As a lead-in to writing, provide as much opportunity as possible for students to listen to and participate in discussions relating to the topics they will be writing about. Make prewriting an important part of every writing activity.

- Read stories and poems to the students. This is effective for kindergarten through high school. Reading aloud provides students with models for story writing by giving them a sense of story form, characterization, plot, drama, and so on. It also sparks their imagination, giving them ideas to write about.

- Brainstorm as a class, generating lists of ideas and possible topics.

- Take field trips.

- Listen to speeches.

- Show films, videos, or filmstrips.

- Allow students to talk about their work with you or with each other.

- Allow students to draw, either as a preparation for writing or as an enhancement to their writing. Drawing is a valid form of communication and often gives students time and ways to formulate their thoughts before they set words to paper. Drawing also lets them demonstrate what they are thinking, but cannot yet articulate.

a.

b.

Figure 6.4a-b. When encouraged to draw, students' responses are more varied, personal, and rich than when simply given fill-in-the-blanks on lined paper. Stan vividly captured the difference between life in rural Central America and life in the U.S. (a). Rhody's drawing depicts the Hmong folktale *The Lady and the Tiger* (b).

2. Drafting

Everyone produces crummy first drafts. For beginning writers in any language, this stage often produces a great deal of what can only be called "junk." Students are often far afield of what they need and want to say and need careful guidance through this process:

> *What is the Americans?*
>
> *Since the Americans have diverse culture, ethnicity and broadly widened land, i cannot find any specific definition of the Americans. In the urban area like New York, Chicago, or Los Angeles, people seem not to be afraid of meeting foreigners because of many opportunities to see them on streets. On the other hand, in the rural area, the Americans are conservative, ignorant and friendly. The average Americans are conservative and ignorant about world geography and words news, contrast to the recognition by the other countries that the United States is the only super power in the world.*

This rough, unedited draft was written using notes taken from the chalkboard. Students had listed their perceptions of Americans, which included the ideas that Americans are ignorant and conservative. Noboru was simply writing without thinking through what had been stated. The paper is filled with unsupportable generalities and vague prejudices. Most of the essay needed to be heavily edited, substantiated with examples, or just plain thrown out.

Beginners often copy straight from the text. This is NOT plagiarism. It is a useful strategy for thinking through what it is they want to say. As students get older and more proficient they can begin thinking about paraphrasing, consolidating information, and putting thoughts into their own words. Enforcing it at the beginning level is counterproductive.

P6

I BELIEVE THIS NATION SHOULD COMMIT ITSELF TO ACHEIVE A GOAL BEFOR THIS DECADE IS OUT, OF LANDING A MAN ON THE MOON AND RETURNING HIM SAFLEY TO EARTH. SO SAID PRESEDENT JOHN F. KENNEDY IN AN ADRESSE TO CONGORES ON MAY 25 1961, HIS WORD'S POSED A CHALLENG TO THE AMERICAN PEOPLE. AT THAT TIME AMERICAN SPACE EFFORTS LAGGED FAR BEHIND.

a.

Apollo 11 Facts

Apollo 11 was the 11 group to go into space but the 1st group of men to set foot on the moon.

The men who set foot on the moon were Neil Armstrong and Buzz Aldrin. Michael Collins stayed inside the rocket ship. Apollo 11 took off on July 16 1969 and made it to the moon 4 days later on July 20.

The Rocket was built by 300,000 workers and had five million separate parts. Apollo had three parts: a command module, the Columbia, the Lunar module, the Eagle and a service module. The two space ships separated and Neil Armstrong said, "The Eagle has wings."

b.

Figure 6.5a-b. One can only wince at the enormous amount of effort put in by this small boy. He clearly did not understand what he was reading and did not know how or where to start when confronted by the assignment to "write an essay on Apollo 11" (a). He went on doggedly to fill seven pages by copying. He should not have been allowed to go on that long in the wrong direction. In the end, Barb asked the child to tell her what he had learned about Apollo 11 and typed his ideas into the computer (b). (At that late stage of the game when his frustration was very high, this approach was the only way of salvaging anything from the assignment.) Through careful questioning and showing him where the essential information was, he could read for meaning and write an adequate paper.

Advanced beginner and intermediate ESL language learners can be especially vulnerable to copying information when attempting to work on content-based essays for assignments. Trying to locate and then juggle information gleaned from text or reference material can be overwhelming to a student not fluent in English. Students at this level are proud to assemble the information they have found and may simply not have the ability to reformulate it for their essays.

The tree element of african culture is food soul food in the south of u.s is very similar to food in africa and dance is same like african s africa america .throughout the natrative,music to place in socio cultural context,which include the author perspective on how cultural implerialism particulary in the united states has excted a toll on person of african descent and negatively impacted the culture of the larger societ.although recognize that african american music is a syncretic creation primary involving african and european roots,she stresses both the importance of the african heritage author perspective,then offers a distinct contribution to our understanding about the essence of african music.

Figure 6.6. Here's another writer who is struggling in his first draft to put his own thoughts into a paper using support from outside sources. The copying is blatant and very apparent in the sudden shifts in style and sophistication of prose. He needs direct instruction in paraphrasing.

There is a certain point, however, when writers need to become aware of the concept of plagiarism. This cannot be left to chance. Raimes (1999) writes that in Western society we take the "ownership of works and text" very seriously and therefore it is important for students, as they grow accomplished and fluent, to know what plagiarism is, when it occurs, and how to avoid it.

Reid (1993) notes that it is our responsibility to give students "frequent, carefully monitored opportunities to practice the skills of paraphrase summary, quotation and citation" so that they can develop an awareness of other authors and texts.

3. Revising

Revising is very hard for many students. Spandel (1997) asks, "Why is revising so repulsive?" For one thing, many beginners, either first- or second-language writers, "have enough trouble getting the copy written in the first place. They're still working on motor skills, pacing, balance, margins, letter orientation, and other complex skills which come naturally and automatically to older writers." For our second-language writers, finding the words they want, groping in a language they're not yet fluent in, can be an exhausting enterprise. Many beginning writers believe that once they have put their thoughts down on paper, they have reached the end; they are finished, and aside from correcting a few spelling errors they have nothing more to do. Students need to learn that authors often write passages many times before they are satisfied. Intervention by the teacher at this stage is critical. This is the stage when changes should be made that affect meaning. Guide your students by making suggestions for changes, by asking for clarification, and so on. Later in this chapter, we provide writing examples and discuss ways to help students revise their work.

Yet, not everything needs to be revised!

Spandel advises: change things ONLY when the piece is going to be formally published and when the student writer has gone as far with the editing as his skills permit. For many of our ESL students who are novice writers, getting the words on paper is enough. As we demonstrate below, the purpose of the writing determines whether it needs to be revised or not.

4. Editing

As difficult as revising is for students, editing is just as difficult; it demands close attention to details such as grammar, punctuation, and spelling that they have not mastered yet. As teachers, we have to resist the temptation to correct everything on every paper. We discuss editing in more detail on page 180.

5. Publishing or Bringing it to Closure

Closure can be achieved by

- Posting work.
- Taking it home.
- Checking off that something is completed.
- Due dates.

a.

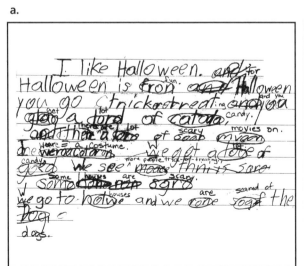

b.

Figure 6.7a-b. This student's writing was carefully revised, illustrated, and proudly displayed.

On Sunday, the camper arrived at camp. He was very hungry.

On Monday, he ate many nature vegetables and squishy banana. Then he played basketball, but he didn't played well.

On Tuesday, he ate his favorite beef stew rice and two rabbits which he hunt in the forest. Now he felt full.

On Wednesday, he found a big hole under a tree. Soon, he went into the hole. That's a good place for him living in. At night he ate two hamburgers which brought from his house.

On Thurday, he got up very early and investigated the dragonfly. Then he went back to the hole and will cook his lunch. He haven't ate breakfast. At lunch he ate five packages of instant noodles. taisty

On Friday, he went into the forest again, but he got lost. He didn't ate anything all day. He was very very hungry again.

On Saturday, he found some bird eggs on the top of the rocks. He try to climb on there. But he was lost. Finally, he fell on the ground and got did. The End.

Figure 6.8. Unlike the younger and less proficient students who wrote *The Very Hungry Camper* stories, Hunter did not want to illustrate his. However, he still enjoyed writing his own version and displaying his considerable skill with the language. There would be no point in editing this, unless he, or his teacher, wanted to display it somewhere, which he chose not to do. Compare Hunter's story to the other versions of *The Very Hungry Caterpillar* examples in this book. It serves to illustrate that a well-chosen task can be fun and appropriate for many ages and levels of proficiency.

Figure 6.9a-c. This paper was revised with a great deal of effort and help from Laura, her teacher (b). The finished product was something that this child could be proud of (c).

a.

b.

c.

a.

I am going to talk about when they tooke me to the U.S. When they tooke me to the u.s. they tooke my in a big boat. When they tooke me to the u.s. it was bad becoase ther was not enough of room for all people in a small boat. I the ship ther wher a lot's of frinds from different trib's and one day I ran in to a family having a pick nick and I saw a girl. And that girl I seen her on the ship to. Ther is a afew people from the village like my best frinds ho work whit me. No I didn't almost now one until we talk to each other when we laid a plan to kill the white man. In the ship is very stuffy because we didn't have a bathroom we have to use the bathroom were we wher. We didn't have enough space we wer dunch upand we didn't have enough food for along time travelling on the ship. The ship is taking use to the U.S. We didn't stop nowere we when't strat ther. The white man treat use very bad because we are black. I get sick for a little whil but most of the other people did.

It is so nasty on the boat because they have childern that have dirty pants. Some people are dead, and some people don't have clothes. Some slaves are sick and throwing up on their people. I have a friend that is on the slave ship with me. She was raped by men and she was crying. We eat some bread and salt water. We didn't have much space until alot of people died The ship is going to South Carolina. We stopped in Florida before we got to South Carolina. The white men were hitting us. They broke the skull of a little girl that was crying. I am so sad because I am going to another country.

b.

Figure 6.10a-b. Examples of students' writing from a sheltered social studies class about slavery. These students wrote journal entries as if they had actually been slaves. These entries gave them opportunities to showcase what they had learned, as well as practice in their writing.

This may or may not involve publishing. Spandel (1997) writes, "Do not feel compelled to publish everything. It's exhausting for everyone and completely unrealistic. No one publishes everything she or he writes. Encourage students to be selective about what goes all the way through the process."

Writing—An Everyday Activity

Make writing an everyday activity. For learners to advance their writing skills, they must have constant opportunity to practice. Setting aside a block of time each day or several class periods per week for reading, revising, and seeking feedback is critical to learning advancement. Second, embed writing in every part of the day, or at the secondary level, into every subject.

- Make writing "real." The writing must be authentic, with real audiences.
- Write letters to the principal, to real authors, to heroes.
- Produce newsletters, or even full-fledged newspapers about class or school activities.
- Prepare invitations to Parent's Night and school concerts.
- Maintain two-way journals with other students.
- Keep records of events, such as field trips, pet care, growth charts for plants, daily schedules, and so on.
- Make writing meaningful. In other words, find topics your students can "sink their teeth into," frequently allowing them to choose their own topics. All students write best about things they care about. Everybody knows how boring the "My Summer Vacation" assignments are, and how little one has to say. But students who are captivated by the need to say something about a topic that interests them will be carried along by their enthusiasm.

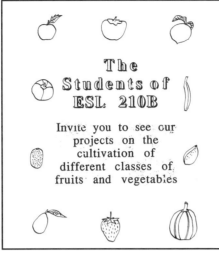

Figure 6.11. This was an invitation produced by one ESL class to a display of their hard work on agricultural products of California.

Figure 6.12. This masterpiece in salesmanship was written by a fourth grader.

cool dood baby herd on the news that a kide got shote by a cowboy in black stone canyen so he floo over thar at the speed of light and he saved the kide he put the coyboy in jale. once again cool dood baby will never end.

Cool dude baby part 13
cool dudes first advencher

cool dude was on vacation to zombie island for two days but he didint no that it was a hontid   Island kas it loot like all the other islands but there are sand monsters and ghools also dragons to wen cool dude got thar he sat down in the sun on the beech to rest from the long trip to zombie island well he was lying on the beech he herd somthing creeping up behind him then he jumped up swung his arm around and hit the sand monster writ in the head and killed the sand monster but he herd another sound behind him and he peeked in back of him and he sawe a sand dragon uh no said cool dude the sand dragon is the powerfullist monster alive it bloos any heart full thing at you to kill you im getting off this island whit now so he flu off zombie island but when he was in the air he saw another island so he flu down to get on that island but he didint no that that island was called ghool island when he landed all these ghools came charging at cool dude yikse said cool dude now I got to get off this island to so he flu off ghoul island. And flu to Hawaii where there is not that much troubel to spend the weekend resting from the long trip to Hawaii The end.

Figure 6.13. This third grader wrote very little, and resisted writing, until he found a computer program in which he could superimpose a small baby upon a series of different scenes. With the picture in front of him, he could invent a story about the scene. His stories grew increasingly complex as the saga of *Cool Dood Baby* developed. In all, he wrote 22 stories.

At both the elementary and secondary levels, teachers have collected "Stories We Brought With Us"—tales from the homeland. These old tales, fairy stories, legends, and myths had special meaning to the students who wrote them and gave their fellow students a greater understanding of the rich cultural heritage the newcomers had brought to their adopted country (figure 6.14).

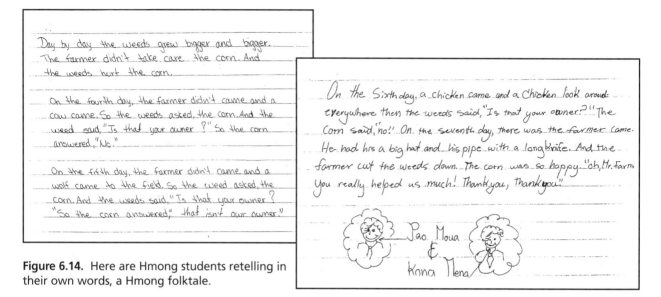

Figure 6.14. Here are Hmong students retelling in their own words, a Hmong folktale.

- Allow students to explore all forms of writing, from poetry, to persuasive essays, to advertisements. Audience, topic, and purpose change with every new composition, as do form and style. Academic writing differs from writing in personal journals, as a letter to a friend differs from a letter of complaining about problems in the school. Students need practice in all areas.

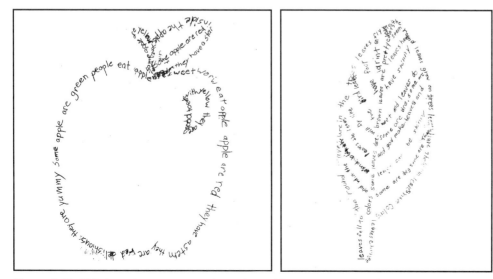

Figure 6.15. Third graders were experimenting with poetry, writing their poem in the shape of their subject.

The following example of a persuasive letter is written tongue-in-cheek. The letter exhibits a very strong voice as well as the linguistic and mental dexterity of the writer.

> *Dear Mr. Detwiler,*
>
> *I am sorry I was unable to come to school last week owing to mental illness. My constitutional defect didn't prevent me from yielding to a disease. I also enclosed herewith a certificate from the doctor, who is attending me. Yesterday he said to me "Health is the most precious. Without health, you can not work or study to the full. In order to maintain health, it is important to take moderate exercise and to take a fresh air" and then he wanted to go with me to the shopping center. For this reason, I visited a shopping center and met you, but you didn't give me a chance to explain my situation. I think that something seems to have gone wrong with us, you and me. For mercy's sake, don't misunderstand my position. In addition, I was very busy last week because of taking three exams. This has been my first time.*
>
> *Therefore, I was afraid that I made a bad record in exam, and then couldn't get a sleep all night. So I couldn't go to school. If I go to my country according to your unreasonable demand, I won't come back to America to study for good. The reason is that Korea is something of a stern country. If you give me a chance once more, from now on, I will study without absence and concentrate my energies on only studying English. I humbly ask for you pardon.*
>
> *Sincerely yours, Kibong*

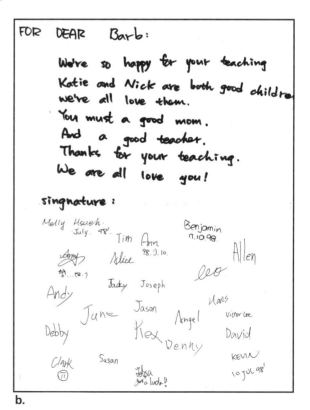

Figure 6.16a-b. These letters, unsolicited, were written from the heart.

■ Provide time for both intensive and extensive writing. *Intensive writing* is structured and written for a specific purpose. This is writing to be revised, writing where the specific skills of organization, mechanics, and editing can be taught. *Extensive writing* is not to be revised or corrected; it is used to articulate thoughts, explore ideas, and gain fluency without the need to stop and worry about correctness. Journals, diaries, and learning logs are all examples of extensive writing.

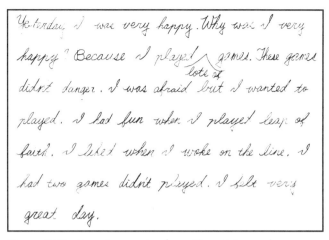

Figure 6.17. Here is an entry from Sherry's journal, a reflection on how the day went and how she felt about it. There is no reason to correct or edit it.

Provide a Supportive Environment

You need to be concerned not only with the act of writing, but the setting in which students write and the response to their writing. Cunningham et al. (2000) write that feeling is the energizer of reading and writing. "Thinking is the essence of what we do when we read or write, but feeling determines how much and how often we choose to read or write, and whether we will persist in reading or writing when we have difficulty." Students must feel that they can learn to read, write, and speak English better. They must feel self-confident in their ability to use strategies. Reading and writing must be pleasurable, not something that causes anxiety or pain. We can help make these things possible in the following ways:

■ Create a comfortable atmosphere.

Set up a climate of trust in which students believe that writing is important and that their writing is valued. Encourage them to take risks as writers, to experiment with different forms and styles without fear that their mistakes will be punished. Give them authority over their writing by allowing each of them to choose topic and style. Encourage students to exchange ideas and share drafts, to get feedback and ideas from each other. Above all, help them to understand that writing is a meaning-making event. Enabling students to become better writers also means making reasonable demands to help them become better writers. Calkins (1994) writes that we should not set up editing expectations that put extraordinary demands on writers who are beginners, or who are second-language learners. "If these children know they must find every single misspelled word in a dictionary, they will write with safe words, choosing *big* when they wanted to say *enormous*."

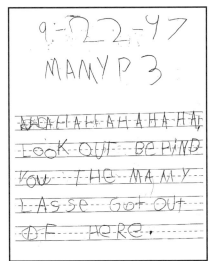 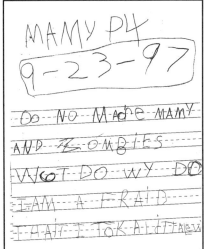 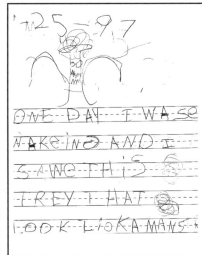

Figure 6.18. This is the first time Nick sat down and seriously wrote something that showed a discernible structure. He had been fascinated with the Goosebumps series, and each page of writing was in an episodic, cliffhanger style that clearly showed attention to the structure of the Goosebumps books.

- Make reading an integral part of the writing program. Opportunities to listen to and to read good-quality literature is a critical component of becoming a competent writer. Only those who have been exposed to good models can become good writers. You can see the reading reflected in the writing of students. Galda et al. (1997) write, "If children spend time exploring and discussing books, if we help them notice the structures and patterns they encounter, and if you let them know that many writers experiment with innovations, they will borrow from their reading when they want to."

- Make writing a collaborative act. There is a myth that writing is a lonely act, done in solitude; this isn't necessarily true. Language is a social act and writing can be too. In observing writers truly engaged in writing, researchers have noted how they talk while they write, sharing their thoughts and their writing with other writers to get more ideas. Bilingual and non-native-English speakers often talk and write more when allowed to interact with their peers. Galda et al. (1997) write, "Beginners talk to themselves to guide their writing and to others to seek and get help or to collaborate. They also use talk to get ready to write, exploring ideas to write about with peers or simply saying them aloud to themselves. They also frequently read aloud as they write." Encourage this interaction by promoting collective writing of stories or plays.

For instance, Barb was continually frustrated by a class in which a research paper was required. By the end of the semester, she didn't have a class anymore, she had a bunch of frustrated individuals mooning about the library searching for information. To keep the class together, to demonstrate the need for revision, and to bring out one of the hardest traits to learn—voice—she introduced dramas. The students wrote plays together. They brainstormed a list of possible settings, voted on one, chose and developed characters, then, in small groups wrote dialogue. The collaboration produced an electricity she had never experienced in a writing class, and the ideas generated together were beyond any an individual could have produced. Even the titles were inspired.

And although Barb announced up front that she was not going to be in the plays, somehow she ended up being the worst bad guy. In *Air Force II: Disaster in the Skies* she played Tiffany, the flight attendant who planted guns in the bathroom for a mere $50,000 so the terrorists could take over the airplane. In *A Time to Sing*, she played Layla Love, an intern who, jilted by the president, let the bad guys (disguised as a rock and roll band called "The Bomb in the Guitar Case") into the White House so they could blow it up.

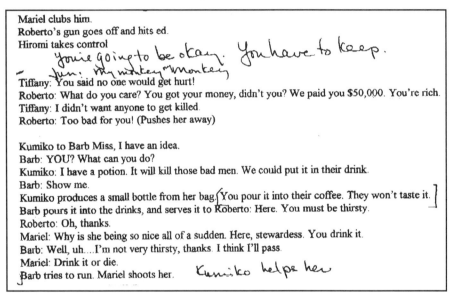

Figure 6.19. Scene from *Air Force II*. Every day Barb typed revisions. On the next day, she would hand write what the students, in character, suggested.

- Provide time for sharing writing and ideas.
- Encourage and train peer editors.
- Celebrate their writing. When students write, they need an appreciative audience to read their writing and to offer them encouragement. The feedback students receive in response to their writing has a significant impact on how they perceive the writing process and how much they improve. Edelsky (1986) noted that writing assignments that emphasize quantity alone, with no honoring of the writing by publishing or discussion, could be destructive—what it promotes is the idea that quantity is more important than quality. To recognize student writing, we suggest you employ some of the following strategies:
  - Display students' writing on the wall for everybody to read.
  - Have an "author's chair" as the seat of honor.

- Have an "Author of the Week" in which one student's writing is celebrated and pinned on a special area of the wall. Have students interview the "author."
- Publish the writing in the form of books, with hard covers the students make themselves.
- Create a special library of books written by the class.
- Provide a time for public reading of students' writing. At both elementary and secondary levels, students need to have the opportunity to be recognized and applauded for their efforts.
- Provide mailboxes for the students to write letters to you, or to each other.
- Produce Readers Theater, using excerpts from students' writing.
- Build in time for students to read their work aloud. This gives them a chance to practice their reading skills, as well as the opportunity to proudly display their stories to an attentive audience.

- Allow the students to write in their own language. If they speak and write in a language you don't know, then, of course, you cannot read it. However, as with reading, writing in one language improves writing in another. Encourage them to write in English, but allow them to start in their own language, making the transition to English as they grow more confident in their abilities. Researchers such as Edelsky have noted that there is often no clear break from the ESL students' native language to English. Often these students will write in both languages within the same piece of writing for a while, until they feel safe or confident enough to write totally in English. Even fluent English speakers will substitute words in their own language during first drafts.

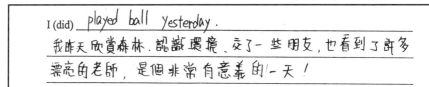

Figure 6.20. This student seemed to need to express what she had done the previous day, in Chinese.

Use Computers

Computers can be very helpful to beginning writers. For some ESL students, it's easier to practice writing on a computer than on paper. Word processing programs print the letters of the alphabet perfectly, in neat straight lines. Students' compositions, no matter how short, can be printed in a professional manner.

All steps of the creative-writing process can be learned and practiced on a computer by individuals or groups. For example, a small group of both ESL and native-English speakers can work cooperatively on one computer. After brainstorming for prewriting ideas, they can write their story without fear of making mistakes, not only because errors are seen as part of the writing process, but also because their errors will be so easy to correct. Revising and editing, when it is possible to delete and/or rearrange words, sentences, and paragraphs simply by pressing keys, is simple, and most students find it satisfying and fun. Writing a second or third draft of a paper is no longer tedious. Students are usually proud of their professionally printed final product and eager to start the next one.

Ensure Guidance and Feedback from Interested Readers

Beginning writers, developing writers, and fluent, experienced writers all need help with the writing process. They need guidance in making some of the larger decisions of writing related to such things as topic, style, and form. All writers need feedback on how effectively they are communicating, direction as to how to improve, and help with specific points such as mechanics, spelling, and punctuation. Your role in implementing a supportive environment and helping writers grow is critical.

Note: For help in evaluating student writing, we have included the Test of Written English (TWE) Scoring Guide in appendix H. The guide prioritizes the elements of good writing, making assessment easier.

Provide Good Models

Modeling means supporting the writing. Just as we can't expect a child to learn to swim by simply throwing him in the deep end of the pool, we can't expect students to become good writers simply by placing a sheet of paper in front of them and telling them to write.

Beginning writers need to see that writing is more than just worksheets and outlines, a chore to get through; writing is a wonderful way to articulate thoughts, one that can be enjoyable and exciting. Watching a teacher working on a draft of a letter or essay can demonstrate that writing isn't a tedious task or a meaningless activity, but a satisfying, creative act.

Atwell (1998) writes, "We need to find ways to reveal to students what adult, experienced writers do—to reclaim the tradition of demonstrations that allows young people to apprentice themselves to grown-ups. Observing adults as they work is an activity of enormous worth and power when it illumines what is possible." For all writers, you are formulating ideas, giving the writing organization, making it interesting, providing an ending, and punctuating. You are also demonstrating how all writers reread what they have written and how to add the necessary changes to improve it.

By modeling the writing process, we give students insight into how to take an idea and move through the process from start to finish. Not all writers need the same amount or kind of support. As they gain independence, strategies, and skills, they need you less and less to show them how to start, write, revise, and edit. There are five levels of support you can give your students (Fountas and Pinnell 1996; Tompkins 2000). These stages don't necessarily mean that beginners are limited only to shared writing, or skilled writers to the process of writing. You can use all levels at all grades, depending on what you are teaching.

1. **Modeled writing:** You write in front of the students, composing and transcribing, while you think aloud about word choice, organization, and ideas. When you are writing for beginners, you are demonstrating all the literate behaviors that they must learn in order to write: left to right with a return sweep, shaping letters, and so on.
2. **Shared writing:** This level of support includes the Language Experience Approach. You and the students create a text together. Everyone is doing the composing, you are doing the transcribing. Students add ideas, but also contribute to word choice, spelling, and so on as they are able.
3. **Interactive writing:** This level is much like shared writing, but you are letting the students take more control of the transcribing side of the writing process, as well as of the creating side. You and the students create the text together, sharing the pen or the chalk. At the lower or elementary level, students take turns writing the words and letters they know. At the upper levels, they are equal partners in writing a text with you. This can be true collaboration. When you allow yourself and your students freedom to experiment, this method can be very exciting. You never know where you'll end up. The results can surprise everyone, as shown in figure 6.21.

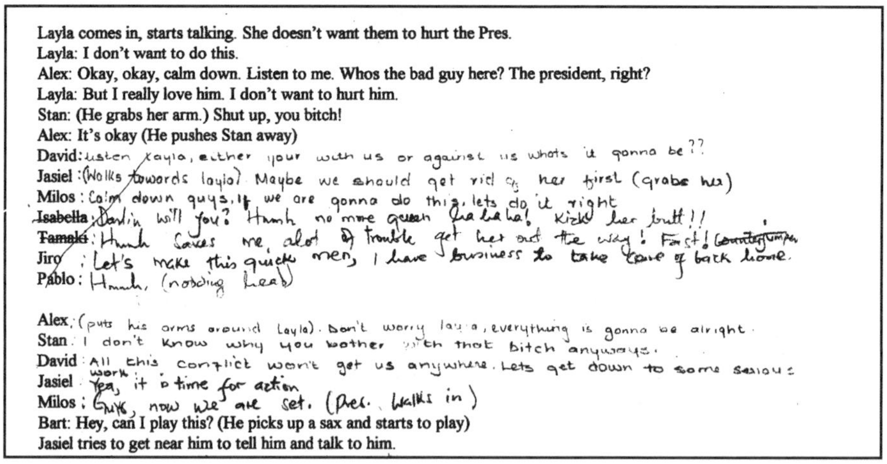
Layla comes in, starts talking. She doesn't want them to hurt the Pres.
Layla: I don't want to do this.
Alex: Okay, okay, calm down. Listen to me. Whos the bad guy here? The president, right?
Layla: But I really love him. I don't want to hurt him.
Stan: (He grabs her arm.) Shut up, you bitch!
Alex: It's okay (He pushes Stan away)
David: listen Layla, either your with us or against us whats it gonna be??
Jasiel: (Walks towards layla) Maybe we should get rid of her first (grabs her)
Milos: Calm down guys, if we are gonna do this, lets do it right
~~Isabella~~: Darlin will you? Hmph no more queen ha ha ha! Kick her butt!!
~~Tamaki~~: Hmph Saves me alot of trouble get her out the way! Fast! ~~Countryjumper~~
Jiro: Let's make this quick men, I have business to take care of back home.
Pablo: Hmph, (nodding head)

Alex: (puts his arms around Layla). Don't worry layla, everything is gonna be alright.
Stan: I don't know why you bother with that bitch anyways.
David: All this conflict won't get us anywhere. Lets get down to some serious work
Jasiel: Yea, it is time for action
Milos: Guys, now we are set. (Pres. walks in)
Bart: Hey, can I play this? (He picks up a sax and starts to play)
Jasiel tries to get near him to tell him and talk to him.

Figure 6.21. Here is a piece of the script from *A Time to Sing.* The parameters for the play was that everybody had an equal role, there were no stars, and no goldbricks. At this point, the general plot had been formulated and class members were writing dialogue for each other (to forego one-word answers from shy violets).

4. **Guided writing:** You present a structured lesson, then the students write as you supervise. This can include teaching one of the rhetorical modes, such as how to structure a comparison-contrast essay, or how to formulate poems. It also means teaching a writing strategy or a skill, such as the functions of punctuation, literary craft, or conventions of writing. (Atwell (1998) discusses mini-lessons in detail.)
5. **Independent writing:** At this stage, if not before, students work through all the stages of the writing process. Students do all composing and transcribing, while you monitor and help revise and edit.

Working With Beginners

My students are illiterate. They don't even know their alphabet much less how to write a whole text. What do I do to help them?

Here is where modeled writing is necessary. Write for them. Many students have never held a pencil before. The fine motor skills required for writing demand much effort on the part of beginning writers. Often just the act of trying to put letters on paper is so taxing it frustrates their efforts to express coherent thoughts. The temptation is to have them practice their ABCs until they have learned them correctly; however, these skills should be practiced only within the context of real writing. Practicing meaningful phrases, rather than words in isolation, reinforces meaning as well as skills. Don't wait until students can form sentences before allowing them to write. Even though they can't write, students have plenty to say; everyone has a story to tell. Encourage them to jump right in.

Researchers studying first-language learners have noted that children pass through a sequence of broad stages: scribbles; only a few letters, words, and illegible squiggles; a sentence or a series of several unrelated sentences; two or more related sentences. While we cannot apply these stages on a wholesale basis to non-English-speaking students, we can be aware of them and allow our students the freedom to experiment and learn, without imposing the need for perfection and precision immediately.

In chapter 5, "Reading," we discussed the Language Experience Approach (LEA), in which the teacher writes the students' thoughts first, then has them copy what you have elicited. The word *fireman* might be a whole text for one student; accept it as such. After you have written their thoughts down for the students, they can copy your writing onto their own paper. They will make the transition to writing on their own when they are ready—when they have gained enough confidence to try, learned some vocabulary, or just simply learned that writing has meaning.

First-grader Rebecca, for example, did not seem to understand the basic speech-print connection. After many months of watching LEA in action, she began to copy the words the teacher provided on the chalkboard as springboards to thought. One day her teacher wrote the words *playground*, *soccer*, and *hopscotch* on the board. This is what Rebecca wrote:

Figure 6.22. Translated, this means, "I love hopscotch because of the kids. I love soccer because of the kids."

For a first try at a real story, her piece is impressive. She shows that she understands the functions of print, and that she is aware of syntax, sentence structure and boundaries, as well as punctuation. Rebecca is also making a personal and lively statement about the topic. She loves soccer and hopscotch because of the kids who play the games with her. There is much to be praised and encouraged.

My students are novices. They don't know where to start, or if they do, they aren't organized. What can I do?

A scaffold is a framework on which students can hang their ideas. Scaffolds allow students to concentrate on content. Since scaffolds provide the forms, they help students learn how to organize at many levels: the grammatical level, the sentence level, the paragraph level, and the text level. Students model the scaffold, imitate it, and gain control over their writing.

There are many different types of scaffolds:

- Patterned poetry, such as haiku, cinquain, diamante, and sonnets.
- Frame sentences. For example, in one elementary school classroom, after a unit on occupations, students made little books about themselves, each in occupational roles they thought they might enjoy. They wrote sentences according to the framework worked out together on the chalkboard: "I am a _____. I wear a _____ uniform. Here is where I work. This is me working." They illustrated their books with pictures of themselves in their various roles (figure 6.23).

Figure 6.23. Yoshi, in second grade, choosing an occupation.

Models are especially important in the upper grades and for the content areas as writers need to have examples of good writing in order to write well themselves. Find good examples—textbooks are one source—for them to use as guides. Provide them with positive models such as sample research reports or science results. With some instruction on how the sample is organized, students can follow the same format for clearer, more readable papers.

Some writing-process advocates feel that teaching structure, such as the rhetorical modes (narrative, descriptive, argumentative, comparison and contrast, and so on) removes students' control over their written work. However, we believe that for ESL students, it is important to focus directly on organization. Most students born in North America have been exposed to writing from early childhood. After many years of reading stories, magazine articles, newspapers, and so on, they have internalized the organizational patterns that are common to each type of writing. So, when we ask them to write a story or compare two objects, for instance, they can do it with little difficulty. Many ESL students have not had the benefit of these years of reading and writing. While we can hope that our students will learn these patterns incidentally, without explicit instruction, we cannot leave this to chance. In addition, many cultures and non-Western societies have different ways of organizing essays and stories. Students

Figure 6.24. Using *Rosie's Walk* by Pat Hutchins as a framework, Jeff and Mimi wrote about their own day using prepositions they knew.

from these backgrounds need to be shown directly that, while their patterns are not actually incorrect, the structure can be confusing to English-speaking readers searching for a familiar pattern of organization. Form should not be imposed arbitrarily without regard for purpose or audience (for example, "Today we're going to write a five-paragraph essay"), but neither should we leave organization to chance.

Giving Constructive Feedback

My students make a lot of grammatical errors. What should I do?

The answer depends on the level of the students and the purpose of the assignment. With younger children and newcomers, it is, at first, best to accept any effort on their part. If the language is totally garbled, the essays unstructured, and the main ideas obscure, don't correct the grammar.

Correcting Errors

Instead, talk to the students about their ideas to help clarify what they really want to say.

Yesterday last night of the teacher Mary Eckes gaven would one to student all student in class-person doesn't get to have to know. This when student dd to get befor big one the squash all way came back to school at reach home family and neighbour. that right your are want to see becouse yours are doesn't have. doesn't know.

Using the example above, find out what Cham is trying to say and how she wants to say it. In this case, Cham was telling a story about a squash. Mary used to bring in produce from her garden and hold a lottery to determine which student would get the vegetables; no one knew who was going to win. Cham won on that occasion, and the prize was such a large squash that she shared half of it with her neighbor. With a little prompting, the story became clear and Mary could help her focus and clarify. Pointing out Cham's grammatical errors at this point would have been harmful because she would have been discouraged.

This does not mean that errors should be completely ignored. We cannot focus solely on the process at the expense of the product. We must show a clear concern for mechanics. Quality and correctness are important issues because, ultimately, we are writing to be read—and understood! Here again, it is a matter of priorities. As with reading, accuracy and skills should be secondary to meaning. We've all read the story or essay that is perfect mechanically and yet says nothing, while we've read others that are riddled with errors and yet are spritely and creative.

Stress content more than correctness. Initially, getting the ideas out is the important thing; then they must be shaped until the writer achieves what he wants to say. Students need the chance to rewrite—nobody writes the first draft perfectly. If students are worried about perfection, they will be afraid to be creative and experimental, sticking only to what they are sure of. Ammon (1985) noted that writers who feel they need to invest much of their time and energy to spelling and other component skills tire quickly and eventually give up before they have finished. If your students are concerned both with mechanics and getting their ideas out, they may be forced into a trade-off, paying more attention to one to the detriment of the other. In other words, as Frank Smith writes in *Reading Without Nonsense* (1997), "Emphasis on the elimination of mistakes results in the elimination of writing." Allow students plenty of time to make tentative efforts and sort out their ideas before asking them to wrestle with the problems of getting their writing to look and sound like native English.

Errors are not random, but are strategies students employ when they have not yet learned or mastered a new form or concept. They show courage in trying something new. Celebrate mistakes; applaud students for daring to do something difficult. Errors can demonstrate both what the students know and what they have not yet learned. As with reading, we can view errors as valuable insights into the students' development and use them to pinpoint areas they need to work on. For example, if Wei Xia writes, "I am a youngest student in the class," it is clear that he needs to learn more about articles.

Publishing students' work in the form of newsletters and so on will motivate them to correct and revise. If they have a stake in what is written, if their names are noted as authors and their work is out there for the world to see, they will be more concerned with perfection.

What should I correct?

Limit yourself to correcting one type of mistake only and ignore the rest for the time being. Marking every error students have made can be defeating; they won't know where to start and will get so bogged down trying to correct all their errors that they may give up, and any momentum gained will have been lost.

Ravi Shorey (1986) lists a hierarchy of error categories:

1. The most serious errors are verb forms (agreement, tenses, and so on).
2. Next in importance are word-choice errors.
3. Less serious errors are articles and prepositions.
4. Spelling errors are the least serious of all.

We shouldn't expect total perfection, nor should we expect that if we correct a type of error once, it will never reappear. Unfortunately, it isn't that simple. Mastering English is a long, often slow process. The English article system, for instance, which we native English speakers take for granted, is a second-language learner's nightmare. What seems to work in one sentence is totally inappropriate in another. Often prepositions make no logical sense at all, so they must simply be memorized. For example, we speak of *in the street* as well as *in the box*, and *on the table* as well as *on time*. Before they can master English forms, non-native speakers need a great deal of exposure to the range of structures and meanings possible.

When allowing time for revision, remember the law of diminishing returns. When we are striving for fluency, working for perfection on each paper fosters frustration. Many times it is appropriate to allow the student one or two rewrites, then go on to something else. It is also appropriate to give them many opportunities to write for fluency alone, without correction, such as in journal-writing.

At what stage should I make corrections?

Correcting, if done at all, must be done with the idea that the student will continue to work on the paper. Proett and Gill (1986) write, "Correcting involves pointing out students mistakes; if it is done by the teacher with no further response from the student, it is probably a useless activity." Instruction and correction in mechanics are most effective at the editing stage, in response to a particular need. For ESL students, error correction

Along the way there were many families camping by the side of the road. These families were either resting due to long hours of traveling, or they were simply stuck because of the car trouble.

Figure 6.25. These two sentences are from an essay written by Annie, a proficient speaker, on *The Grapes of Wrath*. Yet, she still struggles with the article "the"—when to use it and when not to. Care to explain the rule on this one?

too early in the process (for example, during the first revision) is liable to curtail their creativity, because they feel forced to concentrate on being "right." Gadda, Peitzman, and Walsh in *Teaching Analytical Writing* (1988), point out that correcting the mechanical points of a paper is like fine-tuning an engine, something you do only after you have replaced and repaired the major parts. Why should someone work hard to fix something when it may be completely overhauled or even scrapped altogether? If they correct the language first, they will be unwilling to change the content. Only after the paper is clear, well-organized, and thorough, should the student work on fine-tuning grammar, spelling, and so on.

Revising and Editing With ESL Students

The most logical way to make corrections is to allow two revision stages, one for content, the other for mechanics. Thus, the writing process for ESL students would look like this:

1. Students compose.
2. Teacher or peers respond. This first response is for content alone. Ideas, organization, and clarity are the priorities here. You can train your students to work as peer editors for this stage, to respond to the impact of the work, ask for more ideas, clarification, and expansion.
3. Students revise to clarify, add detail, and reorganize.
4. Teacher or peers respond. This response is for mechanics. What has not been cleared up through a second reading and self-editing can be worked on here, on a topic (such as articles or verb tenses) agreed upon by you and the student.
5. Teacher teaches grammatical points as necessary.
6. Students edit for mechanics.

With this sequence, students know when you will be focusing on the form of their papers and won't be wasting their creative energy trying to remember the rules of grammar at stage 2 (although they can ask for and receive help in grammar at any point of their writing).

Andre, for instance, was writing about what it was like in his country. He wrote a paragraph about his journey here from his country (figure 6.26). The links between the sentences, that he came because his grandparents lived in America, are only inferred by their juxtaposition, and the use of the word *but*. He gives a quick travel itinerary and ends up where he is living now. His errors are mostly in grammar and spelling. He spells *deseme (the same)* and *a vael (a while)* phonetically, according to how

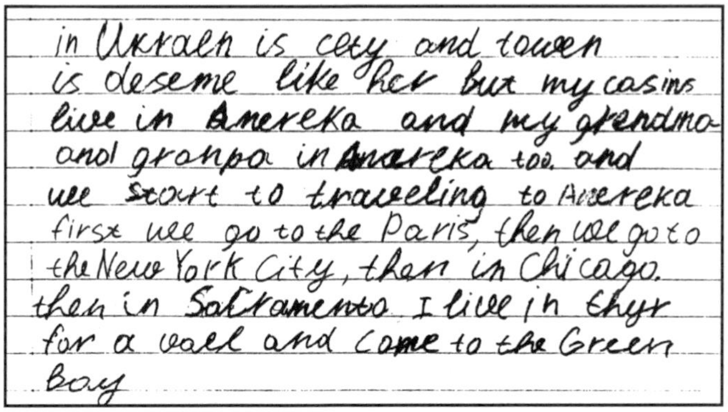
in Ukraen is cety and towen
is deseme like her but my casins
live in Amereka and my grendma
and granpa in Amareka too. and
wee start to traveling to Amereka
first wee go to the Paris, then wee go to
the New York City, than in Chicago.
then in Sakramento I live in thyr
for a vael and come to the Green
Bay

Figure 6.26. Andre's first Draft.

he has perceived the words. His revision consists simply of retyping what he had written before (figure 6.27). He makes mistakes in the retyping, such as *first* and *paris,* that he did not make in his handwritten draft. This is typical of novice writers, who, without direct intervention, do not know how to improve. He does not seem to have a sense of form or purpose. If the purpose of the second draft was to get Andre to practice typing, then it can stand as is, with some lessons on how to use the spell-check and some help with grammar. Should his teacher ask him to revise, they could focus in on why he came to this country, and specifically what the journey was like. The teacher could help him brainstorm a list of details to use in his next try. Or he could focus on why he came here if the cities and towns are alike. What did America have to offer?

Abdullah wrote the following paper in response to the question, "Which English language skill is the hardest one for you?"

> *Which english language skill has been the hartest on. English is funy longuage that we sey some the and read o the such as secret, sure or surprise. That meen riting is the hardest one for me so I thik that I'm still week in spilling and I need riting coure, also I don't knew much vocapulary that hard for me, spilling or riting needs memorise t learn but my memory is not good so it is hard to rite will wheth outrong in spilling or problems. If I tell about the easiest one, I seylistening is more easy for me I have good improvment in it so not prob in it also me gramar is good one easy enough for me to learn but the pig broplem is vocapulary and spilling onthing is easy I can speek will and understand will with proctes every thing become easy sometimes I rite pregraph to improve my riting but still need it might be next term it becom brety good any how I don't like this laguage*

An understandable first reaction upon seeing such a paper is shock, followed by a feeling of helplessness, if not despair. How does one respond when the problems are of such magnitude, when the spelling is clearly out of hand, the punctuation practically nonexistent, and the meaning, in many places, is obscure? How does one untangle the various problems without overwhelming Abdullah and destroying whatever self-confidence he has?

Many of his errors may be performance errors—errors made because he was inattentive, careless, or preoccupied with getting the meaning out. For instance, Abdullah writes *language* once, then *longuage,* and further on *laguage; hartest on* then *hardest one.* Upon rereading, he will probably correct these errors. One strategy you might employ is to have your students read their papers aloud to a peer or have the peer read it back. Many times they will correct themselves because what they write does not jibe with what they hear. Abdullah may hear where the sentences should begin and end and put periods in their appropriate places. If he doesn't, you have an indication of where the gaps are in his knowledge. Those errors are the competence errors—made because he has not learned a particular grammatical point, word meaning, spelling, or rhetorical form.

MY JOURNEY

In Ukrain cetys and towen deseme like her. But my casins, Grandma and Grendpa live in Amereka. and we start to traveling to Amereka. ferst we go to paris. Then we flie to tha New York City. Then in Chicago. And after we flie to the Sacramento. and live in ther for a vael, and com to the Green Bay.

Figure 6.27. Andre's story, second draft.

Responding to Students' Written Work

Once he has had a chance to rethink his paper, it is your turn. Your response is critical and should be on content alone. Ideas, organization, and clarity are priorities. There is a logical order of thinking, which leads to clear statements. In answer to the question, "Which skill has been the hardest one?" he answers that writing is and gives a graphic example of why: we say things one way, and then we write them another. (There is an /s/ sound in *secret* and /sh/ sound in *sure* and a /z/ sound in *surprise*, and yet we write them all with the letter *s*.) He states that he has trouble with spelling and vocabulary, an accurate assessment of his problems. Through his examples, one can sense his frustration at learning this difficult language. There are two important ways to respond to his paper, and you should employ them both:

1. As a reader. It is important for Abdullah to see how his paper has an impact on you personally. You can make inter-lineal comments, such as "I have trouble with spelling too!" and "Good examples!"

2. As a teacher. On a separate sheet of paper make specific suggestions as to how to improve.

Guidelines for Written Responses

Gadda et al. in *Teaching Analytical Writing* (1988), give guidelines for commenting on students' papers:

- Skim the entire paper before writing comments. You may make comments, only to find the student has answered your criticisms further on in the paper.

- Address students by their names. With each communication, you are responding to a real person, and starting out this way establishes a connection between the two of you.

- With each student, begin by stating a major strength of the student's written work, then pinpoint the nature of major weaknesses. Don't negate your praise with a *but* or *however*. Praise without reservation.

- Be supportive in tone. These essays are true accomplishments for those who are struggling to articulate their thoughts in a new language. Don't dampen their enthusiasm. The students are likely to try harder for someone who they know understands and is in their corner.

- List text-specific questions and suggestions for change. Note the places that worked particularly well. Notes at the bottom of their papers like "tighten" or "reorganize" will not help them. If the students knew how, they would have done so.

- Phrase your comments tentatively when appropriate. Students need to understand that there are often many ways to solve problems. On occasion you may mistake the intent of a student, and if you make rigid pronouncements about changes required, you could be destroying the entire paper and its worth. And, most important, remember that these are the students' papers, and they need to maintain authority over their own writing. They need to have the right to change as they see necessary to make their papers fit their plans.

- Don't solve their problems for them. Direct them, find the problems, but let the students work at solving them.

- Close with encouraging remarks. Show that you have confidence in their ability. For example: "Abdullah, your examples of the problems we have with spelling are very vivid. English is a funny language that frustrates many English speakers too. Your paper would be more readable if you reorganized. Your thoughts jump from spelling to writing to vocabulary to listening and back to spelling again. Why don't you look for your weaknesses in spelling and writing first, and try to figure out why you have those problems. Then move on to what you are good at. End on a positive note! You are very accurate when you look at your own problems, and your examples demonstrate just how difficult English can be."

- Give them a chance to revise again. On this draft you can edit for grammar and mechanics. This does not mean doing the work for him. Show Abdullah what is wrong, why, and then direct him in the most productive way to give him a better understanding of English usage. Don't correct every error he has made. (With a paper like this, you would wind up marking nearly every word, and Abdullah would be so defeated he might give up altogether.) Choose one. If he has not corrected his sentence boundaries by inserting periods and starting the next sentences with uppercase letters, that might be a good place to start.

  Many students want—in fact insist—on having every error corrected. If this is the case, it is often fruitless to mark the spelling errors and tell them to look up the words. If they don't know how to spell the words in the first place, looking them up won't help. How can you tell Abdullah to look up *with* when he has spelled it *wheth*? Telling students how to spell words is not cheating, nor is it encouraging them to be lazy. You can incorporate the worst errors into each student's personal spelling plan discussed below.

Their spelling is terrible! If it is a low priority, should I ignore it altogether?

Spelling

The following examples show how third-grade first-language learners spelled the word *policeman*.

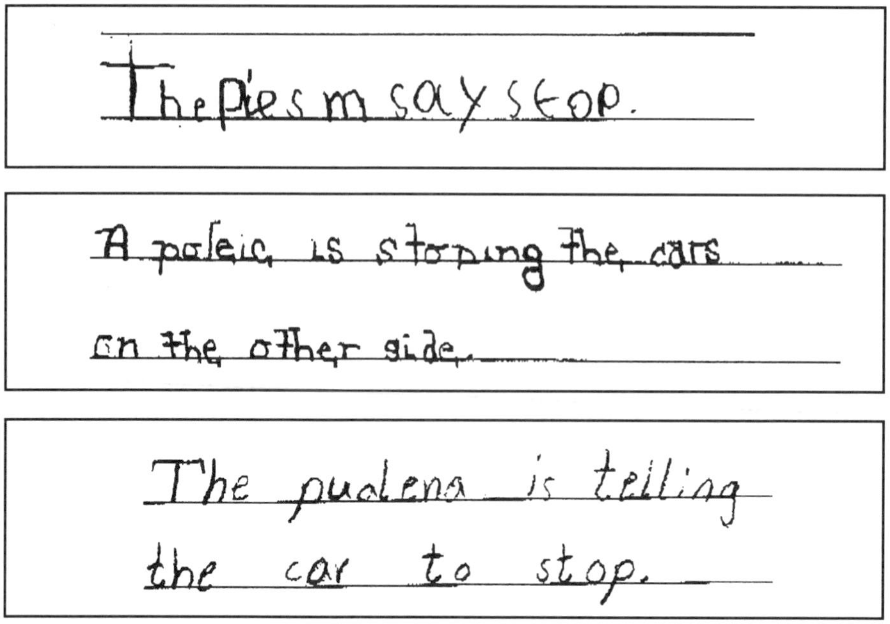

> The Plesm say stop.

> A poleic is stoping the cars
> on the other side.

> The pualena is telling
> the car to stop.

Figure 6.28. These sentences were written in response to a picture prompt of a policeman.

Here's how second-language learners spelled the same word (from the Language Assessment Scale): *palesman, polisoe, polcole, offsur, plecoman.*

Poor spelling is one of the most noticeable errors that writers make, and it is also one that we are most inclined to condemn. Thus, many teachers feel that teaching spelling is important and perfection is critical. Many educators also feel that allowing children to spell spontaneously and incorrectly will lead to bad habits down the road. Experts, however, emphatically disagree. The McCrackens (1987), for example, state: "If conventional spelling is required initially, the [writing] program will fail, because the children will be inhibited from expressing their ideas in writing. They will fail to learn the alphabetic principle of written English, because conventional spelling obscures the sound-letter relationships."

A good reading program, again, complements a writing program, and vice versa. It is in the act of writing that learners figure out the sound-letter correspondences.

Susan Sowers (1985) writes, "Inventive spellers' errors don't interfere with their learning to spell correctly later. Like early attempts to walk, talk and draw, initial attempts to spell do not produce habits to be overcome. No one worries when a child's first drawing of a person is a head propped up on two stick legs. As the errors become more sophisticated, two stick arms protruding from the head where the ears should be—no one fears this schema will become a habit, though it may be repeated a hundred times... [These errors] are greeted as a display of intelligence and emerging proficiency."

Errors in spelling are not random. They are based on a student's stage of understanding of sound-letter correspondences. As with any other skill, children begin with gross approximations, improving their accuracy. For example, when Rania draws a silly picture of Atosa and labels it *I am cucu*, or when Enrique writes *chack* for *chalk*, or Sabina writes *wich broom* under a drawing of a witch, they are demonstrating that they know a great deal, if not the finer points, of English spelling (figure 6.29).

The McCrackens (1995) advocate making a chart of "doozers," words that are very common and yet resist phonetics, such as *once, the, of*. Keep this list displayed on the wall for easy reference.

Some schools use the "guess and go" approach, in which the child writes an approximation of what he wants to say, and comes back later with the correct spelling. This was what Rebecca (page 175) used. *Bksakids* was a very good try at *because of the kids*, and she wasn't hampered by the necessity to get it perfect the first time.

Here are some methods teachers use to support spelling development:

- Daily opportunities to write.
- Word walls.
- Personal dictionaries.

Conventional spelling is important. As time goes by and competence increases, conventional spelling should be expected. By the time English-speaking students reach the fourth grade, they should be conventional spellers. Such an expectation cannot be held out for our ESL students who enter school at all levels of literacy; however, we can expect them to reach for that goal.

The most important things to remember when looking at a student's writing are: (1) there is a logic to the errors, and you can see through them to the meaning if you look hard enough, and (2) the student knows what he is trying to say, and can tell you if you ask.

Written responses to writing are well and good. However, they only go so far. How many times have teachers given up on an entangled piece and simply written, "See me," on the bottom, because there is no way to make headway in the paper without talking to the student?

Conferencing is not for writers who have finished their pieces. It's for writers in the middle of their work, and its purpose is to help with ideas, language, format, and so on. Atwell (1998) writes, "Young writers want to be listened to. They also want honest, adult responses. They need teachers who will guide them to the meanings they don't know yet by showing them how to build on what they do know and can do. Student writers need response while the words are churning out, in the midst of the messy, tentative act of drafting meaning." When conferencing with students, it's important not to take ownership of their work. It's very easy to fall into that trap, and it often happens because they are hesitant about their work.

Figure 6.29. Sabina's picture.

Guidelines for Conferencing

They know less than you do, and it seems easier to just fix it yourself than have them struggle. Resist that temptation.

- Sit next to the student, not across, so that the conference is personal.
- Let them keep the paper in their hands. It's their paper.
- Begin with a general open-ended question. Calkins suggests, "How's it going?"
- Ask them to comment on parts they are struggling with, or are proud of.
- Listen.

For more advice on conferencing, see Atwell (1998) and Calkins (1994).

Using Peer Tutors

Peer tutors can be a valuable asset in a writing classroom because they provide real audiences for students' work. But peer responses can often fall flat or fail altogether because students don't know what to say: they can't get beyond "I liked it," or can find nothing but fault. Train your students to know what to look for, and how to give specific suggestions. Have them look at the content, not the grammar, finding parts they liked and parts that confused them or could have been written in more detail. It may help to give them a worksheet with specific tasks for them to complete, such as those suggested by Karen Yoshihara (1988):

- Summarize your classmate's paper in one sentence. Your sentence should be your own version of a good topic sentence for his paper.
- What did you like best about the way your classmate wrote his paper? Why? Be sure that you mention something that he can continue to do on future papers.
- What are the three best questions to ask about your classmate's paper? If you don't have three good questions, you should have three separate comments about what you liked best (number 2, above) and at least one question.

Time

One of the most important things we can give our second-language learners is time. Time to write and time to learn at their own pace. The only way to become a better writer is to practice, practice, practice. Hoffman (1998) writes that one of the bad things that happened to good ideas was the writing process became "proceduralized, ie, that one Monday we do prewriting, Tuesday we draft, Wednesday we revise, etc." Beginning or limited-English writers need much time to grapple with all the complexities of the process, and it can take much longer for some than for others. Students need time to learn the rhetorical structures, to learn spelling, and to learn strategies. Students need you, the teacher, to spend time talking and writing with them.

Conclusion

The major assumptions we operate under when we teach writing are

- We learn to write by writing.
- All writing must be done for real purposes with real audiences.

Writing is an important part of the school day. Writers learn by interacting with print and by experimenting with thoughts and forms, without being forced to worry about correctness. Younger or newer ESL learners should not be excluded from writing merely because they have not yet mastered orthography, sentence patterns, or a large vocabulary. They need to be allowed to practice communicating thoughts, expressing feelings, and learning how to organize their thoughts on paper through the process of writing whole texts. Spelling and grammar will be learned during the act of writing. By providing a rich and supportive environment for students, you can help them grow as writers.

CHAPTER 7

SPEAKING AND LISTENING

Chapter 3, "Language Learning—Students and Teachers," included a detailed discussion of the ways in which you can provide input that is both meaningful and useful to the second-language learner. In this chapter, we look further at the listening and speaking components of acquiring a language. We focus on

- The importance of oral language in learning and personal growth.
- Phases of language acquisition and what these look like in the classroom.
- How to treat errors.
- How to develop the skill of listening—an end in itself.
- Talk in all parts of the curriculum—opportunities to talk and listen.

The Importance of Oral Language in Learning

Franco, who took his name from a Franco-American truck driving by when he and his brother were choosing new American names, was twelve when he arrived from Taiwan and was enrolled in junior high. His family owned a Chinese restaurant in a nearby shopping mall. Although Barb (his ESL teacher, who worked with him three afternoons a week) and his classroom teachers were conscientious and patient, Franco's progress seemed very slow. Conversations with him were usually one way; he seldom managed more than a phrase or two here and there. More often than not, his response was either a shrug or an "I don't know." He could not do the regular work in his content-area classes. He hardly seemed to be learning at all.

And yet outside the classroom, things were different. He consistently beat Barb at Monopoly and Risk. These are by no means easy games, and Barb explained the rules painstakingly in English. When they played Monopoly at the end of each session, they each kept their own property and money so that they could continue the next session where they had left off.

Barb would read out the Chance and the Community Chest cards that Franco drew, and more often than not he could follow the instructions without further explanation.

Although he was not a break-in artist, Franco gained the respect and admiration of the eighth-grade boys by demonstrating that he could open any combination lock in the school. Another demonstration of his ability to understand was when the other students would tell him, "Go tell Mrs. Mitchell, 'F____ you.'" And with a wide grin on his face, Franco would obligingly go to Mrs. Mitchell and say, "F____ you, Mrs. Mitchell," to the howls of his classmates.

Franco was a lot smarter and knew a lot more than he let on. He used his English (and his lack of it!) to his advantage. He selectively misunderstood what he didn't feel like doing by pretending he didn't know what he was saying, but clearly comprehended things that were important to him, such as the rules of games and instructions from classmates.

One of the most interesting things about Franco was his ability and willingness to use the limited English that he had to great advantage to get by and make friends: he didn't let his lack of English stand in his way. On top of that, his intelligent use of strategies more than made up for his lack of fluency and proficiency.

Not all of our students are as outgoing (or as naughty) as Franco. He was able to use what he had to his best advantage—much shyer or less outgoing students may not be so willing. Franco used interactions to increase both his status and his friendships. If he had so chosen, he could have used interactions to increase his learning. His teachers could have placed him in situations that took advantage of his natural social nature and increased both his proficiency and his ability to function throughout the curriculum.

Angel and Beverly are on the opposite end of the spectrum. Angel is very shy and will not attempt to speak English at all. She and Beverly converse together almost entirely in their native language. It is often difficult to gauge how much they actually understand or are learning; they never raise their hands, or volunteer, and they only speak to each other. This is frustrating for their teachers. It also presents a dilemma for them. They want to encourage the use, growth, and maintenance of their home language. The teachers know that allowing Beverly and Angel (as well as Fernando and Salvador) the chance to talk things over in their first language aids significantly in their comprehension. But, because no adults speak Chinese, they cannot distinguish between real learning and idle chatter.

a. 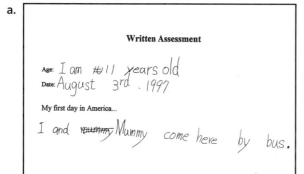   b.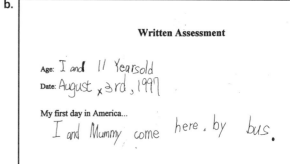

Figure 7.1a-b. It was impossible to tell from Beverly and Angel's writing who had generated the work and who had copied.

As with reading and writing, competence in both speaking and listening is best acquired in a setting that encourages students to talk, experiment with language, and respects and values their contributions, however slight, hesitant or faltering (Brock 1997; Martinez-Roldan and Lopez-Robertson 2000). The environment Franco was immersed in was conducive to learning. He was not isolated in a language lab, learning "Hello, Mrs. Mitchell, how are you?" and "Please pass the pencils." He was surrounded by people using English for real purposes—to further relationships, to get homework done, to harass poor Mrs. Mitchell. Franco was strongly motivated to make friends and used the language skills he had to further that end. Having him spend his time working on pronunciation and grammar would not have helped much.

Beverly and Angel need to be encouraged to open up to others. However, you have to accept the fact that some students simply aren't ready. It is important not to fall back on drills to get them to open up, or force them to speak English to each other. It is very easy to simply give up, overlook them, and decide that they are non-participants in conversations and discussions. This is a trap we cannot allow ourselves to fall into. As we state below and in other chapters, there are multiple means other than speaking to demonstrate competence and understanding. But we also have to keep the door open. Sooner or later, when they are ready, one or the other will begin to talk in English. Hnuku, for instance, had been silent the entire autumn. One day, she was informed that girls from the fifth-grade class were going to come in and perform an ethnic dance. Suddenly, loudly and clearly, she said, "Aw, I already know. I don't wanna do that. I know how to play that," surprising her teachers.

It is easy to undervalue the importance of oral language in learning because we spend so much time inside and outside the classroom doing just that. However, we need to recognize the centrality of talk and capitalize on a natural tendency. Both talking and listening, write Barr et al. (1989, 36) "cut across the curriculum…Within the classroom contexts, the quality and range of oral language opportunities will significantly affect the child's progress and development as a talker, listener and learner…Opportunity for oral language use across a full range of informal as well as formal contexts must be afforded throughout the day." These authors go on to assert that how children use language to explore experience and how they express what they understand "is at the crux of learning."

In fact, the California English Language Arts Content Standards goes so far as to state that "speaking and listening skills have never been more important. Most Americans now talk for a living at least part of the time. The abilities to express ideas cogently and to construct valid and truthful arguments are as important to speaking well as to writing well" (CLAF 1999).

To develop competency in both the listening and speaking areas of English, newcomers need

- Teachers who understand the stages of acquisition and adjust their input to fit each student's level.

- Teachers who are tolerant of errors, enabling students to learn without being labeled or punished for their pronunciation or word-choice errors.

- Many opportunities to talk, listen, and interact with others—real talk, real questions, rather than inquisitions with a predetermined answer that the teacher owns.

- Time.

Language Acquisition and Classroom Input

While acquiring a language is an individual process, we can make generalizations about the phases the learner goes through. Comprehension often precedes production. What Franco, for instance, said—or was able to say—was by no means indicative of the learning that was taking place. He could understand the complex rules of Monopoly, and while he would never have been able to explain them back, he could certainly follow the directions well enough to win time and time again.

We see this with our own children learning their first language. Children recognize their names at five months, and phrases such as "Here's your Mom," and "Wave bye-bye" at about seven months, long before they say their first word. By the time they speak, they have had nearly a year of listening, and their ability to understand spoken messages far exceeds their ability to produce.

For second-language learners, our priority as teachers should be "fluency before accuracy." Getting things done supersedes getting things right. As they gain competence and confidence, students will work out the details of grammar and pronunciation.

The Three Stages—
A Continuum

Researchers Burt and Dulay (1982) found that language learners progress through three general stages as they gain communication skills. These are not necessarily discrete stages; they represent more of a continuum from no language to full participation:

STAGE 1. One-way communication. The learners listen to the target language, but are not able to speak it.

A common question we hear from teachers goes something like: "Beverly and Angel aren't saying anything. What can we do to make them talk?" Some researchers, such as Stephen Krashen (1982), claim that language learners go through a silent period, which can last between one and six months. Others have questioned this idea and found the time frame to be closer to two weeks. Still others say there is no such thing. But we have found that teachers often tell us of students who have been in their classes for weeks without saying a word, leading them to believe that these students aren't learning.

This silent period can be caused by several things, or a combination of things. It could be a period of silent noncomprehension in which the new language simply seems like a stream of sound. It could be due to psychological withdrawal as a result of culture shock. Or it could simply be due to a particular student's personality; perhaps he or she is a shy person. The student's learning style could affect production. This student may prefer to learn by rote memorization of rules, remaining silent until a number of structures are learned, rather than relying on intuitive knowledge and making the most of the skills already acquired. He or she may have come from a school in which asking questions indicates misunderstanding, an insult to the teacher and a dishonorable thing to do.

Mai Lor, for instance, came to Cinda's classroom when she was in the third grade. Records from her former school informed Cinda that Mai Lor had said but two words throughout her schooling thus far; in fact, the kindergarten and first-grade teachers had both remarked that she never said a word in school. Following up on what she observed with Mai Lor, Cinda had conversations with Mai Lor's mom. She found out that Mai Lor spoke only in Hmong at home.

Whether your students are silent for six months or begin to communicate the first day, they need to be allowed "listening time" without being forced to speak. Research has shown that the emphasis in learning a new language should be on listening first, and that forcing a student to speak can be detrimental to his learning. Granted, waiting until your student is ready to speak can be difficult. Going day after day speaking to a student who doesn't respond is frustrating; the temptation to force this student to say something—*anything!*—just to see if you are getting through can be strong. It may be easier to resist the temptation if you are aware that this is a passing stage. Igoa (1995) remarks that "there is a lot that goes on in the silent stage. Beyond our comprehension, they comprehend."

STAGE 2. Partial two-way communication. The learners listen to the communication and respond with either gestures or in their native language.

Students can demonstrate comprehension in ways other than by speech. Allow them to respond by nodding their heads, pointing, drawing, gesturing, or pantomiming.

Over the course of the year, Mai Lor began to join in with the rest of the students while in a small group outside of the mainstream classroom. It was a big day when, in science, Mai Lor pointed to pictures of the full moon, the quarter moon, and the crescent moon, to indicate she understood.

STAGE 3. Full two-way communication. The learners listen and respond effectively in the target language.

Research has revealed that people first learn a language in chunks. Their first utterances consist of unanalyzed wholes, such as "What's the matter?"

or "That's mine." What these chunks do is allow a learner to participate in a conversation or game without having completely mastered the grammar of the language. From these chunks, they can move toward complete sentences as they figure out the rules of the new language.

By the end of the year, Mai Lor would even volunteer to read aloud: "I want to read. Can I read first?" The mainstream teacher insists that she still does not know how to speak English, but Cinda has observed her in many different situations and knows better.

Burt and Dulay state that the three phases of language acquisition are important for the classroom teacher to understand for several reasons:

- By understanding these stages you won't be overly concerned if your students' production does not match their ability to understand.
- Students are best able to succeed if the level of activity matches their current stage of development. Therefore, if your students are capable of uttering only simple sentences, use activities that require minimal language skills.

Four Levels of Questioning

In chapter 3, we discussed ways of adjusting your speech to make it easier for your students to understand. Good questioning techniques also encourage the students to respond in English, at their own levels. Here are four levels of questioning with some examples:

LEVEL 1. The teacher asks questions that require only *yes* or *no* answers. For example: "Are you standing?" "Can you hear me?" "Did Maria open the window?"

LEVEL 2. The teacher asks either/or questions, and the students respond with one-word answers using either a noun or a verb. For example: "Are you walking or standing?" "Is she sitting on the table or on the chair?"

LEVEL 3. The teacher asks questions using *where* or *what*, and the students are able to respond with a single word or a partial phrase. For example: "Where is Baldo sitting?" Answer: "On the floor." "What is Rocio doing?" "Sitting."

LEVEL 4. The teacher uses no content vocabulary to ask questions, and the students are able to respond in full sentences. For example: "What is Sabina doing?" "She's dancing." "What will Salvador do?" "He's going to shut the door." "What did Anna do?" "She climbed on the chair."

This hierarchy of questions is an important concept to remember. In the teacher's rush to communicate, it is easy to overlook the complexity of question-asking. Yet, questions that are above the students' comprehension levels can be confusing for them. When the students' problem is the grammar used, not the vocabulary, rephrasing the question often creates more confusion. For example, you might start out with the question: "What time is it?" Then when the students fail to understand, you may try rephrasing the question, "What time do you think it is?" or "What do the hands on the clock say?" believing that stating it another way might help. If the students understood the concept, however, they would have been able to answer the question in the first place. If they didn't, rephrasing would only confuse them further, because they are hearing three questions they don't understand, not one. If the students are confused at one level of questioning, revert to the previous one. For example, if the student doesn't understand "Where are you going?" revert to "Are you going home or to Mrs. Smith's class?"

Tolerance for Errors

Perfect comprehension and production are not realistic goals for second-language learners. Students need to be encouraged to express themselves. A casual attitude toward oral mistakes, in which one accepts all attempts at communication and does not pounce on errors, will foster confidence and the willingness to speak up. However, this doesn't mean ignoring mistakes altogether. Grammatical and pronunciation errors often do get in the way of communication. The goal, if not to eradicate a foreign accent, is to move the student toward speech that a listener does not have to struggle to understand.

My students make a lot of mistakes in grammar. Should I correct them or not?

Grammatical Errors

Just as we discussed in the chapters on reading and writing, emphasize communication and meaning, not correctness. Most parents recognize that acquiring language is a process that takes several years. A two-year-old does not come out with perfectly formed grammatical sentences. His speech is apt to be limited to only one or two words, such as *Mommy, juice*, or *big dog*. Instead of looking for mistakes, parents focus on the meaning and content of the child's speech. They are confident that these "mistakes" will disappear as the child matures and communicates. Parents don't correct their children for their linguistic inaccuracies. If a child says "Daddy goed to work," the mother accepts this as communication and responds to the truth of the statement. However, if a child points to a dog and says "cat," the mother will correct this error in fact. Parents will also use correct language in response, thereby modeling correct usage.

As teachers, however, we often feel it is our responsibility to point out errors. We feel constrained to correct every mistake the student makes, feeling that if we don't, the student will continue to make that error.

If we view second-language learning as a process that takes a number of years and recognize that students need time to hone and refine the rules of our language, we can view these mistakes not as faults, but as stages of development the students have reached on their way to mastering English. Whatever they say, and however they say it, we need to recognize, understand, appreciate, and support their attempts to communicate by responding to the message.

Research has shown that pointing out mistakes seems to do very little for language learners and may serve more to distract them from their meaning than to help them get meaning across. Pointing out mistakes may even impede their progress, because this approach focuses more on form than on meaning and also undermines their confidence in their attempts to communicate.

Krashen (1982) advises that the focus of language should be on communication, not on grammatical structure. As you observe your students relax and begin to make attempts at communication with you and with other students, encourage them to move beyond silence and focus on continued language interaction. This focus relieves you of the expectations that students must produce "perfect English" and allows students to make their own generalizations. Gradually, through time, practice, and the process of error-making, they will come to approximate the English they hear spoken around them every day.

Use errors as benchmarks to a student's progress, and use your knowledge of these errors for subjects to work on at other times. In chapter 4, we discuss how to use patterned language to focus on specifics such as tenses. Another option is to give brief mini-lessons on these specifics during the editing stages of writing.

Modeling, as parents do, is another way of giving students input about their speech. For instance, if Lupe says, "I no like broccoli," you can respond with, "Oh, you don't like broccoli. What *do* you like?" Thus, she can hear the correct form in the context of a statement that has immediate relevance to her.

If a student has expressly stated the wish to have his grammar corrected then it is best to do so, but only *after* he has finished talking. You can say, "You said 'losted.' The correct form is 'lost.'" But make these corrections only if invited. The long-term efficacy of corrections is dubious and usually only satisfies the individual student's need to know.

We want to emphasize that error correction is not a one-shot solution; you cannot correct or work on an error once and expect the student never to make the same error again. Sorting out the grammar of a language is a long, slow process. For this reason, we reiterate that a lenient attitude toward errors in grammar is the wisest course to follow while the students sort out the intricacies of grammar for themselves.

Trouble With Pronunciation

My students have difficulties with pronunciation. Shouldn't I work on these?

Pronunciation is another matter altogether. While we still advocate getting something said is more important than getting it right, there are times when you may have to take steps to help a student with pronunciation.

A controversy exists among authorities in second-language learning as to whether or not this is important. Many experts feel that the language learner will correct pronunciation problems later in the acquisition process. However, others—ourselves included—believe that some language learners are not able to do this. Frequently, students whose native language has tones (such as Chinese, Vietnamese, or Thai) or a different stress and pitch system, have great difficulty speaking English that can be easily understood. Because they respond to tones, in speaking they often drop the endings of words. For example, "You like some bread?" will sound like "You li' so' brea'?" or "His wife is at home," will sound like "Hi' wi' a' ho'." The focus for teaching pronunciation should be on helping the students to communicate—to get their meaning across accurately—not on the correct reproduction of minimal pairs (sounds produced in the same place in the mouth, in the same way, but that nevertheless differ, such as /p/ and /b/, /f/ and /v/).

Every language uses a certain number of sounds to make up words, and they are not always the same. Some languages have sounds we don't have. Spanish, for instance has two *r*'s, the rolled /r/ in *perro*, and the /r/ in *pero*. Farsi and German have the guttural /h/ as in *khoshamedi* and *ich*. Other languages don't have sounds that we have or "hear" only one sound where we hear two. Arabic speakers, for instance, do not distinguish between /p/ and /b/; Spanish speakers don't distinguish between /sh/ and /ch/. The Navajo language doesn't distinguish between /p/, /b/, and /m/. Often these speakers cannot hear the difference.

Differences are not only confined to different languages, but different dialects within a language as well. In her speech, Mary, a northern California native, doesn't distinguish the difference between the vowel sounds in *cot* (kät) and *caught* (kôt). To Barb, from the Midwest, this is incomprehensible. Barb can hear it; why can't Mary? How pointless it would be for Barb to stop everything and drill Mary in this difference! If Barb said, "I was sleeping on a cot in the tent when my husband caught two fish on Lake Oroville," no one would have any doubt about which word Barb was using when. To label Mary as stupid or slow because she can't hear the difference would be ridiculous. And yet this has been done time and again to students whose dialects or languages do not contain certain sounds we use in our own dialect. One of Barb's student teachers, for example, discovered that the students he was tutoring couldn't distinguish between /f/ and /v/, and spent an entire week helping them articulate the different sounds. Drilling them endlessly on sounds they cannot distinguish is pointless, and more often than not extremely frustrating. What's more, in the face of the whole task of learning English, it is a waste of time.

But we must address the problems created when students speak English structures correctly, but still have problems being understood because of their pronunciation. Mary had a student, Thien, who went to a fast-food restaurant and ordered "free hamburgers." He immediately got a lecture on how "We work for things in this country; if you think you're here for a handout, then go back where you came from." What Thien really meant to order was three hamburgers, but as he was not able to articulate the aspirated /th/, he was misunderstood. This particular sound is difficult for students of many language backgrounds. These students compensate by using /f/ or /t/ in the place of /th/.

Working with minimal pairs within the context of words, for example, *hit* versus *heat, free* versus *three, very* versus *berry*, is often not very productive, but it can work more effectively if the minimal pair work is part of a natural sentence structure. Try using as examples idioms that students find useful or puzzling and want to know the meaning of, such as "save your breath" and "through thick and thin," or common phrases like "Thanks a lot."

Mary found it helpful to alert students to the problems they would encounter when they tried to pronounce English words. Some students preferred to be told that it would be difficult for them to say certain sounds; they then were able to spell, write, draw, and so on in order to communicate.

Pronunciation is more complex than simply mastering minimal pairs. Students from other countries often have a difficult time with the stress and pitch system in the English sentence. As a result, these students can often sound angry, excited, or emphatic to a native-English speaker, when to their own ears they are being solicitous and polite.

Another facet of pronunciation that eludes many ESL students is the clipped, de-emphasized English spoken in informal conversation (often referred to as "reduced English") in which we drop endings and slur our words together. Mary once spent a period of time with her students explaining the have + to (*havta*) construction, when one of her students asked, "When are we going to learn about gotta?" Imagine how frustrating this type of language is to the students who, when speaking in their own language, were rewarded for consistent clarity!

Activities to help improve the students' sensitivity to the nuances of English can be enjoyable. Focus the students' attention on listening to differences in pitch patterns by comparing the pronunciation of words that occur in several languages, like *chocolate* or *coffee*. Have the students pronounce their names with you, pronouncing them the way North Americans would tend to. This helps them focus on the differences in pitch or minimal sounds. Sometimes students discover that a word they have heard frequently but didn't understand is actually a North American approximation of their names!

Students' inability to hear sound differences often show up in writing as well as their speech:

However, we should take notice there are not only regal immigrants, but also illegal immigrants.

In addition the taxes which are corrected from American workers control the welfare that sustain poor illegal immigrants.

After the war Japan became to most successful minority grope in the U.S. because of Pearl Harver.

These examples show how reception and pronunciation spill over into other areas of their work and skew the meaning of what they are trying to communicate.

As you can see, we believe that drilling on sounds in isolation is counterproductive; pointing out troublesome sounds and having the students practice them within words is more helpful. Work on pronunciation only when the students express a wish to focus on improving their language "delivery" or when their pronunciation of certain words gets in the way of being understood.

Using Talk to Explore and Gain Understanding

Talk is an important part—a critical part—of learning. Students need to talk in order to learn and to become competent language users. Barnes (1986) states: "Talk is a major means by which learners explore the relationship between what they already know and new observations or interpretations which they meet." We should, as Barr et al. (1989) emphasize, promote the social aspect of learning as an important dimension of learning and development.

Cullinan (1993) points out several of the roles that talk plays in and outside of the classroom:

- Students learn by talking because talking helps clarify thoughts. Have you ever found yourself talking out loud to yourself when you're trying to figure out something that's hard? Putting something into words helps people give form and shape to the thoughts they have in their heads.

  For example, Mary and Barb email chapters back and forth to each other to read. But it isn't until we actually sit down and talk through each chapter and each paragraph that we can be sure that what we are saying is what we really mean.

- Talk aids comprehension. "Students who talk about a topic understand it better than students who don't talk about it."

  Talking in their own language is especially important for second-language learners. They can go straight to the subject matter, unimpeded by their lack of mastery over English. For example, Barb began a lesson involving animals. She brought in a large number of picture books on animals and allowed the students to peruse them. Then she handed out 3" x 5" cards upon which the name of an animal had been printed; one student had "ant," another "octopus," "deer," "lizard," and so on. Students who could not identify their animal rushed back to the books to find out what it was. Other students knew more English and could help identify and explain. When students were asked to group themselves according to classifications such as height, number of legs, eyes, omnivorous/ carnivorous, nocturnal/diurnal and so on, they could discuss these different traits in their own language. To force them to speak entirely in English would have been pointless; it would have lessened the learning experience as well as diminished the fun, since the object was learning, not necessarily simply learning English.

- Talk provides a window into students' thinking.
- Talk supports reading.

Peterson and Eeds (1990) write,

> The spirit of collaboration is essential in constructing meaning [in reading]. Teachers work together with children, and children with children, to initiate responses, share interpretations, and construct meaning. This messy process involves a certain amount of groping, questioning, and putting forth of promising beginnings in the hope that others will contribute to the completion. This way of working encompasses both inquiry and critique as the basis for comprehending a text is broadened. Children practice making meaning as they make personal connections to the text and benefit from the insights of others.

All of us know that when we read, another reader might have a different interpretation of the story. Book clubs, literature circles, and dramatic readings are all means of increasing both our enjoyment and our understandings of the books we have read. For example, Kari wrote in her journal, *When I read the book, I wasn't impressed with it. It wasn't that I hated the book, it was more of a feeling that I could take it or leave it. Listening to the other class members' feelings about the book gave me a greater acceptance of it. I think if I read it again and thought about it more I would appreciate it in a new light.*

- Talk supports writing.

Galda et al. (1997) write, "Talk that explores ideas can have a profound effect on learning...exploratory talk creates and transforms knowledge."

Second-language learners who are not strong writers can tell us what they mean and the point they are trying to get across when faced with essays or stories that they cannot get the thread of.

Talking with students before, during, and after they work on a piece of writing helps writers clarify their thinking, decide where to go, and furthers their options and choices.

For example, Enrique was a competent English speaker, but could not read or write well in either English or Spanish. Mary helped him prepare to write an essay about "Sir Gawain and the Green Knight" by being his scribe. As Enrique related what the story was about and articulated what he understood, Mary wrote what he told her. Telling it out loud allowed him to clarify his grasp of the story; then Mary typed up exactly what he had said and printed it out. Reading it through gave him successful practice at reading and an opportunity to review the story. He then felt more prepared to tackle the actual writing of the assignment.

It is often necessary to sit and talk with the author about what it is he is trying to convey. Sometimes ESL students' writing is so impenetrable that this is the only way to get the meaning.

Barb once received a composition from a student that was supposed to be a descriptive piece. It was a jumble of "I saw..." sentences that seemed to have neither a central theme nor cohesion. Puzzled by the essay, she returned to the author. The student said she was using, as a model, an essay by a famous author about what he saw in Central Park. Only then did the student's paper make sense to Barb; together, they looked at the original and shaped her essay in ways that made it better.

Glory wrote, *I felt swimming can learn a/the bull's eye a target still more to be fond of. I would like to shopping as can buy very oneself like a/ the bull's eye a target east to west.*

Jim wrote, *Communication is a system formed by the relationship of emotion. Thus, if a partner is the strong silent type, the result of conversation may often be useless or formalistic. Because, the conversation partner feels the simultaneously uncomfortable. In general, the silent moment in conversation comes from the many aspects: the indifferent issue, the linguistic problem, and the unfamiliar relationship with the partner, for example. However, the moment came from such a reason is the instant or temporal problems, perhaps.*

In Glory's case, we can simply ask and go on. In Jim's case, however, we need to untangle with him exactly what he wants to say so that it comes out in a coherent way, understandable to readers. It is obvious that this writer has sophisticated and deep thoughts about the problem, even if what he writes is not altogether clear.

How many times have we heard a student tell us easily and succinctly what they meant to say that did not come anywhere close on paper? And when we ask, "Well, why didn't you write that?" they shrug helplessly.

■ Talk supports growth in the content areas.

"Collaboration to solve problems and make sense of new information is supported by talk. And, because as we talk we become aware of what we think and know and wonder about, talk provides that foundation on which we can build by relating new information to existing knowledge and ideas" (Wollman-Bonilla 1989).

Katrina's second-grade class was studying matter. For several weeks she set up a variety of experiments. Students, working in pairs, added effervescent tablets to water and to vinegar, mixed salt in the water, and then evaporated the water on the windowsill. Water was always spilled, and arguments about who got to do what were rampant, but the second graders were intensely interested and engaged, predicting what was going to happen and writing up the results. A silent classroom, in which everyone was expected to sit still and keep their mouths shut, would have been a sterile atmosphere with the learning curtailed.

Opportunities to Talk and Listen

Studies have revealed that second-language learners and others from diverse backgrounds can engage in meaningful talk; they benefit a great deal from being included in discussions, whether they contribute or not (Brock 1997). Therefore, we need to create as many opportunities for them as possible.

Rashid wrote in his journal,

> *It is no doubt that my surrounding has far fecting implication on a person. I strong believes that morden to learn a language fluently you have to go there to live by so doing you apply the language daily learn new vocabulary your proficiency in the language is test and over all your command inthe language is refined on a daily basic. I realised that my english improve by socializing with different english speaking people. I had a good incident were a girl asked me if it was first time to see snow, I responded back by saying that it may my second time to see snow, I explained to her that I hae seens now before in london. The bad incindent was when I was telling my friend about the fin I had in altant he did not understand me, although I repeated what I wanted to tell him twice. From these two incidents I concluded that I have to learn the american accent well enough and try to keep my accent from interfealing. I hope that by the time I graduate I will master well in my english.*

We need to give students as many opportunities to interact with their English-speaking peers as possible. It is sometimes difficult for older students to overcome the shyness and awkwardness to make attempts, but it's worth the effort.

We also feel it is important to promote listening as an end in itself, not merely as a means to speaking. We spend much of our time listening; we listen to conversations, radio, TV, and so on. Listening is a critical skill, particularly in the content classes where sophisticated listening skills are demanded—following directions in a science lab, listening to lectures in history and government, rules in phys. ed., or explanations of procedures in math.

Here are some strategies you can use to promote listening and speaking skills.

TPR-Total Physical Response

"Total Physical Response," developed by James Asher (1965), is one of the richest and most successful activities you can use. It can involve one student or the entire class. You can turn the responsibility for this activity over to an aide, a native-English speaker, or even a proficient student. The underlying premise is that listening to and understanding English language must come before the actual attempt to speak. The strategy is based upon the belief that language acquisition can be greatly accelerated through the use of body movement; therefore, each lesson includes commands and actions that help the student learn through doing. By listening and responding physically to instructions or commands, students are involved to a greater extent than when they respond only verbally. In the relaxed, fun atmosphere of a TPR lesson, students learn very quickly and efficiently. In TPR, students are not required to respond orally, they are simply asked to follow the directions given by the teacher.

A typical TPR lesson proceeds as follows:

1. The teacher gives a command, modeling if necessary. For instance, say "Stand up," and at the same time stand up yourself. Remember to speak in a normal tone of voice at normal speed. Do not speak too slowly or the students will quickly become bored and inattentive.

2. Students respond physically by standing up. Slower learners can watch and imitate the actions of others who have caught on more quickly.

3. When a number of commands have been given and learned, you can combine them to form a series. For example, "Mario, stand up, walk to the window, and open it."

As students pass through the stages of acquisition, and their ability to speak English develops, TPR gives them the opportunity to take control and use their newly acquired vocabulary by acting as the TPR leader. You can now have them give the series of commands to the class, motivating them to speak clearly and enunciate correctly. You can use this time to pinpoint pronunciation problems your students might have. You have a natural opportunity for working on strengthening those points within a meaningful context.

Use TPR to introduce important survival verbs such as *walk, go, stop, turn, close, open, lock, unlock, sit, stand*. You can embed other important vocabulary within the commands in sentences such as, "Francisco, pick up the blue book and put it under the fire extinguisher."

TPR is primarily a listening activity, but can become a very rich and enjoyable activity involving the four language-arts skills. Language learners are helped to make the speech-print connection if, once a series of commands is mastered, you write the series on the chalkboard for students to read and, if possible, copy for themselves. Realizing that the words they have just heard and responded to are the words they now see on the chalkboard is an important step.

If you find your high school students are reticent about marching around the classroom, or you think that the TPR activities described above would not be appropriate in your class, then adapt TPR to your specific situation. If you are working with a small group of students within a larger class setting, try working with manipulables. For example, place cut-outs of a square, circle, diamond, star, and triangle in front of the group of students.

Point to a shape and say, "This is a star. Now you point to the star." Do the same with one other shape, then review with the star. As the students understand what you are doing, you can have them vary the activity by picking up the shapes and giving them to each other. You can expand this activity to a string of directions in which they listen to your commands and draw the shapes on a piece of paper. For example: "Draw a star in the upper right-hand corner, draw a triangle in the middle," and so on. Then have them circle, underline, check, or cross out the items they put on the paper. You then show the students a model of your instructions, repeating what you said so they can check their papers to see if they followed the instructions correctly. The students are learning listening skills without having to respond verbally. They are also learning to follow a sequence of directions with vocabulary they will be expected to know.

You can use these types of modifications in the content areas, such as science and math, to help students learn to follow instructions or master basic vocabulary. Have your regular students model the appropriate actions. Pair a newcomer with a native-English speaker when following maps or a procedure in science.

Use games to review content-area knowledge. Games are very useful for encouraging student participation and, ultimately, language growth. Best of all, with games, the focus is on the activity, not on language structure. Here are some easily adaptable games:

Games

- Bingo. This game, played with words instead of numbers, is appropriate for all levels and all classes, since it focuses on important vocabulary. Have each student list vocabulary words on prepared grids much like bingo cards. Have another student pull the same vocabulary words, which have been written on slips of paper, out of a bag and read them out loud. The students then cover the words on their grids with slips of paper, poker chips, kidney beans, or some other token. The object of the game is to see who gets bingo first.

- Go Fish. This game is good for reviewing content vocabulary by matching pictures and new vocabulary, or simply by having students supply the vocabulary words from memory when shown the pictures. You can make the game cards out of index cards. If you do not have the time, have an aide, a native-English speaker, or even an ESL student make the cards. You can use this game as an icebreaker for new students, because, along with the vocabulary, students can learn each other's names in a relaxed setting.

- Categories. In this game, have students write a word relevant to a particular topic across the top or down the side of a page. The students must then list words that can be categorized beside each letter of the topic. For example, a lesson in nutrition could require the students to think of food words to fill in beside the words "good health" (figure 7.2).

This activity is a lot of fun when done as a group. It can last as long as the students can think of words to fit into each column. This exercise works best when the topic word has a variety of letters and when the category the students use to find the words is very general.

G	grapes	**H**	ham
O	oranges	**E**	eggs
O	onions	**A**	apples
D	dim sum	**L**	limes
		T	turkey
		H	hamburger

Figure 7.2. "Good Health" was the category in this word game.

■ Hangman or Password. Always favorites with students, these are good games for vocabulary review and also help reinforce spelling. They can be played with either simple or difficult words.

■ Memory. For about two minutes, show the class a detailed picture of a place or an event, or a tray filled with items. After the students have studied the picture or tray, remove or cover it and ask questions about the contents to see how much they remembered. (How many cats were in the picture? What color was the one by the door? What was next to the spool of thread? How many crayons were on the tray?) Or have children draw the objects, labeling them when they know the words (figure 7.3).

Figure 7.3. This student drew these objects from memory and labeled items he knew the words for.

■ Interviews. Make a list of about twenty statements. Draw a line in front of each statement. For example:

_____ has been to Disneyland.

_____ wears glasses.

_____ has a sister.

Have the students interview each other to find out whose name(s) is/are appropriate for each blank. Set a time limit for this activity. Students enjoy finding things out about each other and have an opportunity to use English in the process.

- Silent films. With silent films, students do not need to struggle with language to understand what is going on; this is a purely visual experience. After viewing a film, the students respond to questions about it. If showing an action film, stop the projector at a critical turning point in the plot, and ask students to suggest their own preferred endings, orally and/or in writing. You can use these activities with beginning, intermediate, and advanced students.

- Tongue Twisters. Students enjoy tackling the old favorites such as "She sells seashells by the seashore," "Peter Piper picked a peck of pickled peppers," "How much wood could a woodchuck chuck if a woodchuck could chuck wood?" or "Rubber baby buggy bumpers."

- Drama. Again, we feel that drama is central to any curriculum, whether it be primary, secondary, or adult. One of the strongest contributions that drama makes is to oral language proficiency. Noble, Egan and MacDowell (1977) remark that "oral language is pervasive in adult life, but the...language arts curriculum too often gives only minimal attention to further development of students' oral abilities." They have shown that verbal fluency increased among primary-age minority children as a result of systematic training in creative drama.

The facets of oral language facility that drama encourages are

- Spontaneous speaking.
- Basic listening skills.
- Understanding paralinguistic elements such as pitch, stress, and juncture.
- Vocabulary development.

The beauty of drama is that the vocabulary, the discussion, and the listening are embedded within a real context. The learner is engaged in accomplishing a task as well as solving a problem, such as "Where do I stand?" "How should I move across the stage?" "How do I say this sentence to give the desired effect?" Students must attend to what is going on in order to say or do whatever comes next.

For days before the production of *Lon Po Po*, Eve could be heard practicing "Be sure and lock the door, and do not open it while we are gone" while shaking her forefinger in warning. Tommy labored over the word "unfortunately." Even as the cast was assembling onstage, Jim was whispering "How do you say this?" while pointing at words such as "bought" and "built." He wanted to make sure he had them right. The necessity for clarity and correctness was unmistakable.

Conclusion

The major assumptions we operate under concerning speaking and listening are

- Learners acquire language in an environment that is full of talk that invites response.
- Students will speak when they are ready.
- Fluency precedes accuracy.
- An acceptance of all attempts, whether correct or incorrect, will promote confidence.

Provide opportunities for the students to develop these skills. Present lessons consisting of content that is meaningful, while asking questions appropriate for the students' level in an atmosphere that encourages students to take risks. The interaction you encourage allows for language experimentation and, ultimately, leads to language acquisition.

CHAPTER 8

CONTENT AREA INSTRUCTION

In this chapter, we discuss some of the problems ESL students face in content-area classes and, through the experiences of two teachers, show how they

- Approach curriculum, standards, and benchmarks.
- Develop overall plans.
- Present lessons in an organized, comprehensible way.

Kelly Sturm, a science teacher, was faced with teaching "simple machines" to a class of sixth-, seventh-, and eighth-graders who had minimal English and literacy skills. Written materials consisted of definitions such as the following:

Lever: There are three basic types of levers, depending on where the effort is applied, on the position of the load, and on the position of the fulcrum...

This material was too difficult for the students to read on their own and took a great deal of explaining. The school provided "realia" in the form of packages of plastic gears. The students were led through a series of exercises: Put gear A in the slot. Place gear B so that it interlocks with gear A. Predict what will happen when you turn gear A. Put gear C... Boring! The students were learning little more than if they turned gear A as fast as possible it would clatter loudly as it hit the floor. Or worse—they may have been learning to hate science. The hours Kelly spent making the overheads to explain the various machines seemed an exercise in futility.

Sandy Maxwell's class of fourth- and fifth-graders had twenty-eight students, only four of which were native-English speakers. The proficiency level of the second-language students ranged from no English at all, to fluent, but reading several years below grade level. The social studies and science curriculum for these grades included units on Wisconsin and Climate. Under Climate, Sandy had skipped the lesson on "heat" the previous year; concepts such as therms seemed to be beyond the range of the students' abilities and her ability to get the ideas across. Even the general introduction seemed too technical:

> Heat is a form of energy. Atoms and molecules, the tiny particles that make up everything that exists, are constantly moving and the amount of heat within any substance depends on how much and how fast its atoms move. When more heat energy is given to something its temperature rises, it expands, and it may change from a solid to a liquid or from a liquid to a gas. Heat can be transferred from one place to another in three ways, conduction, convection, or radiation, but it can only move from a hotter area to one that has a lower temperature.

Yet, Sandy recalled what a struggle it was every year to get winter clothes for many of the poorer children; parents from subtropical or tropical countries simply did not understand the dangers of frostbite and hypothermia. Winters are particularly severe in Wisconsin, and last year school did not close until the temperature reached –35° F. Despite repeated warnings, working parents were often forced to drop their children off at school, sometimes an hour before classes started. Sandy decided that a lesson on "heat" was a priority.

The situations these two teachers found themselves in has become increasingly common in North American Schools. Out of a class of twenty-five, many teachers—particularly those in inner-city urban classrooms—have seven or more ESL students. As more and more non-English speakers flood the border states and provinces, just as many are moving away from these port-of-entry points into the midlands and heartlands. This means that more and more mainstream teachers are teaching content to ESL students.

Content-area learning begins in earnest in the upper-elementary grades. In the lower grades science is often embedded in thematic units, but it becomes increasingly compartmentalized as students get older. From about the fourth grade onward, students are no longer only learning to read, they are reading to learn. This means they must have the requisite fluency and skills in reading and the background knowledge required to gather information from a text. Because many of our non-English-speaking students come to us with poor reading skills and many gaps in the kind of background knowledge that we take for granted with our mainstream students, these requirements pose special problems for teachers of the upper-elementary grades. The problems are even more acute for those junior high and high school teachers who specialize in one subject.

In the past several decades, teaching English has shifted from teaching it as a subject, to teaching English *through* other subjects. This is an about-face from when the students had to learn English first; only when the students had enough oral proficiency could they begin learning content in earnest. One supervisor recently visited the high school English classroom of one of her student teachers. Khae, a Southeast Asian Student, sat in the back of the room. Khae was not given anything to do and did not participate in classroom activities. The supervisor asked why he was not included. The student teacher replied that she had been told by the school counselor not to worry about trying to include Khae until he had learned English. (How this was supposed to happen had nothing to do with her!)

Imagine Khae's progress. He is allowed a year of oral development: listening, speaking, working on his language competence. If all goes well, within that year he might speak fairly well, be able to communicate his needs, relate to his friends, and produce a passable English sentence. Along the way, he might begin to read and may even be able to write a few sentences. He might be promoted to the next grade.

In the meantime, his classmates are reading and writing at grade level, taking the content classes such as history, geography, math, and science required for graduation from high school. As the years go by, Khae will be left further and further behind. The gap in background knowledge will become wider; study skills will not be learned. The lag is cumulative; success breeds success, but failure breeds failure.

Integrating Language and Content

The above scenario does not have to happen. Recent research has shown that students can learn content and language at the same time. In fact, we know that integrating language and content—learning the content material and the language needed to understand the content at the same time—is more effective than simply learning language and only then trying to learn content (Short 1991; Crandall 1995). There are several important reasons for this:

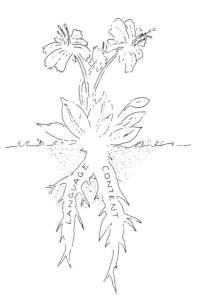

- Integrated instruction brings both cognitive development and language.

- Content provides real meaning, not just structures of language that are abstractions and may seem to be of little value to the learner. "Rather than introducing a series of isolated units, language instruction is most effective if it teaches language that provides access to subject matter texts, discussions, and class activities" (Echevarria 1998).

- When students learn subject and language together they are more motivated because the content is interesting and valuable to them.

- The language used in school is different from the language used outside the classroom. James Cummins (1981) distinguishes between basic interpersonal communication skills (BICS) and cognitive-academic language proficiency (CALP). Within a year or two, a student might have mastered the BICS. He might be a competent speaker, have friends, and be able to carry on conversations in English. But while these interpersonal communication skills are important, they are not enough to succeed in school. They do not carry over into the content areas where other kinds of language demands are made, for several reasons:

  - Basic interpersonal communication skills are inadequate to attain the higher-level skills of problem solving, inferring, analyzing, synthesizing, and predicting—skills required for academic success in the content areas.

  - Conversations are embedded in meaningful context. Students can pick up clues (body language, gestures, facial expressions) to gain meaning. They can also ask for clarification if they don't understand. But academic language is usually "context reduced"; a student is often asked to obtain information by reading texts that have few pictures to help guide comprehension. Cummins suggests that these cognitive academic skills (CALP) require five to seven years to acquire.

Many students come out of ESL or bilingual programs with good oral skills, but have either undeveloped academic language skills or need help transferring to English the knowledge they have acquired using their native languages. The TESOL ESL Standards (1997) state: "In school environments, ESL students need to be able to use spoken and written English both to acquire academic content and to demonstrate their learning."

Potential Problems

The academic language of content-area classes can pose many problems for ESL students. Knowing what these problems are will help you help your students bridge the gap between their first language and the linguistic demands of the lesson. Students in content-area classes are likely to have problems in the following areas: vocabulary, syntax, and pragmatics.

The core content areas are built around certain concepts and certain essential vocabulary. Students often can't understand lessons without knowing this vocabulary. Bobbi Jo Moore, for example was teaching a sixth-grade science unit on "matter." Her students had heard the word before in sentences such as "What's the matter with you?" and "It matters to me." Introducing the concept of matter was difficult, especially the idea that air can take up space and have mass.

With Vocabulary
- Each subject has its own particular set of terms that the students may not yet have learned, such as *synthesis, microorganism, abolitionist, impeach, coefficient, addend*.
- Many words used in everyday language have a specialized meaning within specific content areas, such as *product* or *square* in math, *kingdom* and *energy* in science, or *primary* and *inflation* in social studies.
- Many words are abstract and can't be explained simply, for example, *democracy, justice*.

With Syntax
Textbooks commonly use the passive voice, reversing the normal word order, a form students come to understand and use only later on in their acquisition of English. For example, "This polarization is reinforced by the mass of contradictory evidence that seems to lend support to both sides." (Many native-English speakers will have trouble with that one!)

Texts often use complex sentences whose meanings hinge on transition words like *because* or *although*, which students may not understand or notice. For example, "Both the Puritans and the Pilgrims left England because they felt the Anglican Church should become more like the Catholic Church," or "Although her business was unfinished, she left."

With Pragmatics
Pragmatics involve the larger units of discourse beyond the word, phrase, and sentence level, such as the text itself and your lectures.
- Students may not have enough English proficiency to understand the textbook or your lectures.

- They may not know how to read difficult material for various purposes or have strong enough study skills to extract information from their textbook or reference materials. Many times they read narratives the same way they read expository prose, or editorials as if they were facts.

- They may not have the general knowledge we assume with our North American students. For example, they may not understand the concept of democracy or the meaning of ecosystems, or may be unfamiliar with animals such as mountain lions and armadillos; or they may not have learned of the Challenger space shuttle.

Bridging the Gap

Bobbi Jo wrote in her journal,

> *If there is one thing I learned while agonizing over this unit and discussing it in class, it is that I need to set up more of a bridge from where the kids are to where I want them to be. As of now, I am standing on the other side of this huge chasm yelling, "JUMP!" hoping they are strong enough to make it.*

A typical period in a traditional content-area classroom consists of a lecture, discussion of the assigned textbook readings with students, then tests based on these lectures and readings. Until they achieve full proficiency in English for academic purposes, ESL students simply cannot succeed in such circumstances.

In order to succeed in the content areas, students need

- Clearly defined goals.
- Comprehensible input.
- To be engaged as learners and as investigators.

Your overall goals for teaching are

Your Goals

- To help your students learn English. This means helping your students "to use English to achieve academically" in your content area (TESOL 1997). They need to learn the specialized vocabulary of your particular discipline as well as be given the opportunity to learn such skills as explaining, informing, describing, classifying, and evaluating.

- To teach your content area.

- To teach the higher-level thinking skills.

- To promote literacy. No longer is teaching reading and writing solely the job of the English teacher. These teaching skills belong in every classroom where students need help understanding lectures, making presentations, reading for information, and writing reports.

With mandated standards and benchmarks in most content areas, skills and bodies of knowledge have been laid out in detail. How to operationalize these standards and benchmarks for students who have not mastered the language and may have huge gaps in their learning is a unique and complex challenge. Yet, the standards and benchmarks are an advantage to ESL teachers—we can set up opportunities for students to learn *by doing* rather than by listening to lectures and retrieving facts.

As states implement standards and benchmarks, teachers must begin to consider what these mean for ESL students. Standards are "broad curricular goals, while benchmarks are specific knowledge and skills identified at grade levels or grade ranges. They are the 'what' we are seeking to impart to our students" (Sargent and Smejkal 2000).

Standards and Benchmarks

For example, Kelly, teaching sixth-grade physical science was teaching toward the following four standards for science in Wisconsin:

- Standard 1: Understands the nature of scientific inquiry.
- Standard 2: Understands the interaction of science, technology and society.
- Standard 3: Understands personal and social perspectives of science.
- Standard 4: Understands the history of science, people and technology.

Given what we know about the nature of inquiry and our beliefs about how students learn best, simply manipulating gears was pointless to students without reference to the "why's" and the "what's." Kelly searched for a new approach.

What to Do

The big challenge is to make the content-area lessons comprehensible while meeting the needs of both your regular students and your ESL students—challenging the native-English speakers while making content meaningful and accessible to the others. At the same time, you need to align your teaching to the standards and benchmarks set for your particular grade level.

The following strategies will help your ESL students and, at the same time, enrich learning for your regular students. Strategies to make content easier for ESL students often achieve the same result with *all* students. Again, good teaching is good teaching, and good teaching techniques are especially important for teachers of ESL students.

You can embed content within meaningful context by involving all four language arts skills—reading, writing, listening, and speaking—in active ways. Strategies include grouping, modifying textbooks, and setting priorities.

When you're faced with ESL students and hardly know where to begin, it's easy to get bogged down in the day-to-day problems and lose sight of the overall picture. Here are some steps to help you manage.

Before You Teach

- Choose a topic of study. This may or may not be chosen for you. Some teachers have more leeway than others in specifying the topics they are going to focus on. Some of the issues you may wish to consider in making your choices include the following:
  - Importance in the curriculum. Is this topic so esoteric or so abstract that no matter what you do your ESL students aren't going to get it?

If it's not absolutely central to the curriculum, you might want to discard it.

■ Is the concept "big" enough? According to Wiggins and McTighe (1999) there are four criteria to determine whether a concept is worth studying in any depth:

1. Is it enduring, in other words, will it add value and meaning to your students' lives?

2. Is it at the heart of the discipline, or on the periphery?

3. Does it need "uncoverage," that is, exploration in any depth?

4. Is it potentially engaging? Will your students be actively involved?

For instance, Prentice Halls' *American Journey: The Quest for Liberty to 1877* lists in its table of contents

Unit One: The Americas: Geography of the Americas; The First Americans, European Exploration.

Unit Two: The Colonies Take Root: Colonizing the Americas; The 13 English Colonies; Colonial Life.

Knowing these ideas is undoubtedly important in an overall understanding of the nation's history. Can your students handle them at the level they have attained is another question altogether. You need to carefully select what they can understand in any depth.

■ Possibilities for extension into other areas of the curriculum. Not every topic has to be theme based and include math, history, social studies, and so on, but if you can bring in other areas and make connections, so much the better.

■ "Richness." The possibilities inherent for language use and learning that extends beyond the narrow topic itself.

■ Latitudes for "Ups" and "Downs." Can the lesson be tweaked so that all levels of learners in the class gain something from the lesson, and succeed? Can the assignments be adapted so that each student is working to his or her linguistic and intellectual capacity?

■ Develop a plan. If you have established an overall plan for the course as we suggested in chapter 1, you are way ahead of the game. You have goals and learning targets for your students, competencies they must develop to succeed, and themes to build the course around so that with each successive spiral, the students better understand the material. Now you can go on and work out the fine points of your particular subject matter.

When looking at the standards and benchmarks, it's easy to think you have to abandon everything you have taught. Don't. That's throwing the baby out with the bath water. Sargent and Smejkal (2000) caution that, "Vital connections are lost when benchmarks are taught in isolation. Students end up possessing isolated skills, without the larger concepts and skills to apply them...For students to construct meaning, the benchmarks must 'fit' together in a way that makes sense to them."

Much of what you did before naturally fits under these standards and benchmarks. Don't think that all those years of training and teaching were lost and you have to start over.

- Analyze the textbook. You may or may not use a textbook. For many classes a textbook is the main resource for classroom learning, and reading this book is integral to understanding the content of the course. But what you expect when you say, "Read the following pages for tomorrow's class" and what your students actually do are often very different. For this reason we discuss the use of textbooks, including some strategies for modifying the text to meet the needs of your students.

For instance, the first paragraph in *History of the United States* (1993) begins, "An early scholar to think seriously about the origin of the Indians was Thomas Jefferson. The man who would become the third President of the United States had a consuming interest in all things far and near, past and present." This passage would prove difficult for many students because of the complexity of the sentences, the knowledge of Jefferson and the presidency that's implied, and the vocabulary such as "consuming interest."

We are not in any way suggesting that textbook publishers are at fault. They have, in the past several years, incorporated substantial use of literature, media tie-ins, and extension activities. Many of our students, however, simply do not have the skills to read this sort of text.

You can't take for granted that the students in your class have either adequate study skills or sufficient language proficiency to meet the objectives you have laid out for them. Many students, English speakers included, are poor readers and have poor study skills. Many texts assume that students are all reading on grade level, which often is not true of ESL students (or many others!). They may take the book home, they may not; they may skim it with comprehension, or they may read every word and still not understand what they have read.

When reviewing a textbook, consider the following points:

- Does the subject matter covered match the priorities you have set? When you check this match, decide what to cover and what you will be able to gloss over. If a chapter or section doesn't fit into your scheme, skip it.
- Analyze the textbook from the ESL students' viewpoint. What problems might your students have? What concepts and vocabulary might be new and unfamiliar to them?

Textbooks presume a great deal of background knowledge. For instance, most North Americans know a lot of history. We may not know all the facts behind historical incidents, but most of us have a general idea of our history; we have watched countless westerns, mini-series, and dramas on television and in films, trudged through museums, and visited historical sites on field trips.

We cannot, however, presume ESL students have this background knowledge. Many students from other countries were extremely successful in school and have rich experiences to bring to the learning task. Others know of nothing outside their refugee camp or their village. Knowledge of their native country's role in world affairs may be nonexistent, much less their knowledge of the history of the U.S. or Canada.

But they *do* understand the concept of immigration and change. Many have firsthand knowledge of war, many are now experiencing cultural conflict and the challenge of adjusting to new technology and new ways to make a living. They all understand the concept of freedom. These are critical issues in their lives. You can capitalize on these things by using what they *do* know as a starting base.

Goals for your students consist of both language and content objectives. Decide what, specifically, they need to know. From this list of requirements, you will have a clear idea of what they have attained.

Goals for Your Students

- When teaching English-language learners, you need to support their language development, including essential vocabulary. "Vocabulary is critical for English language learners because we know that there is a strong relationship between vocabulary knowledge in English and academic achievement" (Echevarria 2000). Every subject has its own special content vocabulary. For example, the words *population, community, ecosystem, biosphere, tissue, cells* are fundamental vocabulary to science. This is vocabulary you cannot simplify and which must be specifically taught. Students need to know these words to read the text and to go on to more specialized or broader knowledge in that particular field. For instance, your language objectives may be that at the end of the lesson the students will be able to
  - Understand the essential vocabulary for the unit. For example: *solid, liquid, gas, matter, mass, space.*
  - Follow directions accurately in conducting experiments, such as
    1. Tie string to the middle of a straw to make a hanging balance scale.
    2. Blow up two balloons, and tie a piece of string to each balloon.
  - Write the results of their findings:
    What did you observe?
    What does the experiment prove?
    Was your hypothesis correct?
  - Present findings orally.

Content objectives are what students should know and be able to do at the end of the lesson. Kelly, for example, wanted her students to
  - Practice observation and recording skills.
  - Demonstrate an understanding of the basic concepts of the unit (the simple machines and their functions, forms, and uses).

Provide Comprehensible Input

- Modify your strategies for teaching. In other chapters, we have discussed how to change your speech for English-language learners. Ditch the lecture format.

- Actively involve learners. This means providing as many hands-on materials and/or manipulatives for students as you can think of. Simply asking students to write the list of vocabulary words in their notebooks and looking up definitions for the words is not actively engaging them. Echevarria (2000) writes, "Although all students benefit from guided practice, English language learners make more rapid progress in mastering content objectives when they are provided with multiple opportunities to practice with hands-on materials and/or manipulatives... Practicing by manipulating learning materials is what is important for ELLs because it enables them to connect abstract concepts with concrete experiences." Nobody forgets the time they had to dissect a frog, a cat, a baby pig, or a cow's eye. Years after, we can still recall the excitement or being "grossed out" and yet captivated. We also will never forget Mr. So and So droning on for an entire semester about "Government"—we don't remember the content, simply the drudgery.

- Organize the material into easily attainable and sequential steps. You can organize your lesson in a structured way so that you can teach study skills at the same time as content. We demonstrate how in the next section.

- Provide many opportunities for interaction. This promotes language development, as well as supports the development of content knowledge, especially for language learners. If you do not have bilingual support teachers, there may be other students in the class who "get it" and who can explain concepts in the native language. You can set up group configurations and class projects that promote peer interaction and talk.

- Give students the chance to apply the knowledge they've gained. This is the way they learn best: building, practicing, performing, and doing. Kids never forget the plays they put on, the store they owned in *Sim City*, the edifice they built with toothpicks or Popsicle sticks, or the boat they designed out of aluminum foil.

When You Teach   Expanding on the familiar "preview, view, and review" format, Chamot and O'Malley (1986), who developed the Cognitive Academic Language Learning Approach, suggest the following five steps:

1. Prepare   2. Present   3. Practice
4. Evaluate   5. Follow-up

Follow the same procedure for each segment or unit.

We demonstrate these five steps by returning to Kelly's lesson on simple machines. Kelly knew she had to give up on the pre-packaged gears lessons and start over. While keeping the five steps in mind, she focused on the following benchmarks for Standards One to Four:

- Identifies questions that can be answered through scientific investigations.
- Designs and conducts a scientific investigation.
- Uses appropriate tools and techniques to gather, analyze, and interpret data.
- Develops descriptions, explanations, predictions, and models using evidence.
- Thinks critically and logically.
- Designs a solution or product.
- Implements a proposed design.
- Knows the potential for accidents and the existence of hazards.
- Knows scientists formulate and test their explanations of nature, using observations, experiments, and theoretical and mathematical models.

1. Prepare

What Kelly did first to prepare the students is what the Learning Cycles Framework (1993) terms "engage." We are particularly attracted to this term because it embodies the idea that students (particularly middle-schoolers) need to be engaged and interested in a topic before they learn it. To engage the students Kelly showed the first long, marvelous scene from Charlie Chaplin's *Modern Times*: his day in the factory. The kids were so enchanted with the movie, they talked the substitute teacher (Kelly happened to be away the day of viewing) into showing it three times. Since *Modern Times* has the barest minimum of words they could understand everything. They talked nonstop about the movie when Kelly returned, a total about-face from the silent, disengaged class who had woodenly put gears together.

2. Present

Kelly gave a quick overview of the simple machines—wheel and axle, pulley, screw, inclined plane, wedge, and lever—to show students what they were and how they worked. The students' job, on the next viewing of *Modern Times*, was to identify as many simple machines as they could in the movie.

The next step was to have the students look around their environment. The class took a tour of the school. They went down to the boiler room and up and down halls looking for simple machines. It was hilarious to hear someone shout, "Look! A wedge!" as if he had discovered gold. To reinforce the concepts, students were judiciously divided into groups (more proficient with less proficient, calmer among the more rowdy) with each group in charge of finding as many examples of their simple machine as possible—one for wedge, one for pulley, and so on.

Students were given a worksheet to complete to keep them on task and responsible for recording what they saw, as well as to promote reading, writing, and oral skills (figure 8.1).

Homework consisted of going home and finding as many examples as possible of the seven machines in their own environment.

3. Practice

The students were given the task of inventing their own carnival ride using at least three simple machines. Kelly brought in scraps of wood, metal, cloth, string, and so on. She priced the different materials so that the "contractors" had to budget their money and buy their supplies. The "contract" students had to fulfill is shown in figure 8.2.

4. Evaluate

In this case, Kelly's baseline evaluation was simple: Did the ride work? She added specific criteria on how to judge the rides. She also gave the students responsibility for evaluation by having them judge both the other groups' rides and their own rides (figure 8.3).

The key component of the final evaluation was a Polly Pocket doll to ride in the machine. If "the baby died," (in other words, flew out of the ride and landed on its head), then it was not safe. During this evaluation, one student, Kong, tested the performance of each ride. After placing the doll in the seat, Kong would shout, "Hey, man, see if she flies out!" There were several occasions where "the baby" soared across the room, and the students had to rethink not only how to keep her in, but how to keep the seat from spinning so fast that she was inclined to fly out in the first place.

5. Follow-Up

The class went to the carnival and rode all the rides. Nobody flew out.

The unit was a resounding success on several levels. Not only did Kelly set up a situation in which the students were deeply engaged in what they were doing, it was a "rich" situation: rich with talk, inquiry, and the need to understand in a very real way the principles they were talking about. The concepts and the vocabulary were embedded within the situation and were learned through carrying out of the assignments. In addition, less-proficient students could use what skills they had in their own language and culture in the project. One student in particular, whose English was very low, was extremely gifted in math. Vang could visualize what needed to be done and implement tasks in ways other students couldn't. He brought in a motor and battery from a remote control car. Kelly watched as he hooked it up to his ride, made a few adjustments, and turned it on. It worked! When asked how he knew to do this, Vang replied, "I just, you know, experiment with stuff."

Simple Machines

Date: _____

Names:_____　　_____　　_____

1. In your group, brainstorm where in school you might find the simple machines we have been
   studying. What form will they take?

   _____

   _____

   _____

2. Take a tour around the school. You must find three examples of each.

   Pulley:　　　　　　_____　_____　_____

   Lever:　　　　　　 _____　_____　_____

   Wheel and Axle:　 _____　_____　_____

   Wedge:　　　　　　_____　_____　_____

   Screw:　　　　　　 _____　_____　_____

   Inclined plane:　　_____　_____　_____

3. Report back to the class.

   What did you find?　_____

   _____

   Where did you find it?　_____

   _____

   What was it used for?　_____

   _____

   _____

Figure 8.1. Worksheet for simple machines.

Building Contract

CONTRACTOR'S CURRENT JOB   Date: _____

Your job is to design a carnival ride.

The carnival ride must use at least three simple machines.

The ride must have a name. Your team must agree on the name.

Each member of the team must be able to explain how the ride works.

PROPOSAL

This is what we are going to build: _____

_____

We will also provide a drawing of what the completed carnival ride will look like.

Here is a list of the parts we will need:

Part	Amount Needed	Price Per Part	Cost
Part 1:			
Part 2:			
Part 3:			

Estimated Cost $_____

BUILDING CONTRACT

Names of Building-Team Members:

1. _____

2. _____

3. _____

We will build _____.
(Name of Carnival Ride)

It will have these three simple machines: _____,

_____, _____.

Cost for Labor and Materials: $_____

Upon completion:

Signatures: _____, _____, _____

Figure 8.2. Student contract.

Carnival Ride Evaluation

Every member of the class will judge each ride. The rides will be evaluated based on the following categories: quality, creativity, safety, structural strength, fulfillment of the assignments, uses three simple machines, functioning of the ride, the ride's name, and whether each member of the constructing team can explain how the ride was made and what it does.

The rating scale will work like this:

3 = Wow! Great job!

2 = Pretty good

1 = Needs improvement

0 = This step was not completed

DIRECTIONS: For each category, circle the number you think best fits the carnival ride you are judging. Use the rating scale above.

Category				
Quality	3	2	1	0
Creativity	3	2	1	0
Safety	3	2	1	0
Functioning of the Ride	3	2	1	0
Structural Strength	3	2	1	0
Uses Three Simple Machines	3	2	1	0
Fulfillment of the Assignment	3	2	1	0
The Ride's Name	3	2	1	0
Each Member Can Explain the Ride	3	2	1	0

Figure 8.3. Assessment criteria for carnival rides.

We can see how Kelly prepared for and achieved her goals in a natural way. She gave her students a problem—build a ride—that could be answered through scientific investigation. Only through careful planning and trial and error could the students build a ride that worked and was safe and structurally sound.

On their own, the students

- Designed and conducted a scientific investigation.
- Used appropriate tools and techniques to gather, analyze, and interpret data.
- Were obliged to develop descriptions, explanations, predictions, and models using evidence.
- Thought critically and logically.
- Designed a product.

- Communicated their design plans and their evaluations based on established criteria.
- Considered the hazards and potential dangers of poorly-designed rides.
- Tested out their theories in real ways.

Meanwhile, Sandy Maxwell was searching for ways to make the concept of heat operational. As discussed before, the definition of heat was too difficult and complex for most of her students to understand. So, Sandy looked through several books on climate and temperature and settled on the following goals for her students to understand:

> What is heat?
> Why is it necessary?
> How do we measure it?
> How does it affect us? How do we notice it? How do we feel it?
> What are the consequences of heat (or lack of it)?
> How do we adapt to it? (Getting warm and keeping warm)

1. Prepare

Whole Class Preparation: As a whole class, Sandy began with a discussion about what it takes to survive in winter: students made lists of what kinds of clothes they needed to wear when it's cold. Sandy read aloud from *On the Banks of Plum Creek*, chapters 35 to the end: Pa, returning home from town, gets lost in the snow. He survives for several days, within sight of the house, on melted snow and Christmas candy.

Some of the less-proficient students did not quite understand the story, so the class did process drama, in which more-proficient students reenacted Pa's days in the snow.

Small Group Background Building: Sandy coordinated with the ESL teacher to work on background knowledge. The ESL teacher found books on the students' native countries. Students looked at picture books, she read stories to them, and they discussed the kinds of houses they lived in and the kinds of clothes they wore. The beginner groups did Language Experience activities in which they drew pictures of their homes in their native country and told about their lives (figure 8.4).

2. Present

Whole Group: Students were asked to respond to the question, "If you were stuck in a blizzard for four days, what would you want to have along with you?" Sandy brought in props (matches, candy bars, water, blankets, and coats) so that the students could see the items they had to choose from and select the ones they thought were the most important. In cooperative groups (carefully selected to include beginners surrounded by more proficient classmates), the students listed five things they would want or need. The group had to decide unanimously and justify their choices. A good deal of rich discussion followed.

Figure 8.4. Amparo's picture of her home.

3. Practice

Pair Work: Pairs of students were assigned to monitor the weather around the nation, graphing the temperatures on a chart designed to show temperature ranges in different climates.

Individual: Sandy had students become scientists, observing weather daily. Students kept a daily record of

- Temperature changes.
- What they saw and felt outside.
- What changes they noticed.
- How they adapted to the weather that day.

  The expectations for the assignment varied according to the proficiency and skill level of the individual student. For example, beginners were expected to write frame sentences, such as:

  The temperature is _____ today.
  It is _____ degrees outside.
  I am wearing _____, _____, _____.

  More proficient students were expected to write complete sentences. Native-English speakers were required to write at least a paragraph.

Large Group: The class took periodic tours around the school and school yard, making predictions, such as which areas were warmest, where it was likely to be coldest, what animal tracks they might find, and so on.

4. Evaluate

Large Group/ Small Group/ Individual: Sandy set up scientific experiments that led students to construct their own theories of heat, how it changes, and how it is transmitted (figure 8.5).

Continuing the science theme, Sandy asked these questions: "Why is winter hard for animals?" "What are some of the ways animals deal with the hardships?" The class brainstormed a list of ways animals adapt. Each student chose an animal indigenous to Wisconsin and researched how it adapts to the cold, where it lives, and what it eats during winter. Students wrote reports and drew a picture of their animal in its habitat on a huge winter mural.

Sandy had many books on winter available in her classroom. While students worked on their projects, she worked with small groups, reading to beginners, teaching specific skills, and rereading language-experience stories. She made as many easy readers, picture books, and books in the native languages available as she could.

From there, Sandy branched out into social studies—she had her students study different climates. She found resources for hot, cold, and temperate regions.

5. Follow-up

The long unit on heat culminated in a Beach Party in the gym in mid-winter.

Sandy's units on Wisconsin and Climate were successful for the following reasons:

- She decided beforehand what she wanted her students to know. By doing this, she eliminated a lot of the useless tangents we can find ourselves getting mired in. She was clear in her goals.
- She made the units relevant.
- She was flexible in her grouping strategies, assignments, and expectations based on the proficiency levels of her students. She balanced group work with independent work.
- Her focus for the lesson was to understand the concept of heat, not memorize rote facts.
- She used a variety of materials.
- She varied her assessment of the students.
- The students practiced and learned many of the procedures necessary to do scientific inquiry, by asking questions, conducting experiments, gathering data, and using this data to give explanations.

Not least in importance, the students learned the value of protecting themselves from the elements and adapting to the climate they now live in.

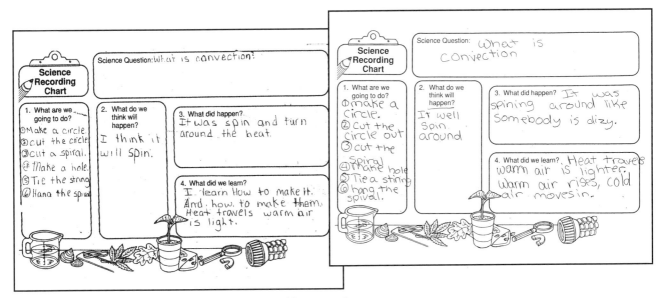

Figure 8.5. Two students record their experiment with convection.

Other Ideas

It is not necessary to always be as ambitious as Sandy and Kelly were. Sometimes we don't want or need to develop an entire lesson. Regardless, you have to ask yourself two basic questions:

1. What content do you want your students to learn?

2. What are the necessary vocabulary words students need to know?

For example, we have been teaching ESL in a summer camp program in the mountains of California for the past several years. When we began planning for our first summer, we chose, as a main theme, the concept of stewardship for our environment and ourselves. When the students arrived, we realized this idea was too ambitious without interpreters and more complex than we had time to develop. We didn't carry through with this part of the curriculum the first year, but we didn't give up on the idea. It struck us how many of our students commented on how clean it was in the mountains and how fresh the air and the water were compared to the dirtiness and pollution in their own country (figure 8.6).

Over the course of the next two summers, we built more science into the curriculum. After all, we reasoned, we were in the mountains, the kids were from the city, and this was probably one of the few chances they would have to camp in the wilds. We wanted to make the most of it. So, revisiting our idea of stewardship (and being more realistic), and keeping in mind that camp was supposed to be fun and lighthearted, we had our students focus on the following goals:

- To wonder.

- To investigate their surroundings in a focused way.

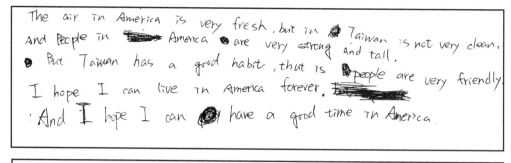

The air in America is very fresh, but in Taiwan is not very clean. And People in America are very strong and tall. But Taiwan has a good habit, that is people are very friendly. I hope I can live in America forever. And I hope I can have a good time in America.

My first day in America...

America is very good, water is very good.

Figure 8.6. Taiwanese students commenting on the air and water in California.

- To learn about nature by experiencing it.
- To care about the environment.

These were modest goals, but we were successful in reaching them. The students enjoyed themselves. They learned a great deal about habitats, about the animals that lived in that particular area, and the accompanying vocabulary. They had the chance to read, write, talk, and be out in the sunshine (figure 8.7a-c). Next year, we'll try again. We'll figure out the next step in making students conscious of their personal role in preserving natural habitats. We didn't do a great job of bringing up the idea of responsibility, but we will keep trying. By looking at what we did, figuring out what worked and what didn't, and keeping in mind our vision, we'll get closer to our original idea. We also made the most of an expressed interest of our students and channeled that interest in appropriate ways.

We included this example to stress that it's okay to stumble, to fall a little short of the mark, to rethink strategies, and try again. It's also okay to go where the interest of the students themselves takes you. And, not the least in importance, if your students are thinking and learning something, the time is not wasted. Whether what they learn is what you state expressly in your goals is only part of the issue. You're adding to their understanding of the world, to their fund of knowledge. It's not okay to beat yourself up about what you didn't accomplish. Analyze it, tweak it, and try again.

Testing for Mastery of Concepts

Testing is a tricky area. Sometimes students' inability to write in English makes it difficult to determine just how much they have learned. Or they may not have enough English proficiency to understand the question, even though they may well understand the concept.

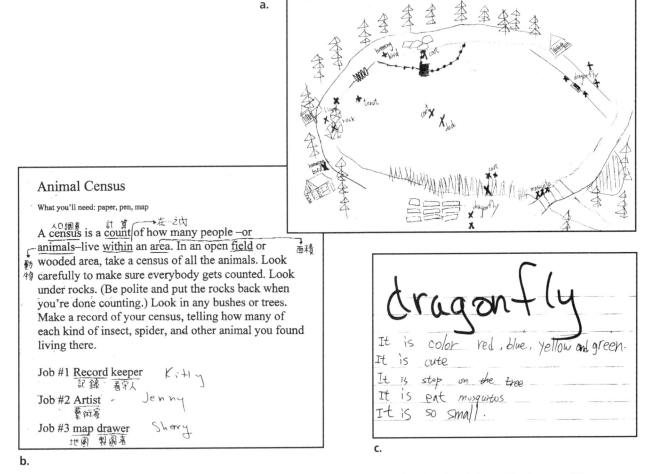

Animal Census

What you'll need: paper, pen, map

A census is a count of how many people –or animals–live within an area. In an open field or wooded area, take a census of all the animals. Look carefully to make sure everybody gets counted. Look under rocks. (Be polite and put the rocks back when you're done counting.) Look in any bushes or trees. Make a record of your census, telling how many of each kind of insect, spider, and other animal you found living there.

Job #1 Record keeper   Kitty

Job #2 Artist   Jenny

Job #3 map drawer   Sherry

dragonfly

It is color red, blue, yellow and green.
It is cute
It is stop on the tree
It is eat musquitos
It is so small.

Figure 8.7a-c. We took the students on a hike around the lake to identify what lived there. The less proficient learners drew maps and pictures of what they saw (a). The higher groups were handed the animal census paper (b) and were encouraged to read it and figure out the meaning themselves. As an extension, they wrote simple reports (c) and made 3-D representations of the animals in their habitat.

Checking Informally for Understanding

There are less stressful and more accurate methods of evaluating student progress than tests. Many of the tasks you set in the evaluation section of each lesson can give you a truer picture of what each student knows. Here are some other informal means of checking for students' understanding:

- Observe students' behavior while they work and interact with others in the practice situation. Does Saif participate or does he sit back and let others take the initiative and do the work? Does Lupe make meaningful contributions? How often and how many? Does Shin-suke look lost and bewildered by the task?

- Talk with the students about their work. Discuss what they've done. Often students are better able to articulate their understanding verbally than in writing.

- Examine the work they have produced. Give credit for any input they have made, whether nonverbal or verbal.

Testing the ESL
Student

If tests are an integral part of your course, here are some suggestions for making tests "easier" for the ESL student:

- Give the test orally. Arrange for a bilingual parent or aide to interpret.

- Simplify the language you use in the test. Unless you are testing vocabulary that is important to your field of study, avoid words you have not taught.

- Simplify the structures. Make the instructions easy to understand and give straightforward commands, such as "Complete the following." Avoid complex sentences.

- Test only the specific skill or concept you have taught; don't test language. For example, here is an answer to a test question given by eighth-grader Chantamala:

New world my father like to go to the new world because you can do everything like the way that know. We can go at the jungle, and cuting the wood to make a house, hunting, killing, growing crop or other thing that you wanted to do best for your life or family, then you can do everything that you want by your own.

It is easy to get lost or overwhelmed by the errors in an ESL student's paper. At first glance, Chantamala's composition might seem incoherent and disorganized, but the student has actually understood quite a bit of the discussion. The students were asked the question: "Would you like to move to the New World? Why? Give reasons." The class had just studied the colonization of America. This student gives very specific reasons why the New World was better. Even with her garbled language, she has conveyed the message that people could do anything they wanted: build their own homes, cut wood, kill animals—rights denied in many Old World countries. She has understood that the New World offered freedom from the harsh restricted life of common people in the Old World. If Chantamala were to be graded on her command of English, her many errors would count against her; however, she has learned some of the basic concepts and demonstrated her understanding of them.

Your criteria for grading might look like this:

- Did she understand the question?

- Did she answer the question?

- How well did she develop her thoughts?

- How thoroughly did she present her case?

- Is she performing to the best of her ability, given her stage of language competency, or is she just goofing off?

With these factors in mind, you can weigh this student's performance against those of the other students in the class and give her a grade that is fair.

Be realistic and honest in your assessment. If your students do less than the basic goals you have mapped out for them, don't give "pity grades." High school teacher Mary Delie stresses that it doesn't help

Briefly define or describe the following terms:

Sea Dogs: they were Sleves

Golden Hind: sailed th rough the strait of magellan

Charter: it document the rules

Armada: a warship

Joint Stock Company: a company

House of Burgesses:

Royal Colony: under complete control

puritans: were reformers

separatist: new churches

pilgrims: or religious travelens

Fundamental Orders: plans of the gov.

proprietors: charters and own eq.

patroons: religious groups

Quakers:

Frame of Government: gave the Colonists a representative

Pennsylvania Dutch: which means Germans

U.S. HISTORY
CHAPT 6. pages 121-124

1. Name two Indians that helped the early English settlers.
Chief Powhatan ara Squanto

2. What was the attitude of the Indians toward land ownership?
they had lot of culturals

3. How were the Indians beliefs about land different from the colonists?
the indians belived that the land belonged to no one person/group

4. What is a pagan?
or people who worshpped many gods rather than...

5. Why were the Indians destined to lose the conflict of cultures?
becausa thire dieing out and poeples are movin in to their land.

6. What was the middle passage?
a voyage across the Atlantic Ocean

7. What were the slave codes?
it made slaves their owners property

8. Describe three of the slave codes?
a. they could not vote
b. if they run away they would be hit or whiped
c. they could not own they thing

9. Who led one of the earliest slave rebellions in the colonies?
did Cato

10. Why was life so difficult for free blacks?
they were not welcome into white coloial society. they had to live in a separate neighbornoods, the even had black pews in churches and they had their own black school.

Figure 8.8a-b. This student defined key terms (a). What grade would you give her for this test? How well did the student answer the short-answer questions (b)? Would you include any "fudge factors" in your grade?

students in the long run. They may pass the assignments and their grade level, but if they haven't mastered the content, they can't move on to the next level and succeed. It is better to assess the students fairly and know up front where the gaps are.

When author Mary received a recent ESL student at her high school, it was evident he had fallen through the cracks throughout his elementary and junior high years. Tomás was a kind, gentle boy, and while his spoken English was excellent, he had many serious reading problems. Mary wondered how he had gotten as far as he had, but suspected, due to his sweet nature, teachers were reluctant to fail him. As a result, he was in high school unable to manage in his content classes. He needed attention, he needed work, and time was running out.

Grading ESL students is difficult; the key is to have goals and expectations for your students and understand what ESL students can demonstrate.

Conclusion

The two major assumptions we operate under when teaching the content areas are

- Language can be effectively learned through content.
- Content language provides students with both useful (in terms of knowledge) and usable language.

Time in a content-area classroom can be productive time for ESL students, even before they become as proficient in the language as their English-speaking peers. They can gain English competency by and through what they learn in class, and even though they cannot always articulate as well as their classmates, there are many alternative ways they can demonstrate their mastery of the concepts.

CHAPTER 9

RESOURCES

In this chapter, we discuss how to best use the resources in your school and the community. We give suggestions on how to

- Coordinate with support personnel such as ESL, bilingual, and reading teachers and paraprofessionals to use them to your and their best advantage.

- Use buddies and tutors.

- Encourage your students' parents to participate in their children's schooling.

- Use interpreters.

Katrina works in an inner-city school that has received a block grant limiting class size to twenty. She has ten Hispanic students, three Hmong, two African American, a Native American, and four native-English speakers. She meets every week with the other second-grade teachers to plan. They coordinate their efforts, talk over problems, and modify the curriculum together to meet the needs of their students. During the day, the lowest ESL students leave the classroom to go to ESL during language arts. The ESL teacher comes in during content science and social studies, the Title I teacher comes in to work with several small groups during reading time, and a bilingual person comes in to work with the Hispanic students during writing and math time in the afternoon.

Katrina is trying to make the most of the personnel in her school. While aligning all her core work to the curriculum and the state's model standards, she is giving ESL students the maximum support during the time they need it most and giving her more proficient students challenging material to work with.

What Katrina has going for her is her willingness—and confidence—to allow other teachers into her classroom to share the load. She also has the support of her principal and other professionals who adapt their schedules in creative ways. This is as it should be.

Solving the major issues concerning placement and configuration of services is not the point of this chapter. For each district, with its own particular problems, populations, and politics, there are unique answers. It is too easy to focus on the things that get in the way of collaboration. This does not make them any less real. Pull-out, push-in, and centers all have their attendant problems. Sometimes the politics of special interests take precedence over the needs of the whole. Other times, budget considerations eliminate the most needed programs or personnel. However, in this chapter, we have decided to sidestep these issues in favor of presenting a model of what *can* be. If you break down how these issues are configured, you have some sense of the choices you have and what you can lobby for. A collaborative model, in which responsibility is shared among the professionals in each building, is best. And again, flexibility is the key. We cannot promote one ideology, because everything might change tomorrow.

We have always stressed that ESL is everybody's responsibility. Just because Bounkham has been assigned to your class does not mean that you should shoulder the entire task of teaching. Nor does it mean that if there is an ESL teacher in the classroom, Bounkham is hers alone. He is in your class for the majority of the day. In addition to the help he gets from the ESL teacher, you need to modify your classroom and your teaching to make the curriculum accessible to him.

Meeting the needs of your English-speaking students is a challenge in itself. Teachers of ESL students are often frustrated because they cannot give their ESL students the time and attention they need.

ESL Teacher

Classroom Support   The ESL teacher is your prime source of support. She has the expertise in language acquisition and in modifying instruction to meet the needs of your students. She is also an extra pair of hands and eyes—another adult to watch, reason, and evaluate what's going on. Making the most of your time maximizes the learning your students get. But it takes coordination and careful planning.

Debbie, the ESL teacher, comes in for science and social studies. The other day she arrived in the classroom ten minutes after school had started and science was about to begin. She had no idea what Katrina was going to do that day and spent most of her time bending and pointing. This was not the best use of her time, and she and Katrina were both frustrated and grouchy.

Katrina thought back to her own days as a bilingual teacher. She was primarily responsible for working with first- and second-grade teachers, and with one teacher in particular. She and Sherry planned for one hour each week. They discussed content and reading in terms of who was going to be in charge and who was going to do what. When Katrina came into the classroom, they already had their game plan worked out and they were on the same page. "It takes time and it takes commitment," says Katrina. But it worked.

Katrina's school devised a Team Teaching Checklist. We believe this list captures what needs to be done to take full advantage of an ESL teacher's skills.

Team Teaching Checklist	
_____ Define your teaching roles.	_____ Agree on common discipline system.
_____ Establish common class goals and individual goals. ■ Groupings (how and where) ■ Modifications ■ Enrichments	_____ Build in time for parent communication.
	_____ Set your routines. ■ Daily teacher tasks ■ Ordering materials ■ Copying lesson plans
_____ Divide responsibilities for subjects.	
_____ Make time for planning.	_____ Work to maintain consistency in schedules and plans while allowing for flexibility.
_____ Decide on who will do grading and report cards.	_____ Do ongoing assessment of past lessons.
	_____ Keep lines of communication open.

Figure 9.1. Team Teaching Checklist.

"But I don't have time!" you say. Make time. It's that simple. First, however, you have to learn how to make the best use of what time you have. You are not making the best use of time when, for example, an aide or ESL teacher asks, "What are we doing today?" and learns on the spot, what is going on that day, or, you respond, "I don't know." Planning together up front eliminates

■ Using the ESL teacher as an aide.

■ The ESL teacher not knowing what students are expected to know.

■ Duplication of services.

■ ESL teachers having to guess what to teach, teaching things that are not relevant or useful, or undermining what you do in the classroom.

Communication is the most important factor in establishing a good relationship with the teachers who work with you and your students.

Flynn (1992) recommends that ESL teachers team with a limited number of classroom teachers. This allows them to work with classroom teachers to plan the curriculum for the entire class. They can then concentrate instruction on the needs of the LEP students as they relate to the instruction in your classroom.

This is the ideal, and perhaps, unrealistic. Bad principals, bad administrators, bad policies, lousy allocation of dollars, and poor planning get in the way. But the ideal is worth working for. When it works, as it did for Sherry and Katrina, it's wonderful. The kids get the best of both of you.

Hiring an Effective Classroom Paraprofessional

Classroom aides and/or ESL aides are often hired in response to a sudden influx of children who speak a language that no one in the school can understand or speak. Many times these aides have no training; they are hired simply because they can speak both English and the language of the new students. In some districts, the minimum requirement for hiring bilingual aides is that they can speak English. Even this criterion is sometimes difficult to meet. If you can't find a bilingual aide who is proficient in both languages, you are probably better off with an aide who is simply a good aide.

The Ideal Aide

The ideal classroom aide has all of the following characteristics:

- Good English-language skills—not just "some" English, but proficiency in reading and writing.
- A positive attitude.
- A working knowledge of classroom management: how to motivate students, how to discipline, how to reinforce what you teach.
- Cultural savvy, i.e., enough understanding of both cultures to work at ease with both.
- Patience.

An aide with all these qualities would be wonderful, but you may not be able to find someone matching this description in your district. Certainly, the decision to hire an aide should not be based solely on his or her knowledge of the ESL students' language. Good English skills are far more essential. Other useful skills are a working knowledge of reading theory and some knowledge of the basic principles of ESL.

Although most of our discussion relates to the issue of working with paid aides, parents or bilingual volunteers may also be used in this capacity.

Using Your Classroom Aide

You must first decide whether the classroom aide is merely to be a clerk, or is to be given a more responsible role within the classroom. We believe that your aide is a valuable resource, and though keeping records, grading papers, and running off copies are all useful tasks, your aide can be used to advantage in many other areas.

Some teachers give their aide complete responsibility for their ESL students. This may be a temptation, as you have many other students to work with, but the aide, who lacks both training and experience, is not the teacher. Your aide should be there to complement your role, not to take over and work exclusively with the ESL students. As the teacher, you must be the driving force. It is up to you to be the role model, to give clear directions, to set expectations and parameters, and to use the aide to your advantage, capitalizing on his or her strengths and personality.

Your main role is to offer guidance and supervision, as well as to provide an environment conducive to rapport and open communication among you, your aide, and your students. Here are some suggestions as to how to go about it:

The Teacher's Role

- Find out the strengths and weaknesses of the aide and what he or she feels most comfortable doing. Here are some questions for the aide to answer; ask for written rather than verbal responses.

    - What do you feel you do, or could do, especially well in the classroom?

    - What do you feel unprepared to do in the classroom?

- Clarify expectations. We suggest that both you and the aide respond in writing to the following four-part question. Provide space on the paper for four or five different thoughts.

    What do you see as each person's responsibilities in the following relationships:

    Teacher's responsibility to the teacher aide.

    Teacher's responsibility to the students.

    Teacher aide's responsibility to the teacher.

    Teacher aide's responsibility to the students.

    The answers to these questions will alert you to your aide's expectations of you and to possible differences between your two sets of expectations. It will also help you define your perception of your own role and responsibilities. There is nothing as destructive to a good working relationship as two people operating under different assumptions about their roles. If these aren't spelled out and clarified at the beginning, frustration and resentment can lead to job dissatisfaction, unhappiness, or an inability to work together, which may lead to the aide resigning his or her position.

- Clearly define duties and responsibilities for both yourself and the aide and draw up a written contract that outlines these. This contract can be renegotiated from time to time and referred to during the term. In "The Aide's Role" on page 239, we give suggestions for appropriate tasks.

- Before school begins, meet with the aide (let's call him Mr. Chun) and help him become familiar with the classroom, the materials, and textbooks. Make sure he also knows the jargon of the school, such as what CTBS, SAT, and so on, mean.

- Give a complete tour of the school and introduce him to the support staff of the school, the secretaries, principal, nurse, counselor, and so on.

- Introduce him to the students. Use the same title they use for you, to demonstrate that they are to treat him with the same respect. If you are known as Mrs. Burton, he will go by Mr. Chun, not Martin.

- Make sure he knows the philosophy of North American education, as well as your own personal educational philosophy. Many aides come from countries that have philosophies much different from ours. To an immigrant from Japan, for example, American classrooms can seem overly noisy and chaotic, children rude and disrespectful, and discipline nonexistent.

- Make sure he has at least a basic knowledge of the principles of ESL teaching/learning. When Barb taught in a self-contained classroom, she welcomed the assistance of an ESL intern from the local university. He worked two days a week for ten weeks, participated in planning sessions, and carried on many conversations concerning learning styles and philosophies of education. But after he had left, his final report to his professor stated unequivocally that there should have been many more drills and that the teacher should have been focusing on grammar. Even after ten weeks of involvement, he was unable to accept established second-language teaching theories and continued to compare Barb's teaching methods unfavorably to those methods used when he was a student in his own country. As a result, Barb was never quite sure how much he had tried to undermine what she had been doing while he was working with her students—a discomfiting feeling.

- Discuss lesson plans, objectives, and the implementation of your long- and short-term goals. Make sure he knows exactly what you want him to do, either in conjunction with what you are doing in the class, or as extension and enrichment. Figure 9.2 provides a sample planning sheet you can use with either paid or volunteer aides. The "comments" section is to be used for observations and perceptions of how the day went, who did particularly well, and who had difficulty with the material. These comments are particularly useful if your time is limited, or if the aide leaves each day before you have a chance to discuss work with him. His assessment will also be useful when planning new activities.

- Make sure your aide knows the why as well as the how to. Often good ideas go awry because the aide doesn't know the reasoning behind the lesson plan. For example, if you ask Mr. Chum to do TPR (see page 202) with some students and, without understanding the principle behind it, he has the students repeat every command after him, he is defeating the purpose of TPR.

- Clarify when it is important to use the first language. Having someone who is able to jumpstart comprehension by explaining in the first language, build background knowledge, clarify misunderstanding, and affirm the validity of the first language is an invaluable asset in a classroom. But there is a fine line between being an asset and being a crutch—one that you and the aid need to work out between you.

- Ask for input. If your aide works consistently with small groups of ESL students, he may know them better than you do and may have a clearer insight into their strengths, weaknesses, and possible reasons for behavior problems.

- Capitalize on his strengths. Find out if he has any special talent. For instance, Barb's aide Emma had abundant artistic talent and enjoyed making posters, wall displays, and awards for the students. Midori was a librarian and could always find a book appropriate for each child.

Teacher-Volunteer (or Aide) Planning Sheet

Name of volunteer (or aide) _____

Name of teacher/grade level _____

Name(s) of student(s) _____

Skills to be reinforced or tasks to be completed by volunteer (or aide):

Time frame _____

Materials to be used _____

Location of materials _____

Procedures _____

Comments of volunteer (or aide):

_____

_____

_____

_____

_____

Figure 9.2. Teacher-Volunteer (or Aide) Planning Sheet. (Reproducible master in appendix I)

- Tap his knowledge of his own culture, traditions, and values. He has the special perspective of someone within a culture, and can bring an understanding and richness to the classroom that would be lacking otherwise. He can help you and the students understand how culture influences people's way of perceiving things, and how different behaviors result from language or cultural differences. For example, when Mary was teaching a lesson on body parts, the students were not responding as enthusiastically as she had hoped. This was suddenly made clear when her aide pointed out that she was touching them on the head and shoulders, sacred areas to Buddhists.

- If he is comfortable with it, allow him to assume responsibility in his area of expertise. Some aides enjoy responsibility, others prefer to be led. Still others are very conscious of what-is-aiding and what-is-teaching and will not cross that line.

The Aide's Role

Your aide's principal role is to complement you in the classroom, to carry out your lesson plans, and supplement and enrich what you have taught. The most helpful areas are

Translating (if the aide is bilingual)

- When there is a breakdown in communication or a problem, acting as interpreter to explain or sort out the difficulty.
- Translating school notices, permission slips, and so on.
- Providing initial orientation and explaining the rules and regulations of the school and classroom to parents.

Working in the school with individual students or in small groups

- Developing LEA stories (see page 124).
- Developing reading readiness skills.
- Reading to students.
- Working on math concepts that the ESL students may not understand.
- Breaking down activities into smaller, more comprehensible units for students who need extra explanation.
- Coordinating with the content area teachers, previewing a lesson, then recapping it for the ESL students in their language.
- Reviewing and reinforcing concepts taught to the class as a whole.

Acting as a bridge with the community

- Attending parent-teacher conferences and acting as translator.
- Getting permission slips signed.
- Accompanying parents to school programs and activities to help prevent discomfort or alienation.

Community Aides

Community aides, who liaise between the school and the community, play quite a different role from classroom aides. They can be a powerful force and exert much more influence on parents and community than you, so English-language skills are not as important for community aides as the ability to command respect. In many Asian neighborhoods, a man who has status as a respected member of the community is far more influential than someone whose English might be better, but who has no status. One elementary school in northern California has an older Hmong man as a volunteer. He is a clan leader, and, therefore, is given great respect and deference by the local Hmong population. When there is a discipline problem, Mr. Lee steps in and the problem no longer exists. He is the community liaison, interpreter, and elder, and is, by all accounts, a man to be reckoned with. His pervasive influence is invaluable to the school; he is an ally they both appreciate and depend upon.

Buddies

We discussed buddies briefly in chapter 1; now we would like to treat the issue in more depth.

Rather than arbitrarily assigning a "buddy" student to help out a newcomer and leaving the buddy to his own devices undirected, it is probably wise to be more systematic. One school has instituted a carefully planned and executed buddy system that has seen great success. This system, as with any successful program, has strong administrative support. It involves the careful selection and training of ESL buddies, as well as parental involvement and the use of contracts.

- Only good students who are patient, mature, tolerant of differences, and wise enough to know when to help and when to let the ESL student work on his own, are selected as buddies.

- A training workshop is given at the beginning of the year to sensitize all student-buddies to the problems of ESL students and to help them learn ways to assist their buddies. Parents of student-buddies are given a form to sign, giving permission for their children to be buddies.

- Each buddy is matched with a student in his class and given a list of fun—and friend-making—things to do. Students sign contracts, which detail things they will do with their buddies. Some suggestions include: going to McDonald's together, calling their buddy on the phone every day, inviting their buddy home once a week.

- Special recognition is given to buddies for their service. There is a Friendship Picnic at the end of the year, and a "Buddies Poster" (photographs of each of the buddies with their newcomer friend) is displayed in a prominent place in the school.

This program makes everyone in the school aware of the ESL students, not as a problem to be overcome, but as a special opportunity for learning and friendship. Being appointed a buddy is seen as an honor. This buddy program is a systematic, well-planned way to ease the transition of new students.

Tutors

For additional one-on-one help for students, tutors are invaluable. A tutor may be another student in the class, a more advanced ESL student, a student aide, a senior citizen, or a National Honor Society student interested in gaining service points. A tutor does not have to speak the language of the ESL student he works with. According to high school teachers Debbie Angert and Jan Booth in a conference workshop in 1987, the best candidates for peer tutors are those who

- Exhibit a willingness to help others.
- Are not overly grade conscious.
- Are not excessively shy.
- Will be good models for appropriate behavior and good study habits.

Working before or after school or during study time, they can

- Take notes during each class, giving copies to the ESL student.
- Explain directions.

- Clarify vocabulary.
- Read the textbook material to the ESL student.
- Make sure the student is following directions and working on the task at hand.
- Give you feedback on the ESL student's progress and problems.

Parents

Contrary to the perception of many teachers, most parents are anxious and willing to help at home and are extremely concerned about their children's success at school. The major hindrance is that they don't know how to help. You can help them help their children by showing them specific ways to encourage and enrich their children's learning experiences. Here are some suggestions that include the family in literacy and language learning. The title of these activities, "home fun," is important. According to Mary Lou McCloskey and Scott Enright (1988), who developed them, home fun activities should

- Be engaging and fun.
- Integrate language learning into all activities.
- Necessitate both parent (or other older persons) and child participation.
- Respect and use the family's native language.
- Allow adequate time for completion.
- Be presented by the teacher with preparation and follow-up.
- Provide variations based on the student's language level.

The most basic and important activity literate parents can do is read to their children. It doesn't matter in what language, whether their first language or English; reading in one helps reading in the other. It doesn't even have to be literature; food labels, newspapers, letters, bulletins—anything in print—will do. If parents are not literate, other family or community members can help.

Home Activities to Promote Literacy

McCloskey and Enright list other activities to promote literacy and an understanding of the value and use of literature:

- Record the ways family members use reading in a day.
- Record examples of environmental print (street signs, bumper stickers, and so on) that students can recognize.
- Collect food labels and/or containers to be used in classroom activities.
- Give ESL students assignments to help them learn about their families.
- Make a family tree.
- Make a personal "what-happened-when" time line.
- Collect funny stories about the student's childhood.
- Collect family stories in a certain category—humor, superstitions, ghost stories.

- Interview family members to study the history of the family.
- Study a particular aspect of the parents' lives when they were children.
- If parents have moved around, make a map of their migration.
- Give them assignments to help learn about their culture
- Write stories about holidays and special events in their culture or homeland, such as New Years, Bon Dances, powwows, fiestas, and so on.
- Write down recipes for ethnic dishes.
- Illustrate traditional costumes.
- Collect traditional fairy tales.
- Interview others to find out traditional ways of doing things, such as how to conduct a Japanese tea ceremony.
- Interview others to find out about skills they had in the homeland, such as carving, hunting.
- Illustrate life as it was in their homeland.
- Involve family members in projects to learn about their communities.
- Sketch their rooms, their houses, their blocks.
- Make a map of the student's street.
- Make maps of routes commonly traveled, such as from home to school and to the store.

Interpreters

There are times when it will be absolutely essential for you to have an interpreter—when things go wrong and you need to clarify why and how to rectify the situation; when you need to discuss with parents how their child is doing in school; when a student is sick or hurt and in need of medical attention. For these occasions, it is important that you have located and approached at least one person who is a fluent speaker of your student's language.

Interpreters are valuable assets to any teacher. If they are from the same ethnic group as your student they know the culture of the person you are trying to communicate with and can provide a bridge between your culture and theirs. They can advise you, for instance, that in their culture it is very impolite to be direct, that one communicates by beating around the bush; or that it is typical to flee from the police when you've been stopped for a violation, because people in their country are often jailed for long periods without knowing why. While the interpreter is explaining something to the student in his language, you have time to think through your next question. Most important, interpreters can verify that you and the other party are actually communicating with understanding.

When you require an interpreter, do not use children in this role. It may be all right to collar a fellow student occasionally in a casual situation, when you simply need to get a point across or understand a student's question, but for major interviews or problems, children should not be used for several reasons:

- Children don't have the experience, wherewithal, or training to ask appropriate questions.

- Using children robs adults of their authority. This is particularly true with parents from traditional patriarchal societies. Giving children such power strips adults of their authority.

- If something goes wrong, the child will get the blame.

- The child may not be old enough to understand the concepts or problems you are trying to discuss, especially when they involve a medical situation.

- Some concepts are not directly translatable, and the child may not have the cognitive maturity to explain in other words.

Using Interpreters

Here are some suggestions about using interpreters and the procedure to follow in selection and training:

Choose the appropriate interpreter for the situation.

- Know your students and have some understanding of their cultures. For example, if you have a suicidal teenage girl, you should not use her father as the interpreter. Be aware of the ethnic antagonisms that exist between groups. One student of Barb's slept with a knife under his pillow for an entire year because he had been paired with a student that his country traditionally shared a mutual hatred with. Regardless of the fact that they liked each other and made it through the year, his learned distrust simmered below the surface. The tensions or discomfort between certain family members or cultural groups can short-circuit any efforts you make.

- Select someone you're comfortable with, someone who you think is reliable, who you can trust to translate your ideas accurately and not undermine what you are saying. For instance, if you are telling a student that keeping a handgun in his locker is a very serious offense, you don't want your interpreter saying, "Don't worry. I have one myself. I'll show you how to use it."

Meet with your interpreter before the session to talk about the situation at hand.

- Explain the purposes and the goals of the meeting. You don't want to shock the interpreter with discussion of a sensitive subject when the client is already present. For example, an interpreter may feel extremely uncomfortable discussing gynecological issues or personal issues that in his culture are inappropriate for him to broach with the other party.

- Make sure he knows that he should not ask questions for you or answer questions for the student. His job is simply to interpret what each of you say; he is not your voice or theirs, but the conduit through which you both talk.

- Make sure that what transpires will be absolutely confidential.

- Make sure you know how to pronounce the names of the persons you are meeting with.

- Establish such basics as

  How you will be introduced.

  Where you will sit—behind your desk or with the others in a circle. (What is the least intimidating arrangement?)

  If it is appropriate to touch the other person.

  If it is appropriate to make eye contact.

  If the interpreter will paraphrase or interpret word-for-word and if he will interpret in short phrases or paragraphs.

  If the interpreter will give you feedback about the other person's feelings and reactions (such as telling you, "He's sad") during the meeting or afterwards.

When the student arrives

- Make introductions.

- Establish immediately that your interpreter is simply there to interpret, not level charges.

- Look at the student, not at the interpreter.

- Establish your student's degree of English proficiency (you don't want to be shocked or embarrassed by finding out that your student has understood many of the comments you have made to the interpreter that were not meant for the student to hear).

- Avoid long discussions with your interpreter while the student waits.

- Simplify your language.

- Plan your next statement while the interpreter is relaying your message.

- Watch nonverbal cues carefully for signs of frustration, discomfort, or anger.

After the session

- Discuss whether you solved the problem or if another meeting is required. How did the student respond to your decision?

- Pay him. Even if it's a nominal fee, make it worth his while to have come. Schools usually have some kind of fund to pay for this, and you must compensate him for his time and effort.

Conclusion

Teachers often express their frustration at the monumental task of meeting the needs of all their students. This chapter has been written to help you tap the resources available.

You're not in this alone. Using available help makes your job easier, reinforces the things you do in class, and helps you establish what you are doing right, as well what needs improvement. The main benefit you gain is support for your efforts.

CONCLUSION

Teachers in today's world juggle a complex variety of concerns. Added to the fundamental challenge of teaching the curriculum to an increasingly diverse population of students are the pressures of accountability, standardized testing, and standards and benchmarks. Another chainsaw in your juggling routine is how to teach the ESL student in your classroom. This is one issue that will not go away. With the growing number of immigrant populations in large urban centers, and the secondary migrations to rural areas, teaching ESL has become everybody's business. If you have had little experience working with these students, you may feel overwhelmed and intimidated. You see the need to help the newcomers at the same time as you are trying to do a competent job of teaching your other students. Perhaps you feel that it is impossible to do both well.

First, recognize that these anxieties are rooted in your desire to do a good job. You can prevail, so don't let the enormity of the situation overwhelm you. Take the job in steps. Find out where your students' starting points are, and take it from there. It is possible to teach the ESL students and the rest of your class at the same time—and in the process they will learn from each other!

Find Support

Most important, be aware that education works best with support systems. This means for your students and for you. Don't allow yourself to become so inundated with work or stress that you feel drained. Find support. It is almost impossible to work continually without any creative stimulus for yourself. Get input. Bounce ideas off other teachers, counselors, ESL specialists, bilingual teachers and mentors, or other professionals who have experience dealing with newcomers. If you have access to education libraries, read articles and borrow books that deal with the topic of educating the ESL student. Surf the Net. There are many wonderful sites that offer terrific ideas and lesson plans to give you starting points (see Internet Resources, page 293). Find a confidant—someone you can share your classroom trials and triumphs with. The important point is to avoid getting walled in and burned out.

Build a Supportive School Program

We have focused mainly on what YOU can do to provide good, solid instruction to your students. But you're not alone and you shouldn't be.

You can't be expected to cope in isolation. Quality programs depend on these factors:

- Quality staffing. This means people who are trained (or willing to be trained) in ESL methodology, and are ready—and willing—to work with ESL students. It means principals and administrators who recognize the need to support you and give you and your students what you need.

- A commitment of time for training. Gaskins (1998) calls this "the cornerstone of instructional programs that produce significant results in student progress." This doesn't mean one Friday afternoon workshop. It means ongoing training throughout the year, time off for attending conferences, and monies set aside for gaining expertise. Lucas (1997) writes that the insufficient preparation of mainstream teachers is a major obstacle for the success of ESL students. This is beginning to change. As the number of limited-English-speaking students has increased, universities have responded with programs to train teachers. There are summer institutes if no school near you offers courses. You owe it to yourself and your students to learn everything you can. Lucas unequivocally states,

  > Educators urgently need more education to increase their sensitivity to and knowledge of their students' cultures and languages. New and different kinds of educators are needed who have a positive attitude toward cultural differences, extensive knowledge about students' cultural experiences, and the technical skills to translate this cultural information into pedagogical practice and who have a positive attitude toward linguistic differences, acknowledge the value of bi- and multilingualism, understand language development and second language learning, and possess the skills to guide students in developing bilingual fluency while they learn language and learn though language.

- Money to buy materials. When Barb started out in her career, her only supplies were books ten years out of print. Every bit of student material was bought with money out of her pocket, and every ditto was made on the back of someone else's castoffs. The next year, she talked her way into a budget. Her office was no longer the Boogie Room, a windowless office above the kitchen at the middle school, but a spare office in the band/orchestra room. The "desks" the students used were the music stands. At one school, she worked with a child for an entire year on the steps to the attic because Will, the speech teacher, would not share his office. Things have gotten better in most places, but not everywhere. You might have to fight to be heard above the clamor for more money, more space, and more materials.

- A willingness to support change. Schools need to modify their priorities, their classrooms, and their strategies to accommodate new students. There are many obstacles, but we have to continue to work to overcome them.

- Congruence between the regular classroom and other programs. Pull-out programs have a bad reputation. There are reasons for this, and some of them are good ones. The main reason is poor coordination with the curriculum and instruction of the regular classroom. No matter how good pull-out instruction is, it's not usually sufficient to create successful students. ESL and other at-risk students have the best chance for success if what you do in your classroom instruction and what the bilingual, ESL, or reading teacher do are not only of high quality, but also mesh in purpose and in particulars. Collaboration, congruence, and good communication between you and your colleagues are essential for your students.

- Time for learning to occur. Gaskins notes that what is missing in most initiatives to teach students who are at-risk (such as delayed readers and many of our ESL students), is sufficient time to accomplish the goal of preparing students to be successful in the mainstream. We have stressed the time factor throughout this book, and we reiterate it here. Students need time to adjust, time to learn the language and the "ropes" of a new culture, and time to find themselves. They bring with them a rich cultural and linguistic heritage, which they will, with our support, meld into their new lives here.

- Willingness to modify programs as students and their needs change. The "one-size-fits-all" approach to educating immigrants is destructive to meeting their needs. For example, the Vietnamese refugees who came in the seventies were, by and large, the elite educated professionals. The wave of Laotians and Hmongs who came later were from rural villages and farms, and were largely illiterate. Those with limited schooling need different kinds of services from those who have achieved a high degree of education in their home country. We need to be flexible and maintain adaptable programs as new and different kinds of students enroll in our schools.

Tolerance

Develop a tolerance for gray. There are few cut-and-dry rules when dealing with language learning. If you can accept that tests may not accurately reflect your new students' knowledge and skills, that your classroom game-plan may need revision, that your ESL students may linguistically regress for no discernible reason, and that there may be times when you rely on your instincts over anything else, you won't lose sleep over things outside your control. And we suggest you keep a sense of humor handy.

Don't be afraid to stumble. If you read this book carefully, you'll see that we have stumbled often. We have found ourselves in uncomfortable situations and with students we weren't sure how to handle. Mary often thought there was nothing but her mistakes in the first edition of this book. That's part and parcel of what this job is all about. Everybody was happy when Boris left. No tears were shed when Abir went home to her country. We've said things we regretted. We've ended some school years with little more than a sigh of relief—and galloped for the door. But when the next year arrived we were up for it, ready to try again. And when the Spencers and the Beverlys and the Floriens move away, we cry. When the Fernandos and the Jeremys and the Robbys and the Andres graduate, we cheer. And when the Salvadors and the Destinys and the Hnukus grow up to take their place as upstanding, decent members of the community, we can feel justifiably proud because we contributed. What more can anybody ask? And so, we, like thousands of other teachers, are in there every day slugging.

Don't give up! The rewards of working with—and including—students with different language and cultural backgrounds are huge. These students broaden the perspective of the class and contribute fresh viewpoints to your class discussions. Students, even when they are unable to speak English, enrich and add immeasurably to each classroom and to the lives of their classmates. We hope that this book is a beginning, a step toward making that richness a reality.

APPENDIXES

BASIC INFORMATION FOR PARENTS

To the parents of _____

The following information will help you to understand your child's new school. Please share this information with your child so that he or she will feel more comfortable at school.

If you have questions, please call _____ and we will be happy to answer them.

Date _____

Identification Information

Name of school _____

School address_____

School telephone _____

Name of principal _____

Name of teacher_____

Grade_____ Room number _____

Other Information
Schedule of school day

First bell for
morning session_____

Tardy bell_____

Morning recess _____

Lunch _____

First bell for
afternoon session _____

Afternoon recess_____

Dismissal time _____

Lunch Options

☐ Eat hot lunch provided at school.   Cost: _____

☐ Eat sack lunch provided at school.   Cost: _____

☐ Eat sack lunch brought from home.

☐ Purchase milk only, to drink with
     sack lunch brought from home.   Cost: _____

☐ Return home for lunch.

Transportation Options

☐ Bus   ☐ Walk

☐ Parents provide transportation

Illness   If your child is ill please do not send him or her to school.

              If your child is too ill to be able to function in class or if his or her temperature is 100° F (37.8° C) or above, we will send him or her home. (If no one is at home during school hours, please make other arrangements with the school in case your child becomes ill.)

Absence   If your child is ill or for some other reason will not be at school, please phone the school secretary or principal at _____

HOME LANGUAGE SURVEY

NOTE: This form is used for assessment and placement purposes. Obtaining this information is required by law in the U.S.A.

Date _____

School _____

Teacher _____

Dear Parents,

In order for us to help your child, we need to know the language(s) you speak at home. Please answer the following questions. Thank you for your help.

Name of student_____

                                     Family name   Given name

Completed years in school_____ Age _____

Native country_____

1. Which language did your child learn when he or she first began to talk?

   _____

2. What language does your child most frequently use at home?

   _____

3. What language do you use most frequently to speak to your child?

   _____

4. What language is most often spoken by the adults at home?

   _____

                                          _____

                                          Signature of parent or guardian

Student Vocabulary Test

NOTE: To be completed when new student is admitted to school. You may wish to make flashcards for this purpose using photos from magazines or catalogs. Drawings are not recommended.

Teacher _____   Student _____

School_____   Grade _____

Have student identify using English vocabulary. Use check marks to note those words the student knows. Leave others blank.

1. Colors
- ☐ red
- ☐ blue
- ☐ green
- ☐ yellow
- ☐ orange
- ☐ black
- ☐ purple
- ☐ brown
- ☐ white

2. Numbers—Kindergarten
- ☐ 1
- ☐ 2
- ☐ 3
- ☐ 4
- ☐ 5
- ☐ 6
- ☐ 7
- ☐ 8
- ☐ 9
- ☐ 10

Grades 1–3, as above plus
- ☐ 11
- ☐ 12
- ☐ 13
- ☐ 14
- ☐ 15
- ☐ 16
- ☐ 17
- ☐ 18
- ☐ 19
- ☐ 20

3. Shapes
- ☐ circle
- ☐ square
- ☐ triangle
- ☐ rectangle

4. Alphabet (present in random order)
- ☐ A
- ☐ B
- ☐ C
- ☐ D
- ☐ E
- ☐ F
- ☐ G
- ☐ H
- ☐ I
- ☐ J
- ☐ K
- ☐ L
- ☐ M
- ☐ N
- ☐ O
- ☐ P
- ☐ Q
- ☐ R
- ☐ S
- ☐ T
- ☐ U
- ☐ V
- ☐ W
- ☐ X
- ☐ Y
- ☐ Z

5. Holiday names
- ☐ Easter
- ☐ Halloween
- ☐ Valentine's Day
- ☐ Thanksgiving
- ☐ Christmas
- ☐ New Year's Day

6. Personal information
- ☐ name
- ☐ age
- ☐ address
- ☐ phone number

7. Body parts

- ☐ eye
- ☐ nose
- ☐ cheek
- ☐ mouth
- ☐ neck
- ☐ chest
- ☐ shoulder
- ☐ arm
- ☐ hand
- ☐ stomach
- ☐ leg
- ☐ knee
- ☐ foot
- ☐ finger

8. Spatial orientation

- ☐ left
- ☐ right
- ☐ in front of
- ☐ out
- ☐ over
- ☐ above
- ☐ beside
- ☐ behind
- ☐ in
- ☐ near
- ☐ far

9. School vocabulary

- ☐ recess
- ☐ hall
- ☐ washroom
- ☐ auditorium
- ☐ playground
- ☐ locker
- ☐ office
- ☐ lunch
- ☐ teacher
- ☐ lunch room
- ☐ principal
- ☐ secretary
- ☐ tardy slip
- ☐ school
- ☐ science
- ☐ phys. ed.
- ☐ math
- ☐ school bus
- ☐ language arts
- ☐ drinking fountain

10. Classroom words

- ☐ desk
- ☐ books
- ☐ paper
- ☐ chalkboard
- ☐ crayons
- ☐ notebook
- ☐ pencil
- ☐ glue
- ☐ chalk
- ☐ clock
- ☐ eraser
- ☐ page
- ☐ rug
- ☐ scissors
- ☐ seat
- ☐ chair
- ☐ table
- ☐ window
- ☐ wastebasket

11. Clothing

- ☐ coat
- ☐ dress
- ☐ jacket
- ☐ hat
- ☐ gym shoes
- ☐ mittens
- ☐ pants
- ☐ shirt
- ☐ shoes
- ☐ skirt
- ☐ socks
- ☐ sweater

12. Safety terms

- ☐ stop
- ☐ go
- ☐ walk
- ☐ don't walk

13. Time

- ☐ morning
- ☐ noon
- ☐ night
- ☐ afternoon
- ☐ tomorrow
- ☐ yesterday
- ☐ year
- ☐ month
- ☐ next week

14. Other vocabulary

- ☐ first
- ☐ last
- ☐ big
- ☐ little
- ☐ small
- ☐ smaller

15. Money
- ☐ penny
- ☐ nickel
- ☐ dime
- ☐ quarter
- ☐ cent
- ☐ cost
- ☐ dollar

16. Transportation
- ☐ bus
- ☐ car
- ☐ truck
- ☐ plane

17. Everyday directions
- ☐ wait
- ☐ sit down
- ☐ stand up
- ☐ sit on floor
- ☐ come here
- ☐ line up
- ☐ pick up
- ☐ open book
- ☐ touch
- ☐ cut out
- ☐ wait
- ☐ copy
- ☐ wash your hands
- ☐ raise your hand

18. Home words
- ☐ address
- ☐ brother
- ☐ sister
- ☐ father
- ☐ mother
- ☐ home
- ☐ sofa
- ☐ chair
- ☐ table
- ☐ bed

BASIC STUDENT INFORMATION

NOTE: This form is to be filled out at time of student's admission to school, with the assistance of parents and/or interpreter. (Health information is retained separately.)

Name of student_____

Address _____

Telephone _____ Birthdate _____ M ☐ F ☐

Father's name _____

Place of employment_____

Business telephone_____

Mother's name _____

Place of employment_____

Business telephone_____

In case of emergency, if parents cannot be reached, call

Name _____ Telephone _____

Other Information

Native country_____

Native language _____

Other languages spoken _____

Arrival date in U.S.A./Canada _____

Arrival date in state/province _____

Number of years in school in first language _____

Number of years in school in second language _____

Previous school enrollment in U.S.A./Canada _____

Previous English instruction before arriving in this country _____

Comes from rural/country background _____

urban/city background _____

Additional Information

_____

_____

_____

_____

_____

CHECKLIST FOR ASSESSING EMERGING READERS

Student Name _____   Date_____

Age _____   Grade _____

	Not yet	Emerging	Yes
Listens to story but is not looking at pages			
Tries to read environmental print			
Demonstrates book handling knowledge (right side up)			
Watches pictures as story is read aloud			
Makes up words for picture			
Demonstrates directionality of written language (left to right, page order)			
Pretends to read			
Recognizes some words from a dictated story			
Participates in reading by supplying rhyming words and some predictable text			
Memorizes text and pretends to read story			
Looks at words and tracks words when reading or is being read to from a familiar story			
Recognizes words in a new context			
Reads word for word			
Reads familiar stories fluently			
Reads unfamiliar stories haltingly			
Uses context clues, phonic analysis, sentence structure, to read new words and passages			
Reads easy books fluently			
Chooses to read independently			
Reads fluently			

WRITING SAMPLE SCORE SHEET

SKILL AREAS	DESCRIPTION	SCORE
Content	☐ theme developed ☐ related ideas and examples supplied	**Fluent**
	☐ thought development adequate ☐ some unrelated ideas used	**Intermediate**
	☐ uneven (or no) theme development ☐ many unrelated ideas included ☐ few (or no) examples given ☐ insufficient writing for evaluation	**Beginner**
Organization	☐ good topic development ☐ opening sentence/or introductory paragraph included ☐ concluding sentence/paragraph included ☐ ideas well organized, clearly stated, and backed-up ☐ transitions included	**Fluent**
	☐ topic or opening sentence included, but no closing sentence provided ☐ weak organization ☐ inadequate back-up information provided ☐ few transitions included	**Intermediate**
	☐ no topic sentence development ☐ no opening or closing sentence included ☐ little or no organization ☐ no back-up information provided ☐ no transitions included ☐ ideas confused or unrelated ☐ insufficient writing for evaluation	**Beginner**
Vocabulary	☐ correct use of word forms (prefixes, suffixes, etc.) and idioms ☐ sophisticated word choice ☐ meaning clear	**Fluent**
	☐ generally correct use of word forms and idioms ☐ word choice correct ☐ meaning clear	**Intermediate**

SKILL AREAS	DESCRIPTION	SCORE
	☐ many errors in word forms and idioms	**Beginner**
	☐ ineffective word choice	
	☐ words selected through direct translation	
	☐ meaning confused or obscured	
	☐ insufficient writing for evaluation	
Language Skills	☐ correct use of verb tense	**Fluent**
	☐ good sentence variety and complex construction	
	☐ good control of agreement, number, word order, parts of speech	
	☐ most verb tenses correct	**Intermediate**
	☐ simple sentence construction	
	☐ errors in agreement, number, word order, parts of speech	
	☐ frequent errors in tense	**Beginner**
	☐ forced sentence constructions	
	☐ many errors in agreement, number, word order, parts of speech	
	☐ insufficient writing for evaluation	
Mechanics	☐ few errors made in spelling, punctuation, capitalization	**Fluent**
	☐ occasional errors in spelling, punctuation, capitalization	**Intermediate**
	☐ many errors in spelling, punctuation, capitalization	**Beginner**
	☐ handwriting unclear or illegible	
	☐ insufficient writing for evaluation	

INDIVIDUALIZED EDUCATIONAL PLAN

NOTE: This form is to be completed by the ESL teacher, the resource teacher, or the classroom teacher three or four weeks after the new student has been assigned to the class, or whenever an IEP is to be updated.

Student's name _____
Family name   Given name

Birth date_____ Age _____ M ☐ F ☐
Mo   Day   Year

Grade level _____ Assessment test _____

Date given _____ Primary language_____

Assessment test given in primary language?   yes ☐   no ☐

Supplemental Testing Observations

Oral production _____

_____

_____

Comprehension _____

_____

_____

Reading skill_____

_____

_____

Written skills_____

_____

Summary of observed testing performance_____

_____

_____

_____

_____

_____

_____

_____

_____

Particular
Learning Needs

☐ Spoken language   ☐ Reading   ☐ Written language

☐ Other _____

Comments _____

_____

_____

_____

_____

_____

_____

Short-Range Goals

_____

_____

_____

_____

_____

Strategy for implementation _____

_____

_____

_____

_____

Long-Range Goals

_____

_____

_____

_____

Strategy for implementation _____

_____

_____

_____

_____

_____

_____

_____

_____

_____

INDIVIDUALIZED EDUCATIONAL PLAN

NOTE: This form is to be completed by the ESL teacher, the resource teacher, or the classroom teacher three or four weeks after the new student has been assigned to the class, or whenever an IEP is to be updated.

Student's name ___Ruyshchenko___ ___Boris___
                              Family name   Given name

Birth date ___January 13___   Age ___13___   M ☒ F ☐
            Mo Day Year

Grade level ___8___   Assessment test ___LAS___

Date given ___January___   Primary language ___Russian___

Assessment test given in primary language?   yes ☐   no ☒

Supplemental Testing Observations

Oral production _Excellent. He held up his end of the conversation._

Comprehension _Understood everything he was asked and could answer easily._

Reading skill _Scores show reading in Russian were at grade level, but he is a level 4 or 5 in English._

Written skills _Could write in English, but had many non-native errors._

Summary of observed testing performance _Boris talked incessantly. He couldn't sit still, answered with questions trying to get you to give him the answers. Very busy even when sitting. Seems to have a chip on his shoulder about the inferiority of schools in America._

Particular Learning Needs

☑ Spoken language   ☑ Reading   ☑ Written language

☐ Other _____

Comments _Continue to develop content vocabulary. Continue to develop reading skills in both English and Russian. Work on fluency. Work on social skills._

Short-Range Goals

Work on content vocabulary in all skill areas. Help Boris adapt to classroom structure. Work on social skills with peers.

Strategy for implementation _Assign Boris an adult mentor to work with him on adapting to new school situation and routine, help with feedback on school assignments and work on content._

Long-Range Goals

Continue to develop cognitive academic vocabulary. Continue reading in Russian. Develop reading content material in English and work towards fluency in writing English.

Strategy for implementation _Work on specific assignments with Boris to focus on vocabulary. Get appropriate books in Russian from home, newspaper articles on Internet, review reading in English. Monitor Boris group activities for success._

INDIVIDUALIZED EDUCATIONAL PLAN

NOTE: This form is to be completed by the ESL teacher, the resource teacher, or the classroom teacher three or four weeks after the new student has been assigned to the class, or whenever an IEP is to be updated.

Student's name _*Thuyen*_ _*Newton*_
                    Family name   Given name

Birth date _*March 4*_   Age _*16*_   M ☒   F ☐
          Mo Day Year

Grade level _*10*_   Assessment test _*LAS*_

Date given _*January*_   Primary language _*Vietnamese*_

Assessment test given in primary language?   yes ☐   no ☒

Supplemental Testing
Observations

Oral production _*Minimal. Frequently unintelligible because of pronunciation. Inaccurate grammar, halting speech, simple vocab.*_

Comprehension _*Knows a few words. Can retell a story on basic level.*_

Reading skill _*Knows a few words. Unable to fill in home language survey.*_

Written skills _*Can write name. Shows limited knowledge of simple vocab. Syntax irregular*_

Summary of observed testing performance _*Newton was born in this country and should be farther along in English than he appears. Seems to have an excellent ability for drawing as he drew a few pictures while waiting for testing to be completed. He is withdrawn.*_

Particular Learning Needs

☐ Spoken language   ☐ Reading   ☐ Written language

☐ Other _____

Comments _Newton needs reinforcement in all four skill areas. Beyond academic skills, Newton will need help interacting with peers._

Short-Range Goals

Involve in group activities. Capitalize in artistic area.

Strategy for implementation _Place in art class. Work with mentor for reinforcement and mediation with content area teachers._

Long-Range Goals

Work on social skills, monitor closely. Continue to develop skills in reading and writing. Observe and develop performance in Vietnamese.

Strategy for implementation _Work closely with mentor, particularly as this type of student can fall through cracks easily. Foster work with art projects inside and outside class, encourage a buddy in particularly difficult classes, try to develop a small group for this student._

INDIVIDUALIZED EDUCATIONAL PLAN

NOTE: This form is to be completed by the ESL teacher, the resource teacher, or the classroom teacher three or four weeks after the new student has been assigned to the class, or whenever an IEP is to be updated.

Student's name *Luckner*   *Spencer*
              Family name   Given name

Birth date *November 2*   Age ___ *6* ___   M ☒ F ☐
         Mo   Day   Year

Grade level *Kindergarten*   Assessment test *Print Awareness*

Date given *April*   Primary language *Non-Standard English*

Assessment test given in primary language? yes ☒   no ☐

Supplemental Testing Observations

Oral production *Very oral and fluent*

Comprehension *Good*

Reading skill *Could not pick out his name from a list of five names.*

Written skills *Wrote 3 letters of his name and random letters in response to spelling test.*

Summary of observed testing performance *This boy tried very hard to do a good job. He was charming and capable of holding a conversation. He displayed intelligence and was quick to find ways to "survive" the test. Didn't know the names of all his brothers.*

Particular Learning Needs

☑ Spoken language   ☐ Reading   ☐ Written language

☐ Other _____

Comments _This child will need support in all areas. Spencer wants to achieve, so this desire needs to be reinforced with success._

Short-Range Goals

Assimilate into class and routine. Make the most of the time left in the year.

Strategy for implementation _Strong 1 on 1 support for this student. LEA, word banks, frame sentences._

Long-Range Goals

Resist temptation to give into shortness of time left in school year, use what time is left. Build self esteem through reading and writing successes.

Strategy for implementation _Paired reading, mentor for 1 on 1, sound/spelling correspondence. Establish home/school connections._

INDIVIDUALIZED EDUCATIONAL PLAN

NOTE: This form is to be completed by the ESL teacher, the resource teacher, or the classroom teacher three or four weeks after the new student has been assigned to the class, or whenever an IEP is to be updated.

Student's name ___*Bill*___ ___*Charlie*___
                              Family name   Given name

Birth date ___*Febrary 20*___   Age ___*6*___   M ☒ F ☐
            Mo Day Year

Grade level ___*Kindergarten*___   Assessment test ___*LAS*___

Date given ___*August*___   Primary language ___*Unknown*___

Assessment test given in primary language?   yes ☐   no ☒

Supplemental Testing Observations

Oral production ___*Minimal*___

_____

Comprehension ___*Difficult to know*___

_____

Reading skill ___*Could not pick his name out of field of five names. Does not demonstrate any knowledge that print has meaning.*___

Written skills ___*Could not write name, does not know alphabet.*___

Summary of observed testing performance ___*Shy and hesitant, did not seem to have experience with print. Did not attempt to read/write, spoke little, seemed unfamiliar with school.*___

_____

_____

_____

Particular Learning Needs

☐ Spoken language   ☐ Reading   ☐ Written language

☐ Other _____

Comments *Help Charlie become comfortable with school and begin reading and writing*

Short-Range Goals

Help Charlie feel part of group in order to participate.

Strategy for implementation *Pair with friendly buddy to get connected. Work on affective objectives first.*

Long-Range Goals

Focus on familiarization with print. Continue to work with Charlie on feeling comfortable at school. Learn about home language. Encourage family to build skills.

Strategy for implementation *Focus on Charlie's participation at all levels, work with LEA, frame sentences, and reading books of his interest areas. Meet with parents.*

INDIVIDUALIZED EDUCATIONAL PLAN

NOTE: This form is to be completed by the ESL teacher, the resource teacher, or the classroom teacher three or four weeks after the new student has been assigned to the class, or whenever an IEP is to be updated.

Student's name ___*Xiong*_____*Hnuku*_____
                   Family name   Given name

Birth date __*June 10*_____   Age ____*9*_____   M ☐ F ☒
           Mo Day Year

Grade level ___*3/4 split*_____   Assessment test ___*LAS*____

Date given ___*October*_____   Primary language _*Hmong*_

Assessment test given in primary language?   yes ☐   no ☒

**Supplemental Testing
Observations**

Oral production ___*Didn't say anything*_____

Comprehension ___*Very little*_____

Reading skill ___*None demonstrated*_____

Written skills ___*None demonstrated*_____

Summary of observed testing performance ___*Hnuku was*___ *very shy and reluctant to respond to any questions. Avoided eye contact and seemed very uncomfortable with the process. Shrugged her shoulders in response to questions.*

Particular Learning Needs

☑ Spoken language   ☑ Reading   ☑ Written language

☐ Other _____

Comments *Need to develop a social vocabulary first. Start with print has meaning, environmental print, labels in classroom. Begin with lists, name, environmental print.*

Hnuku will need intensive work in all areas.

Short-Range Goals *Develop survival and social vocabulary, introduction of reading skills, help with assimilation into classroom and school routine.*

Strategy for implementation *Read to Hnuku, label items, use English to create LEA stories, provide opportunity to draw, copy, and practice writing.*

Long-Range Goals *Participation in classroom work, develop content vocabulary, incorporate Hnuku in classroom routine, continue work in four skill areas.*

Strategy for implementation *Continue to provide appropriate books for reading, place Hnuku in groups to encourage social English. Use LEA stories to reinforce vocabulary and reading skills in content area, use Hmong aide to foster primary language development.*

TEST OF WRITTEN ENGLISH (TWE) SCORING GUIDE

SCORE

6 **Demonstrates clear competence in writing on both the rhetorical and syntactic levels, though it may have occasional errors.**

A paper in this category

- effectively addresses the writing task
- is well organized
- uses clearly appropriate details to support a thesis or illustrate ideas
- displays consistent facility in the use of language
- demonstrates syntactic variety and appropriate word choice

5 **Demonstrates competence in writing on both the rhetorical and syntactic levels, though it will probably have occasional errors.**

A paper in this category

- may address some parts of the task more effectively than others
- is generally well organized and developed
- uses details to support a thesis or illustrate an idea
- displays facility in the use of language
- demonstrates some syntactic variety and range of vocabulary

4 **Demonstrates minimal competence in writing on both the rhetorical and syntactic levels.**

A paper in this category

- addresses the writing topic adequately but may slight parts of the task
- is adequately organized and developed
- uses some details to support a thesis or illustrate an idea
- demonstrates adequate but possibly inconsistent facility with syntax and usage
- may contain some errors that occasionally obscure meaning

3 **Demonstrates some developing competence in writing, but it remains flawed on either the rhetorical or syntactic level, or both.**

A paper in this category may reveal one or more of the following weaknesses:

- inadequate organization or development
- inappropriate or insufficient details to support or illustrate generalizations
- a noticeably inappropriate choice of words or word forms
- an accumulation of errors in sentence structure and/or usage

2   **Suggests incompetence in writing.**

A paper in this category is seriously flawed by one or more of the following weaknesses:

- serious disorganization or underdevelopment
- little or no detail, or irrelevant specifics
- serious and frequent errors in sentence structure or usage
- serious problems with focus

1   **Demonstrates incompetence in writing.**

A paper in this category

- may be incoherent
- may be underdeveloped
- may contain severe and persistent errors

TEACHER-VOLUNTEER (OR AIDE) PLANNING SHEET

Name of volunteer (or aide) _____

Name of teacher/grade level _____

Name(s) of student(s) _____

Skills to be reinforced or tasks to be completed by volunteer (or aide):

Time frame _____

Materials to be used _____

_____

_____

_____

_____

Location of materials _____

Procedures _____

_____

_____

_____

_____

_____

_____

_____

Comments of volunteer (or aide): _____

_____

_____

_____

_____

_____

_____

_____

GLOSSARY

BICS—Basic Interpersonal Communication Skills
The skills involved in everyday communication—listening, speaking, carrying on basic conversation, understanding speakers, and getting one's basic needs met.

CALP—Cognitive Academic Language Proficiency
The skills that are needed to succeed in the academic classroom, which include problem solving, inferring, analyzing, synthesizing, and predicting. They go beyond the BICS, demanding much greater competence in the language.

Context-Reduced Language
Language that has few visual and/or aural cues to help the learner understand. This is demanding language because the learner's ability to understand the spoken or written message depends solely on his proficiency in the language. Examples of context-reduced language situations are lectures without demonstrations or visual aids; math word problems without illustrations; textbooks without charts, diagrams, or photos.

Context-Embedded Language
Language that is most easily understood is embedded in a context that is rich in cues such as concrete objects, gestures, facial expressions, art, music, phys. ed., face-to-face conversations, games, hands-on activities (as with science), math computation problems, and TPR.

Emergent Literacy
Literacy is viewed as the development of the association of print with meaning, something that begins in early childhood and is acquired over time, rather than as skills students are formally taught and learned when they go to school. Most children who grow up in Western society have experience with print long before they come to school. Not so with a host of newcomers. Teachers cannot assume that these students know such things as how to hold a book, or what reading and writing are for.

Explicit Instruction
Instruction that directly explains the what, why, when, and how of certain skills, such as how to write a paragraph, skim a text, sound out a word, or use context and other clues to figure out meaning.

FEP/FES—Fully English Speaking/Fully English Proficient
Students who are able to participate fully in regular classroom activities. ESL students are usually designated FEP after scoring beyond a designated percentile on a standardized proficiency test. Educators must keep in mind that students should not be considered FEP on the basis of their oral language alone—the FEP designation does not necessarily mean that the student will be able to perform successfully in the content areas. Many FEP students struggle with the cognitive academic language in the content areas and may continue to need some support. In addition, many students, no matter how proficient, still write with a foreign accent; in other words, their syntax and word usage show many traits of their first language.

Input
The language the student hears and encounters on a daily basis. This includes directed input in the form of language lessons and ordinary conversation.

Intake

The language the student actually processes and learns, and is able to use and understand when he reads it or hears it spoken.

Integrated Approach

An approach to literacy instruction that links reading, writing, listening, and speaking skills, rather than considering them separate skills.

LEA—Language Experience Approach

A method of promoting reading in which the teacher begins with the experiences the students bring to class (or experience together), and then develops oral and written activities around these experiences. The teacher uses the students' own words to write stories, which are then used in a variety of ways.

LES/LEP—Limited English Speaking/Limited English Proficient

Understands some English, but is not fluent enough to compete academically with English-speaking peers.

Literature Circle

Discussion group based on self-selected books for reading; each group consists of students who independently read the same book (or different titles by the same author or books with a common theme), rather than the lock-step reading approach where the teacher selects the reading, or the students go on to the next story in the basal reader.

Miscue Analysis

A miscue is defined as the difference between the oral response of a reader and the actual words printed on the page. Miscue analysis, developed by Kenneth and Yetta Goodman, is a method of evaluating reading comprehension using a detailed analysis of the types of errors made when reading aloud. Particular strategies are then used to help the reader correct his comprehension errors.

NES/NEP—Non-English Speaking/Non-English Proficient

Speaks little or no English.

Pull-Out

Students are "pulled out" of the classroom to work with the ESL teacher. Often, the ESL teacher supplements or prepares the students for what is going on in the regular classroom. At the high school level, ESL teachers act as a resource, helping students get through their content classes by explaining homework and with understanding the readings. Many times, ESL teachers teach vocabulary that we assume students know: shapes, telling time, colors, parts of the body, or teaching beginning reading skills.

Push-In

In this model, the ESL teacher comes into the classroom to work with the students. In the ideal world, this is a terrific option especially if the ESL teacher is bilingual. The teachers team together to work on content. It's here that the bilingual teacher can translate, add insight into cultural issues or special problems that arise.

Sheltered English

Sheltered English is an approach to teaching the content of science, social studies, etc. through modified language and methods in order to make the information comprehensible to the students.

TPR—Total Physical Response

Introduced by James Asher, this method uses physical actions to develop language skills in second-language learners. Students are asked to respond physically to commands or directions, often in a game-like situation.

Writing Process

The activities involved in producing writing, including prewriting, drafting, revising, editing, and publishing.

BIBLIOGRAPHY

Alatis, Penelope et al. "Learners, Teachers, and Aides/Volunteers: Bermuda Triangle or Synergy?" Paper presented at the 21st International TESOL Conference, Miami, FL, 1987.

Allen, Janet. *It's Never Too Late: Leading Adolescents to Lifelong Literacy.* Portsmouth, NH: Heinemann, 1995.

Allington, R. "The Schools We Have, The Schools We Need." In *Reconsidering a Balanced Approach to Reading*, edited by C. Weaver. Urbana, IL: National Council of Teachers of English, 1998.

Ammon, Paul. "Helping Children Learn to Write in ESL: Some Observations and Some Hypotheses." In *The Acquisition of Written Language: Response and Revision*, edited by S. W. Freedman. Norwood, NJ: Ablex Publishing, 1985.

Anderson, R. C. et al. *Becoming a Nation of Readers.* Washington, DC: National Institute of Education, 1985.

Asher, J. "The Strategy of the Total Physical Response: An Application to Learning Russian." *International Review of Applied Linguistics* 3 (1965): 291–300.

Atwell, Nancie. *In the Middle: New Understandings About Writing, Reading and Learning with Adolescents.* 2d ed. Portsmouth, NH: Heinemann, 1998.

Au, Kathryn. *Literacy Instruction in Multilingual Settings.* Fort Worth: Harcourt Brace Jovanovich, 1993.

———. "Participation Structures in a Reading Lesson with Hawaiian Children: Analysis of a Culturally Appropriate Instructional Event." *Anthropology and Education Quarterly* 11 (1980): 91–115.

Au, K., and A. J. Kawakami. "Research Currents: Talk Story and Learning to Read." *Language Arts* 62 (1985): 406–411.

Barnes, D. *Language, The Learner, and The School.* 3rd ed. New York: Penguin, 1986.

Barr, M. et al. *The Primary Language Record: A Handbook for Teachers.* Portsmouth, NH: Heinemann, 1989.

Bell, J., and B. Burnaby. *A Handbook for ESL Literacy.* Toronto: Ontario Institute for Studies in Education, 1984.

Benesch, S., ed. *Ending Remediation: Linking ESL and Content in Higher Education.* Washington, DC: TESOL, 1988.

Berinton, D., M. A. Snow, and M. Wesche. *Content-Based Second Language.* New York: Newbury House, 1989.

Biological Sciences Curriculum Study. *Developing Biological Literacy: A Guide to Developing Secondary and Post Secondary Biology Curricula.* Colorado Springs, CO: BSCS, 1993.

Bliatout, Bruce et al. *Handbook for Teaching Hmong-Speaking Students.* Folsom, CA: Folsom Cordova Unified School District, Southeast Asia Community Resource Center, 1988.

Briggs, Sandra et al. *Guidelines for Working with Limited-English Proficient Students.* San Mateo, CA: San Mateo Union High School District, 1985.

Brock, C. "Exploring the Use of Book Clubs with Second Language Learners in Mainstream Classrooms." In *The Book Club Connection: Literacy Learning and Classroom Talk*, edited by S. McMahon and T. Raphael. New York: Teachers College Press, 1997.

Burt, M., H. Dulay, and S. Krashen. *Language Two.* New York: Oxford UP, 1982.

Calkins, L. McCormick. *The Art of Teaching Writing.* Rev. ed. Portsmouth, NH: Heinemann, 1994.

Cantoni-Harvey, G. *Content-Area Language Instruction: Approaches and Strategies.* Reading, MA: Addison-Wesley, 1987.

Carbo, Marie. Carbo Recorded-Book Method.™ Syosset, NY: National Reading Styles Institute, 1992.

Chall, Jeanne. *Learning To Read: The Great Debate.* 3rd ed. Fort Worth: Harcourt Brace, 1996.

Chamot, Anna Uhl, and M. O'Malley. *The Cognitive Academic Language Learning Approach.* Washington: NCBE (National Clearinghouse for Bilingual Education), 1986.

Charter, Patricia F. "Special Education/Bilingual Education: A Collaborative Model." *Thrust* 18 (1989).

Chips, B. "Using Cooperative Learning at the Secondary Levels." In *Cooperative Learning: A Response to Linguistic and Cultural Diversity*, edited by D. Holt. Washington, DC: Center for Applied Linguistics, 1993.

Clearinghouse on Languages and Linguistics. "Indochinese Students in U.S. Schools: A Guide for Administrators." *Language in Education: Theory and Practice* 42 (October 1981).

Collier, V. "How Long? A Synthesis of Research on Academic Achievement in a Second Language." *TESOL Quarterly* 23 (1989): 509–531.

Cooper, J. David. *Literacy: Helping Children Construct Meaning.* Boston: Houghton Mifflin, 1997.

Cramer, Ronald. *Writing, Reading and Language Growth.* Columbus, OH: Charles E. Merrill Publishing, 1979.

Crandall, J., ed. *ESL Through Content-Area Instruction.* Englewood Cliffs, NJ: Prentice-Hall, 1987.

———. *Developing Content-Centered Language Learning: Strategies for Classroom Instruction and Teacher Development.* Thailand: Chulalongkorn University, 1995.

Cullinan, B., ed. *Children's Voices: Talk in the Classroom.* Newark, DE: International Reading Association, 1993.

Cummins, James. "The Role of Primary Language Development in Promoting Educational Success for Language Minority Students." In *Schooling and Language Minority Students: A Theoretical Framework,* edited by Charles F. Leyba. Los Angeles: California State University, National Evaluation, Dissemination and Assessment Center, 1981.

Cunningham, P. M., and J. W. Cunningham. "Making Words: Enhancing the Invented Spelling-Decoding Connection." *The Reading Teacher* 46 (1992): 106–107.

Cunningham, P. M. *Phonics They Use: Words for Reading and Writing.* 3rd ed. New York: Longman, 2000.

Cunningham, P. M. et al. *Reading and Writing in Elementary Classrooms.* New York: Longman, 2000.

Daniels, H. *Literature Circles: Voice and Choice in One Student-Centered Classroom.* York, ME: Stenhouse, 1994.

Duncan, Sharon E. et al. *How to Administer the LAS.* San Rafael, CA: Linguametrics Group, 1981.

Dunn, Sonja, and L. Parmenter. *Butterscotch Dreams.* Portsmouth, NH: Heinemann, 1987.

Dyson, Anne Haas. "Appreciate the Drawing and Dictating of Young Children." *Young Children* 43 (1988): 25–32.

———. "Symbol Makers, Symbol Weavers: How Children Link Play, Pictures, and Print." *Young Children* 45 (1990): 50–57.

———. "Transitions and Tensions: Interrelationships between the Drawing, Talking, and Dictating of Young Children." *Research in the Teaching of English* 20 (1986): 379–409.

Echevarria, J., and A. Graves. *Sheltered Content Instruction: Teaching English-Language Learners with Diverse Abilities.* Needham Heights, MA: Allyn & Bacon, 1998.

Echevarria, J., M. Vogt, and D. Short. *Making Content Comprehensible for English Language Learners: The SIOP Model.* Needham Heights, MA: Allyn & Bacon, 2000.

Edelsky, Carole. *Writing in a Bilingual Program: Habia Una Vez.* Norwood, NJ: Ablex Publishing, 1986.

Elley, W., and F. Mangubhai. "The Impact of Reading on Second Language Learning." *Reading Research Quarterly* 19 (1983): 53–67.

Emig, Janet. *The Composing Processes of Twelfth Graders.* Champaign, IL: National Council of Teachers of English, 1971.

Enright, Scott, and M. L. McCloskey. *Integrating English: Developing English Language and Literacy in the Multilingual Classroom.* Reading, MA: Addison Wesley, 1988.

Flower, L. S., and J. R. Hayes. "Problem Solving Strategies and the Writing Process." *College English* 39 (1977): 449–461.

———. "Writing Research and the Writer." *American Psychologist* 41 (1986): 1106–1113.

Flynn, H. C. "A Collaborative Model of Service for LEP Students." Master's thesis, Hamline University, 1992.

Forester, Anne D., and Margaret Reinhard. *The Learners' Way.* 2d ed. Winnipeg, MB: Peguis Publishers, 2000.

Fountas, I., and G. Pinnell. *Guided Reading.* Portsmouth, NH: Heinemann, 1996.

Gadda, George, Faye Peitzman, and William Walsh. *Teaching Analytical Writing.* Los Angeles: California Academic Partnership Program, UCLA, 1988.

Galda, L., B. Cullinan, and D. Strickland. *Language, Literacy and the Child.* 2d ed. Fort Worth: Harcourt Brace Jovanovich, 1997.

Gaskins, I. "There's More to Teaching At-Risk and Delayed Readers Than Good Reading Instruction." *The Reading Teacher* 51 (1998): 534–544.

Genesee, Fred., ed. *Educating Second Language Children.* New York: Cambridge University Press, 1994.

Goodman, Y. "Children Coming to Know Literacy." In *Emergent Literacy: Writing and Reading,* edited by W. H. Teale and E. Sulzby. Norwood, NJ: Ablex Publishing, 1986.

Gonzalez, Josue, and L. Darling-Hammond. *New Concepts for New Challenges: Professional Development for Teachers of Immigrant Youth.* Washington, DC: Center for Applied Linguistics, 1994.

Graham, Carolyn. *Big Chants.* Fort Worth: Harcourt Brace, 1994.

———. *Jazz Chants for Children.* New York: Oxford University Press, 1979.

Graves, Donald. "An Examination of the Writing Processes of Seven-Year-Old Children." *Research in the Teaching of English* 9 (1975): 227–241.

Gudschinsky, Sarah. *A Manual of Literacy for Preliterate Peoples.* Ukarumpa, Papua New Guinea: Summer Institute of Linguistics, 1973.

Gunderson, L. "Second Language Reading Instruction in ESL and Mainstream Classrooms." In *Issues in Literacy: A Research Perspective,* edited by J. Niles and R. Lalik. 34th Yearbook of the National Reading Conference, 1985.

———. *ESL Literacy Instruction: A Guidebook to Theory and Practice.* Englewood Cliffs, NJ: Prentice Hall, 1991.

Hamayan, Elsa V. et al. *Assessment of Language Minority Students: A Handbook for Educators.* Arlington Heights, IL: Illinois Resource Center, 1985.

Handscombe, J. "A Quality Program for Learners of English as a Second Language." In *When They Don't All Speak English,* edited by P. Riggs and G. Allen. Urbana, IL: National Council of Teachers, 1989.

Heath, S. B. *Ways With Words: Language, Life and Work in Communities and Classrooms.* Cambridge, MA: Cambridge UP, 1983.

Hoffman, J. "When Bad Things Happen to Good Ideas in Literacy Education: Professional Dilemmas, Personal Decisions, and Political Traps." *The Reading Teacher* 52 (1998): 102–112.

Igoa, Cristina. *The Inner World of the Immigrant Child.* New York: St. Martin's Press, 1995.

Judy, Stephen, and Susan Judy. *The English Teacher's Handbook.* Boston: Little, Brown & Co., 1983.

Krashen, Stephen. *Principles and Practice in Second Language Acquisition.* New York: Pergamon Press, 1982.

Krogness, Mary. *Just Teach Me, Mrs. K.: Talking, Reading, and Writing with Resistant Adolescent Learners.* Portsmouth, NH: Heinemann, 1995.

Kuhlman, N. A., and J. Vidal. "Meeting the Needs of LEP Students Through New Teacher Training: The Case in California." *The Journal of Educational Issues of Language Minority Students* 12 (1993): 97–113.

Lamott, Anne. *Bird By Bird.* New York: Pantheon, 1995.

Law, B., and M. Eckes. *Assessment and ESL.* Winnipeg, MB: Peguis Publishers, 1995.

Lucas, T. "What Have We Learned from Research On Successful Secondary Programs for LEP Students?" *Proceedings of the Third National Research Symposium on Limited English Proficient Student Issues.* Washington, DC: U.S. Department of Education, Office of Bilingual Education and Minority Language Affairs 1 (1993): 81–111.

―――. *Into, Through, and Beyond Secondary School: Critical Transitions for Immigrant Youths.* Washington, DC: Center For Applied Linguistics, 1997.

Martinez-Roldan, C., and J. Lopez-Robertson. "Initiating Literature Circles in a First-Grade Bilingual Classroom." *The Reading Teacher* 53 (1999/2000): 270–281.

McCracken, Robert, and Marlene McCracken. *Reading Is Only the Tiger's Tail.* Rev. ed. Winnipeg, MB: Peguis Publishers, 1987.

―――. *Reading, Writing and Language.* 2d ed. Winnipeg, MB: Peguis Publishers, 1995.

McMahon, S. "Reading in the Book Club Program." In *The Book Club Connection: Literacy Learning and Classroom Talk,* edited by S. McMahon and T. Raphael. New York: Teachers College Press, 1997.

Met, M. "Teaching Content Through A Second Language." In *Educating Second Language Children: The Whole Child, The Whole Curriculum, The Whole Community,* edited by F. Genessee. Cambridge, MA: Cambridge UP, 1994.

Michaels, S. "Sharing Time: Children's Narrative Styles and Differential Access to Literacy." *Language in Society* 10 (1981): 423–442.

Moffat, J. *Drama: What is Happening.* Champaign, IL: National Council of Teachers of English, 1967.

Mohan, B. *Language and Content.* Reading, MA: Addison-Wesley, 1986.

Moustafa, M. *Beyond Traditional Phonics: Research Discoveries and Reading Instruction.* Portsmouth, NH: Heinemann, 1998.

Newman, J. *The Craft of Children's Writing.* Portsmouth, NH: Heinemann, 1984.

Noble, G., P. Egan, and S. MacDowell. "Changing the Self-Concept of Seven Year Old Deprived Urban Children by Creative Drama or Video Feedback." *Social Behavior and Personality* 5 (1977): 55–65.

Ocean View School District. *Survival Guide for Teachers of NES/LES Students.* Huntington Beach, CA, 1980.

Peregoy, S., and O. Boyle. *Reading, Writing and Learning in ESL*. 2d ed. White Plains, NY: Longman, 1997.

Peterson, R., and M. Eeds. *Grand Conversations: Literature Groups in Action*. New York: Scholastic, 1990.

Philips, S. "Participant Structures and Communicative Competence: Warm Springs Children in Community and Classroom." In *Functions of Language in the Classroom*, edited by C. Cazden, V. John, and D. Hymes. New York: Teachers College Press, 1972.

Proett, Jackie, and Kent Gill. *The Writing Process in Action: A Handbook for Teachers*. Urbana, IL: National Council of Teachers of English, 1986.

Raimes, A. *Keys for Writers: A Brief Handbook*. 2d ed. Boston: Houghton Mifflin, 1999.

Rathmell, George. *Benchmarks in Reading*. Hayward, CA: Alemany, 1984.

Read, D., and H. Smith. "Teaching Visual Literacy Through Wordless Picture Books." *The Reading Teacher* 35 (1982): 924–933.

Reid, Joy. *Teaching ESL Writing*. Englewood Cliffs, NJ: Prentice Hall, 1993.

Rosenshine, B. "Teaching Functions in Successful Teaching Programs." Paper presented at the Center for the Study of Teacher Education, University of British Columbia, Vancouver, October, 1983.

Routman, R. *Literacy at the Crossroads*. Portsmouth, NH: Heinemann, 1996.

———. *Transitions: From Literature to Literacy*. Portsmouth, NH: Heinemann, 1988.

Samway, K., and G. Whang. *Literature Study Circles in a Multicultural Classroom*. York, Main: Stenhouse, 1996.

Sargent, Judy, and A. Smejkal. *Targets for Teachers: A Self-Study Guide for Teachers in the Age of Standards*. Winnipeg, MB: Peguis Publishers, 2000.

Saville-Troike, M. "What Really Matters in Second Language Learning for Academic Achievement?" *TESOL Quarterly* 18 (1984): 117–131.

Schickedanz, J. *More Than the ABCs*. Washington, DC: National Association for the Education of Young Children, 1986.

Schirmacher, R. *Art and Creative Development for Young Children*. Albany, NY: Delmar Publishing, 1998.

Shorey, Ravi. "Error Perception of Native Speaking and Non-Native Speaking Teachers of ESL." *English Language Teaching* Journal 40 (1986).

Short, D. "Integrating Language and Content for Effective Sheltered Instruction Programs." In *So Much To Say: Adolescents, Bilingualism, and ESL in the Secondary School*, edited by C. Faltis and P. Wolfe. New York: Teachers College Press, 1999.

Short, D., J. Crandall, and D. Christian. *How to Integrate Language and Content Instruction: A Training Manual*. Washington, DC: Center for Applied Linguistics (ERIC Document Reproduction Service No. ED 305 824), 1989.

Short, S. *How to Integrate Language and Content Instruction*. Washington, DC: Center for Applied Linguistics, 1991.

Smith, Frank. *Reading Without Nonsense*. 3rd ed. New York: Teachers College Press, 1997.

Soven, Margot. *Teaching Writing in Middle and Secondary Schools: Theory, Research and Practice.* Boston: Allyn & Bacon, 1999.

Sowers, S. "Six Questions Teachers Ask About Invented Spelling." In *Understanding Writing*, edited by T. Newkirk and N. Atwell. Portsmouth, NH: Heinemann, 1985.

Spandel, Vicki. *Seeing with New Eyes: A Guidebook on Teaching and Assessing Beginning Writers.* Portland, OR: Northwest Regional Educational Lab, 1997.

Spangenbert-Urbschart, K. *Kids Come in All Languages: Reading Instruction for ESL Students.* Newark, Delaware: International Reading Association, 1994.

Spiegel, D. "Silver Bullets, Babies, and Bath Water: Literature Response Groups in a Balanced Literacy Program." *The Reading Teacher* 52 (1998): 114–124.

Stewig, J., and C. Buege. *Dramatizing Literature in Whole Language Classrooms.* 2d ed. New York: Teachers College Press, 1994.

Teachers of English to Speakers of Other Languages. *ESL Standards for Pre-K–12 Students.* Alexandria, VA: TESOL, 1997.

Teale, W., and E. Sulzby, eds. *Emergent Literacy: Writing and Reading.* Norwood, NJ: Ablex Publishing, 1986.

Tompkins, Gail. *Teaching Writing: Balancing Process and Product.* 3rd ed. Upper Saddle River, NJ: Merrill, 2000.

Trelease, Jim. *The Read-Aloud Handbook.* New York: Penguin, 1985.

Ventriglia, Linda. *Conversations of Miguel and Maria: How Children Learn a Second Language.* Reading, MA: Addison-Wesley, 1982.

Waggoner, D. "Who are Secondary Newcomer and Linguistically Different Youth?" In *So Much to Say: Adolescents, Bilingualism, and ESL in the Secondary School*, edited by C. Faltis and P. Wolfe. New York: Teachers College Press, 1999.

Wells, G. *The Meaning Makers: Children Learning Language and Using Language.* Portsmouth, NH: Heinemann, 1986.

Wiggins, G., and J. McTighe. *Understanding by Design.* Alexandria, VA: Association for Supervision and Curriculum Development, 1998.

Wollman-Bonilla, J. E. "Reading Journals: Invitations to Participate in Literature." *The Reading Teacher* 43 (1989): 112–120.

Wong, Fillmore, L. "Research Currents: Equity or Excellence?" *Language Arts* 63 (1986): 474–481.

Yoshihara, Karen. Paper presented at California TESOL Conference, 1988.

Zemelman, S., H. Daniels, and A. Hyde. *Best Practice: New Standards for Teaching and Learning in America's Schools.* 2d ed. Portsmouth, NH: Heinemann, 1998.

BOOK LIST

Buss, Fran Leeper. *Journey of the Sparrows*. New York: Lodestar Books, 1991.

Carle, Eric. *The Very Hungry Caterpillar*. New York: Philomel, 1969.

Cisneros, Sandra. *The House on Mango Street*. New York: Vintage, 1984.

Cowley, Joy. *The Ghost*. Bothell, WA: The Wright Group, 1983.

Dahl, Roald. *George's Marvelous Medicine*. New York: Knopf, 1982.

Dr. Seuss. *One Fish, Two Fish, Red Fish, Blue Fish*. New York: Beginner Books, 1960.

Frank, Anne. *The Diary of a Young Girl*. New York: Doubleday, 1967.

Friedman, Ina. *How My Parents Learned to Eat*. Boston: Houghton Mifflin, 1984.

Hersey, John. *Hiroshima*. New York: Vintage Books, 1989.

Hinton, S. E. *The Outsiders*. New York: Dell, 1968.

Hutchins, P. *Rosie's Walk*. New York: Macmillan, 1971.

Ingalls, Laura Wilder. *On the Banks of Plum Creek*. New York: HarperTrophy, 1971.

Lee, Harper. *To Kill a Mockingbird*. Philadelphia: Lippincott, 1960.

Levine, Ellen. *I Hate English!* New York: Scholastic, 1989.

MacLachlan, Patricia. *Sarah, Plain and Tall*. New York: Harper & Row, 1985.

McCunn, Ruthann Lum. *Thousand Pieces of Gold*. Boston: Beacon Press, 1982.

Naylor, Phyllis Reynolds. *Shiloh*. New York: Dell Publishing, 1991.

Paterson, Katherine. *Bridge to Terabithia*. New York: Crowell, 1977.

Rathmann, Peggy. *Officer Buckle and Gloria*. New York: Putnam, 1995.

Rice, Elizabeth. *Jacki*. Chicago: Childrens Press, 1969.

Scieszska, John. *The Good, The Bad and the Goofy*. New York: Puffin, 1993.

Slobodkina, E. *Caps for Sale*. New York: W. R. Scott, 1947.

Taylor, Mildred. *Roll of Thunder Hear My Cry*. New York: Dial Press, 1976.

Taylor, Theodore. *The Cay*. Santa Barbara, CA: Cornerstone Books, 1990.

Tolstoi, Alexei. *The Great Big Enormous Turnip*. New York: F. Watts, 1968.

Tsuchiya, Yukio. *Faithful Elephants*. Boston: Houghton Mifflin, 1988.

Wakatsuki, Jeanne. *Farewell to Manzanar*. Boston: Houghton Mifflin, 1973.

Williams, S. *I Went Walking*. San Diego: Harcourt Brace Jovanovich, 1996.

Yashima, Taro. *Crow Boy*. New York: Viking, 1995.

Young, E. *Lon Po Po*. New York: Philomel Books, 1989.

INTERNET RESOURCES

http://www.ef.com

EF Education Tours is the world's largest language school. It provides programs for high school and adult students as well as for professionals and corporations. This site gives students and teachers the opportunity to discover new places, cultures, and languages through group travel adventures.

http://www.tesol.edu

TESOL on line—Teachers of English to Speakers of Other Languages. This site contains a multitude of services for teachers: an extensive catalog of publications and materials, conventions, ESL standards for preK–12, and information on professional development.

http://www.eslcafe.com

A great site for both teachers and students that make learning English fun. It includes discussion forums, a help center, book store, a job center, and helpful links that will give any surfer the information and assistance they need.

http://www.cal.org

The Center of Applied Linguistics is a comprehensive site that provides information on new publications, current news events regarding language education, and professional development events. The topic areas for the site range from adult ESL literacy, to language testing, to refugee concerns.

http://www.alr.org

American Language Review is a journal of language teaching and learning in the U.S. and around the world. It is an excellent resource for information on new and evolving methodologies, practices, and products in the field of language education.

INDEX